HAGIOGRAPHY IN MARGUERITE DE NAVARRE'S *HEPTAMÉRON*

The Early Modern Exchange

SERIES EDITORS

Gary Ferguson, University of Virginia, author of *Same-Sex Marriage in Renaissance Rome: Sexuality, Identity, and Community in Early Modern Europe*

Meredith K. Ray, University of Delaware, author of *Daughters of Alchemy: Women and Scientific Culture in Early Modern Italy*

Julia Domínguez, University of Delaware, author of *Quixotic Memories: Cervantes and the Culture of Memory in Early Modern Spain*

SELECTED TITLES

Widow City: Gender, Emotion, and Community in the Italian Renaissance, Anna Wainwright

The Age of Subtlety: Nature and Rhetorical Conceits in Early Modern Europe, Javier Patiño Loira

Redreaming the Renaissance: Essays on History and Literature in Honor of Guido Ruggiero, edited by Mary Lindemann and Deanna Shemek

Ordering Customs: Ethnographic Thought in Early Modern Venice, Kathryn Taylor

The Waxing of the Middle Ages: Revisiting Late Medieval France, edited by Tracy Adams and Charles-Louis Morand-Métivier

Hagiography in Marguerite de Navarre's *Heptaméron*

Saints and Debates in Renaissance France

Leanna Bridge Rezvani

UNIVERSITY OF DELAWARE PRESS

Newark

Library of Congress Cataloging-in-Publication Data

Names: Rezvani, Leanna Bridge, author.
Title: Hagiography in Marguerite de Navarre's Heptaméron : saints and debates in Renaissance France / Leanna Bridge Rezvani.
Other titles: Early modern exchange.
Description: Newark, DE : University of Delaware Press, 2025. | Series: The early modern exchange | Includes bibliographical references and index.
Identifiers: LCCN 2025007109 | ISBN 9781644534007 (paperback) | ISBN 9781644534014 (hardcover)
Subjects: LCSH: Marguerite, Queen, consort of Henry II, King of Navarre, 1492–1549. Heptaméron. | Hagiography in literature. | Christian saints in literature. | French literature—16th century—History and criticism.
Classification: LCC PQ1631.H4 R49 2025 | DDC 843/.3—dc23/eng/20250626
LC record available at https://lccn.loc.gov/2025007109

A British Cataloging-in-Publication record for this book is available from the British Library.

∞ The paper used in this publication meets the requirements of the American National Standard for Information Sciences—Permanence of Paper for Printed Library Materials, ANSI Z39.48-1992.

udpress.udel.edu

Distributed worldwide by Rutgers University Press

For the Silverthorn sisters

Contents

Acknowledgments

Just as the *Heptaméron* is rich with a diversity of viewpoints, this volume has benefited from mentors, colleagues, and friends who have shared their perspectives on Marguerite's work and offered invaluable support and advice at various stages of the project.

This book was made possible because of generous support from MIT's School of Humanities, Arts, and Social Sciences, the French Initiatives Endowment Fund, and the Global Languages Section. I want to thank my wonderful colleagues in French, especially Bruno Perreau, Catherine Clark, Sabine Levet, Eva Dessein, and Cathy Culot. Maria Khotimsky has consistently shared ideas and encouragement. I am also grateful for the support and assistance of Per Urlaub, Paula Cogliano, Joe Borkowski, Lisa Hickler, Weiwei Pearl, and Maroua Ouadani.

I want to thank the dedicated community of scholars of Marguerite who regularly present their research at the Renaissance Society of America Conference and the Sixteenth Century Society Conference. I am particularly indebted to Mary McKinley and Nicolas Russell, who generously shared their forthcoming translation of the *Heptaméron*. Scott Francis has invigorated studies of the *Heptaméron* with his tireless work on the Marguerite de Navarre Society. Judy Kem has been a mentor, friend, and source of sage advice from the earliest stages to the conclusion of this project. Matilda Bruckner has offered thoughtful feedback on my work and shared words of wisdom over tea. Conversations with Carrie Klaus and Emily Thompson have helped shape my ideas and lifted my spirits.

I must also express my appreciation for the librarians at the Bibliothèque nationale de France, the Bibliothèque municipale de Toulouse, the Morgan Library and Museum, Boston College Libraries, the Beinecke Rare Book and Manuscript Library at Yale University, and MIT Libraries. I am thankful to have had the opportunity to discuss Queen Claude's Prayer Book with Roger Wieck at the Morgan Library. Ann Marie Holland at McGill University's Rare Books and Special Collections has been a tremendous help on numerous occasions. Tina Chan and the entire team at Interlibrary Loan at MIT have been nothing less than heroic in tracking down obscure references and texts.

Editors and reviewers at *L'Esprit Créateur* and *Romance Notes* have improved my work. I am thankful that these publications have allowed these materials to reappear here.

It has been a great pleasure to work with Julia Oestreich, Gary Ferguson, Meredith Ray, and the editorial and marketing teams at the University of Delaware Press. Their advice and guidance have been invaluable. This volume has been improved by the thoughtful comments and excellent suggestions of two anonymous readers.

I am also grateful for colleagues and friends in France and the United States. While doing research in Paris, I have been inspired by thought-provoking conversations about all things literary with Pierre-Louis Rey. I have also been fortunate to spend time with Françoise Quartier, the Quartier family, Rozen Noguellou, and the Seyfritz family. In the United States, I am grateful for rich friendships with Julie Gingles, Juliana Pirak, Deanna Bennett, Jeanne Douglass, Ruth Kim, and Renée Steinbrecher.

I cannot adequately express my immense gratitude for my family. My mom's love of reading has left me with a passion for literature. The Bridge family, the Javidan family, the Rezvani family, and the Silverthorn siblings and their families have been a constant source of joy and laughter. My husband, David, has provided unwavering love and support and essential backgammon breaks. My daughter, Sofia, has helped me maintain perspective with her artistic spirit and zest for life. My son, Alistair, has reminded me that periods of hard work should always be punctuated with great adventures. I am profoundly grateful that you are all part of my story.

Note on *Heptaméron* Editions

Unless otherwise noted, citations of the *Heptaméron* refer first to the original French as it appears in Marguerite de Navarre, *Œuvres complètes,* vol. 10, *L'Heptaméron,* edited by Nicole Cazauran and Sylvie Lefèvre, 3 vols. (Paris: Honoré Champion, 2013), and second to the English translation in Marguerite de Navarre, *The Heptameron,* edited and translated by Mary B. McKinley and Nicolas Russell, (Toronto: Iter, Centre for Reformation and Renaissance Studies, forthcoming). Citations of the Cazauran and Lefèvre edition refer first to the volume number, and then to the page number. As the McKinley and Russell edition was not published as of the writing of this book, translations from that edition are included without pagination.

Introduction

Marguerite, the Saints, and Renaissance Debates

> Avecques tous les saintz parfaitz,
> Je vous en rends gloire éternelle.
>
> [With all the perfect saints,
> I give you eternal glory.]
>
> —Marguerite de Navarre, *Marguerites de la Marguerite des Princesses*

Marguerite de Navarre was one of the most learned and influential women of Renaissance Europe. Along with her active engagement in politics and religion, she was a patron of the arts and a prolific writer of poetry, drama, and prose. The *Heptaméron,* her compelling collection of tales, offers readers invaluable insights into diverse facets of sixteenth-century French society. Scholars of Marguerite have written extensively on the complexities of her religious thought. Countless books and articles have examined her theological views and the representation of religion in the *Heptaméron*. More specifically, her connection to the evangelical reform movement in sixteenth-century France has received significant scholarly attention. The critical emphasis on Marguerite's ties to reformers has left the substantial influence of Catholic tradition on her writings underexplored. This book will examine the myriad connections between the saints' lives and Marguerite's tales with particular emphasis on how the *Heptaméron*'s intertextuality with hagiographic works bolstered the queen of Navarre's response to various social and theological debates in Renaissance France.

While hagiography is often associated with the Middle Ages, the saints were omnipresent in daily life in sixteenth-century France. Virginia Reinburg underscores the central role of the saints "in the relationship between God and the living faithful" at that time.[1] Regular attendance at Mass was the cultural norm and references to hagiography were consistently integrated into homilies, offices, and liturgical music.[2] Pilgrimages to shrines of the saints and novenas imploring their intercession remained popular devotional practices. Feast days of prominent and regional saints were also widely celebrated. Architectural and artistic features of Catholic churches like side chapels, stained glass, and statues depicted the lives of the saints, contributing to the French population's detailed knowledge of their legends.[3] The iconography of saints was also present in private homes in the form of pious images and devotional books, a significant number of which were printed during the fifteenth and sixteenth centuries.[4] Saints were represented both textually and visually in Renaissance books of hours, a favored genre among the laity during this period.[5]

Marguerite's contemporaries would have been cognizant of the Fourteen Holy Helpers, a group of saints who were invoked for their intercessory powers against various diseases and who rose in popularity during the outbreak of the bubonic plague.[6] They would have also easily recognized the *Quattuor Virgines Capitales*, or Four Capital Virgins. Saints Catherine of Alexandria, Margaret of Antioch, Dorothy, and Barbara were regularly depicted in literature and visual arts as the most excellent among the virgin martyrs.[7] Saint Martin of Tours, the patron saint of France, and patron saints of Paris such as Saint Genevieve and Saint Denis, would have also been well known by the sixteenth-century French population. Saint Francis's stigmata, Saint Catherine's wheel, or Saint Margaret's dragon are just a few of the innumerous examples of saints' attributes that were common knowledge in early modern France. Throughout the Renaissance, the saints were an integral part of daily life, religious practices, and literary culture.

Narratives of saints' lives continued to be a widely appreciated genre in early modern life. The impact of Jacobus de Voragine's thirteenth-century *Legenda aurea*, or *Golden Legend*, on European culture was both widespread and enduring. Not only was his collection of hagiographies one of the most disseminated and influential texts of the Middle Ages, but it was printed even more often than the Bible between 1470 and 1500.[8] Scott Francis has shown that Marguerite would have had access to this work in Latin and in the French translations (*Légende dorée*) by Jean Belet and Jean de Vignay.[9] De Vignay's 1333 *Miroir historial*, a translation of Vincent de Beauvais's thirteenth-century *Speculum maius*, was another popular work that included numerous saints' vitae.[10]

Although the saints' lives composed by male clerics were often marked by the gender bias of patristic writings, the genre was certainly not monolithic.[11] Brigitte Cazelles explains that saints' vitae "constitute a textual corpus of considerable variety."[12] Marie de France's late twelfth- or early thirteenth-century *La vie Seinte Audree* (The Life of Saint Audrey) and Christine de Pizan's *Le livre de la Cité des dames* (*The Book of the City of Ladies*, 1405) illustrate the presence of women's voices in the hagiographic corpus. Mystery plays were also widely appreciated; the extensive number of these texts from the Renaissance highlights the prevalence and diversity of the genre.[13] Marguerite's own *Comédies bibliques* (Biblical comedies, 1535–1546) illustrate both her familiarity with and her respect for these religious plays.[14] Along with the prominence of the saints in religious life and literature in early modern France, the theological disputes over their role in the Catholic Church heightened awareness of the communion of saints.

Saints were also one of many points of contention between Catholics and Protestants in the sixteenth century. Detractors of the cult of saints argued that the role of saints diminished the unique intercession of Christ as the one mediator between God and humanity, and that the cult was a form of idolatry. John Calvin addressed the topic in the *Institution de la religion chrestienne* (*Institutes of the Christian Religion*), which was published in 1536 in Latin (*Institutio christianae religionis*) and 1541 in French. He declared, "Et si on appelle en tesmoing la conscience de ceux, qui s'arrestent à l'intercession des Sainctz: on trouvera que cela ne vient d'autre chose, sinon qu'ilz sont en perplexité: comme si Christ leur defailloit, ou bien s'il estoit trop rigoreux. En laquelle doubte ilz font grand deshonneur à Christ: & le despouillent du tiltre du seul Mediateur" (If you call to witness the conscience of those who fix on the intercession of the saints, you will find that they do so only because they are in confusion, as if they were lacking Christ or indeed as if He were too strict. Caught in that doubt, they do great dishonor to Christ and strip Him of His title of sole Mediator).[15] In Calvin's 1543 *Traité des reliques* (*Treatise on relics*), he emphatically declares, "Pour dire en bref ce qui en est, la convoitise d'avoir des reliques n'est quasi jamais sans superstition, et, qui pis est, elle est mère d'idolatrie" (The desire for relics is never without superstition, and what is worse, it is usually the parent of idolatry).[16] Like Calvin, Martin Luther argued that these practices were a form of idolatry: "How will you endure [the Romanists'] terrible idolatries? It was not enough that they venerated the saints and praised God in them, but they actually made them into gods."[17]

Although reform-minded Catholics commonly voiced concern over certain excesses in the cult of saints, they also demonstrated a diversity of perspectives. In his 1503 *Enchiridion militis christiani,* or "The Handbook of the Christian Soldier," Dutch humanist and Catholic reformer Desiderius Erasmus warned against the external trappings of the cult, saying, "You venerate the saints, and you take pleasure in touching their relics. But you disregard their greatest legacy, the example of a blameless life."[18] However, he also recognized that a sincere devotion to the saints could ultimately glorify Christ: "If you take great delight in worshipping Christ in his saints, then make sure you imitate Christ in his saints and in honour of each saint eradicate one vice or strive to attain a particular virtue. If this is the fruit of your devotion, I shall not be averse to these external manifestations."[19] The French evangelical reformers also displayed a variety of positions on the topic.[20] Some viewed the saints as models to imitate, but they rejected the idea of them as intercessors. Other reformers denounced the falsehoods of certain legends about the saints, but nevertheless expressed a belief in their intercessory powers. For instance, François Demoulins de Rochefort invoked the intercession of numerous saints for the protection of the royal family in the *Petit livret faict à l'honneur de madame saincte Anne et de la royne, sa fille, vierge pure, mere de Jesus-Christ* (ca. 1501–1525), a text that he composed for Louise de Savoie.[21] Given Marguerite de Navarre's keen interest in religious matters and her ties with prominent thinkers from opposing theological perspectives, she would have been cognizant of the wide range of arguments surrounding the controversy over the saints.

The intertextual echoes between Voragine's *Golden Legend,* Christine's *Le livre de la Cité des dames,* and various texts associated with early modern debates over specific saints situate the *Heptaméron* in a long tradition of religious writing. In exploring this period of controversy between Catholics and Protestants over the cult of saints, this study will demonstrate that Marguerite's religious practices and written works illustrated her ongoing attachment to this aspect of Catholic devotion. Considering Marguerite's embrace of this facet of Catholicism and references to saints in her other works inevitably leads to compelling questions about her celebrated novella collection. Did the Catholic literary tradition of saints' lives influence Marguerite's frame narrative and her tales? Did the heroic virtue and unwavering faith recounted in female saints' lives serve as a model for Marguerite's stories? Did the queen of Navarre incorporate elements of hagiography into her tales to lend greater authority to her writing? Did Marguerite simply draw on hagiography or did she transform certain aspects of this genre? And if she diverged from hagiographic tradition, what do these departures tell us about her beliefs? The present volume will examine connections between saints' vitae and the *Heptaméron* to gain further insight into these questions and to illustrate their importance for a more comprehensive understanding of Marguerite's work as a whole.

Many of the novellas share compelling thematic parallels with hagiographic tradition, particularly in Marguerite's representations of rape (or attempted rape), her depiction of women's faith and heroic virtue in response to injustice and suffering, and her portrayal of her heroines as brides of Christ. The fact that these themes, which consistently appear in saints' lives, are incorporated throughout the *Heptaméron*, particularly in stories depicting exemplary women, merits examination. This study will demonstrate that Marguerite portrays several of her most celebrated heroines as saintly figures. By combining a close reading of her tales with an analysis of other literary works, theological texts, and visual images of the saints in connection with Renaissance religious and social disputes, this book will shed new light on numerous connections between hagiography and the *Heptaméron*. Reading Marguerite's novella collection together with hagiographic narratives and images of saints from her immediate family's devotional books will offer fresh perspectives on the *Heptaméron*'s sources, lead to a greater understanding of the queen of Navarre's position on controversies surrounding the saints, and clarify her stance on debates about women's role in the church and in society more generally. By contextualizing the *Heptaméron* this way, this volume will demonstrate how Marguerite borrowed from hagiography to establish greater authority in her writing, strengthen her defense of the female sex, and advocate for women in the Renaissance Catholic Church, the literary realm, and sixteenth-century French society more broadly.

Connections between Marguerite's literary works and Renaissance theology have long fascinated scholars, and recent publications demonstrate the continued interest in the topic. Carol Thysell's *The Pleasure of Discernment: Marguerite de Navarre as Theologian* (2000), Jacob Vance's *Secrets: Humanism, Mysticism, and Evangelism in Erasmus of Rotterdam, Bishop Guillaume Briçonnet, and Marguerite de Navarre* (2014), and Emily Butterworth's *Marguerite de Navarre: A Critical Companion* (2022) all illustrate the enduring scholarly enthusiasm for exploring theological elements in the queen of Navarre's writings.[22] Theresa Brock's *The Visionary Queen: Justice, Reform, and the Labyrinth in Marguerite de Navarre* (2024) explores links between Marguerite's reformist agenda and her work for greater social justice.[23] Elizabeth Chesney Zegura's *Marguerite de Navarre's Shifting Gaze: Perspectives on Gender, Class, and Politics in the Heptaméron* (2016) examines various religious elements in the *Heptaméron,* but only briefly alludes to saints.[24] Marie-Claire Thomine-Bichard and Véronique Montagne's *Marguerite de Navarre,* L'Heptaméron (2020) includes a section entitled "La place accordée à la Vierge et aux saints" (The place given to the Virgin and the saints); however, other than a passing reference to Saint Francis, it primarily focuses on the Virgin Mary.[25] Gary Ferguson has analyzed the role of saints in Marguerite's poetry in *Mirroring Belief: Marguerite de Navarre's Devotional Poetry* (1992).[26] His work illustrates the potential for exploring the presence of hagiographic elements in the queen of Navarre's prose.

While numerous scholars have briefly alluded to resonances of saints' vitae in the *Heptaméron,* in recent years there has been increasing critical interest in the subject. Katherine Kong has demonstrated the parallels between Saint Martha's legend and novella 13.[27] Elizabeth Archibald has explored the influence of the life of Saint Gregorius on the *Heptaméron*'s thirtieth tale.[28] Scott Francis has examined saints' lives in connection with tale 31, as well in an article on pilgrimage and the cult of saints in Marguerite's theater and prose.[29] I have myself published work on pilgrimage and the Prologue and on the second novella and Saint Sebastian's iconography.[30] François Rigolot and Gary Ferguson have both analyzed the thirty-second novella in relation to Saint Mary Magdalene's iconography.[31] Their articles point to the importance of contextualizing Marguerite's entire text in a period when and place where her readers were keenly aware of Catholic narrative tradition and representations of the saints in the visual arts. The present volume's analysis of the *Heptaméron* through the lens of saints' vitae will lead to a deeper understanding of the substantial influence of Catholic culture on Marguerite's text as well as a greater appreciation of her innovative response to sixteenth-century religious debates.

The first chapter argues that the focus on the *Heptaméron*'s connections to Boccaccio's *Decameron* and the scholarly emphasis on her connections to the evangelical reform have left the influence of saints' lives on Marguerite's text underexplored. Through an analysis of selected hagiographical writings, as well as an examination of Marguerite's devotional practices, her other texts, and the *Heptaméron*'s Prologue, this section contends that traditional Catholic saints' lives were integral sources that influenced both the content and structure of the *Heptaméron*. This chapter also contextualizes Marguerite's work in another body of literature that profoundly shaped her collection of tales—the texts involved in the *querelle des femmes,* or Debate about Women. This analysis of the *Heptaméron*'s intertextuality with both saints' vitae and the works in the *querelle des femmes* highlights various reasons why hagiography appealed to Marguerite, and also sets the stage for the close reading of tales in subsequent chapters.

The second chapter examines how Marguerite incorporated elements of pilgrimage and the interrelated concepts of feast days and hagiography into the journey of her *devisants* (storytellers or discussants). It also explores texts associated with the Renaissance controversy over Saint Anne's marriage(s) in relation to Louise de Savoie's widowhood and Marguerite's devotion to the Virgin Mary's mother. The chapter sheds light on Marguerite's views on the female saints and her perception of her mother's spirituality by establishing connections between hagiography's emphasis on Saint Anne as Mary's mother, spiritual teacher, and interpreter of sacred texts, and the *Heptaméron*'s representation of Oisille as a maternal figure and spiritual leader of the *devisants.* Through an analysis of references to saints, pilgrimages, and feast days, this chapter demonstrates how Marguerite integrates hagiography and pilgrimage narrative traditions in the Prologue to prepare readers for other elements of saints' vitae that are consistently integrated throughout her work.

The third chapter explores the physical sufferings of the women in tales 2, 10, and 22, alongside the pain depicted in hagiographical writings and visual images from early modern devotional books to illustrate how Marguerite represents her heroines as saint-like figures. The second tale recounts the tragic story of the mule-driver's wife, a virtuous woman who is brutally attacked with a sword, raped, and murdered. The nature and extent of her injuries and her prayerful response to violence recall Saint Sebastian's persecution. In the tenth tale, the heroine Floride mutilates her face in a chapel to avoid rape, much like Saint Eusebia did. The twenty-second tale recounts how a corrupt cleric brutalizes and humiliates a young nun when she resists his advances; she responds to her persecutions with courage, eloquence, and faith, like Saint Catherine and Saint Margaret. Marguerite draws on hagiography to engage more effectively in the *querelle des femmes* and to advocate for women in debates about their role in the Renaissance Catholic Church by juxtaposing male violence and clerical corruption with women's moral integrity and piety.

The fourth chapter explores how Marguerite incorporates hagiography into her depictions of women's confinement and isolation. The twenty-first and fortieth tales of the *Heptaméron* portray heroines who respond to imprisonment with prayer and exemplary faith in God. More specifically, Marguerite depicts her heroines as saint-like figures whose trials recall Saint Barbara's enclosure in a tower and physical persecution. The thirty-second tale also presents a confined woman; the portrayal of the adulteress and references to Saint Mary Magdalene as a sinful woman serve to contest the Renaissance church's stance on this saint and to question the traditional depictions of clerics and hagiographers. The sixty-seventh tale's marooning of a woman on an isolated Canadian island includes references to the "desert" and "lions," two common elements of Saint Mary of Egypt's iconography, thereby establishing parallels between Marguerite's heroine and this saint. The allusions to saints' vitae in these novellas highlight the injustices that women encountered in the patriarchal society of Renaissance France while they also call into question the gender bias in hagiography and in the Catholic Church.

The fifth chapter examines the life and legend of Saint Francis in connection with Marguerite's emphasis on the corrupt behavior of Franciscans. The nineteenth tale includes multiple references to the religious orders of Saint Francis and Saint Clare, and Marguerite also mentions Saint Mary Magdalene. Several other novellas highlight the clergy's misdeeds by repeatedly evoking the crimes of Franciscans in particular. While scholars have frequently explored clerical abuse in the tales, Marguerite's explicit references to Saint Francis in these stories are noteworthy. This chapter contends that Marguerite draws on Saint Francis's iconography to emphasize the moral divergence between the holy man from Assisi and the clerics, who demonstrate false sanctity. This section also demonstrates how Marguerite uses her knowledge of the saints and her familiarity with pilgrimage traditions in the communities of Blois and Autun to highlight clerical corruption and to avoid polarized depictions of the genders through her portrayal of ungodly clerics and unholy women in tales 60 and 61.

The concluding chapter begins with an analysis of the references to the Virgin Mary and Marguerite's depiction of herself doing a novena in the *Heptaméron*'s final tale. It then considers how Marguerite both borrows from and revises hagiography to formulate a powerful and creative response to the *querelle des femmes*, Renaissance theological debates, and specific controversies involving the cult of saints.[32] Through her revisionist hagiographies, she offers more inclusive models of female sanctity and questions the hierarchy of the sixteenth-century Catholic Church. Despite the countless tales highlighting violence, sexual assault, and gender-based injustices in the *Heptaméron*, this section underscores how Marguerite's text nonetheless offers hope to readers through its repeated insistence on God's faithfulness to women and its portrayal of the power of women sharing stories. This chapter also addresses the relevance of the *Heptaméron* at the present time by highlighting how Marguerite's extensive knowledge of theology and hagiography, and her bold literary response to sexual assault and misogynistic discourse, remain pertinent for today's readers who confront similar issues with widespread sexual abuse scandals still plaguing religious institutions and the continued prevalence of femicide, rape, and gender-based violence.

CHAPTER ONE

Beyond Boccaccio

Saints' Vitae and the *Heptaméron*

Tous anges, sainctz et sainctes bienheureux,
Le sainct esprit de Jesus en eulx crie.

[All angels and blessed saints,
The holy spirit of Jesus cries out in them.]

—Marguerite de Navarre, *Dialogue en forme de vision nocturne*

Marguerite de Navarre was actively engaged in a wide array of theological matters throughout her life. She served as the chief liaison between the French court and the pope, she consistently worked to reform certain aspects of the Catholic Church, and she offered financial support to various religious orders. She worked tirelessly to improve conditions in monastic institutions, and she personally withdrew to convents for solace during times of difficulty.[1] She was an avid reader of religious texts, and her knowledge of theological matters was remarkable, especially for a woman in Renaissance France. In fact, Matteo Dandolo, an Italian ambassador at the French court, suggested that Marguerite was more capable of discussing Christian doctrine than most men: "Questa credo sia la più savia, non dico delle donne de Francia, ma forse anco degli uomini . . . e nella dottrina cristiana è persona e cosi bene intelligente e dotta, che io credo che pochi ne sappiano parlar meglio" (I believe she is the most learned, I do not say only among the women of France, but perhaps even among the men. . . . As for Christian doctrine, she demonstrates so much intelligence and knowledge that I believe that few people know how to speak about it better).[2] Given the many constraints on women in this realm in sixteenth-century Europe, it is hardly surprising that her religious activities and writings were not always viewed favorably.

In 1533, Marguerite's *Miroir de l'âme pécheresse* (*Mirror of the sinful soul*) was threatened with censure by the theologians at the Sorbonne. She avoided more serious repercussions uniquely because her brother, King Francis I, intervened on her behalf. The queen of Navarre remained a practicing Catholic throughout her life. She consistently attended Mass and demonstrated an enduring attachment to saints and pilgrimage, but she also actively worked for substantial reforms within the Catholic Church. Consequently, scholars have espoused divergent views of her religious beliefs. For Pierre Jourda, Marguerite's desire for reform may have been motivated by her love for the Catholic Church.[3] Abel Lefranc goes so far as to claim that Marguerite was a "protestante à sa manière" (Protestant in her own way).[4] Lucien Febvre concludes that she fashioned her own personal religion.[5] More recently, Jean-Marie Le Gall has persuasively demonstrated Marguerite's enduring adherence to her Catholic faith.[6] Jonathan Reid has argued that Marguerite played a leading role in a network of *évangéliques* (evangelical reformers).[7] These reform-minded Catholics were nonschismatic; they longed to implement important changes, but not to break with the Roman Church.[8] Nicolas Russell aptly describes Marguerite's position, saying, "Marguerite never left the Catholic faith but she was nonetheless a supporter of many reformers. Her own stances on theological questions did not fit neatly into any one camp in the religious disputes of the early sixteenth century but rather drew on and responded to a range of different currents in these debates."[9] As a result of Marguerite's engagement in religious matters, both schismatic reformers and orthodox Catholics harshly criticized her, but they also sought to benefit from her influence and position.[10]

Within Marguerite's own family, her religious activities provoked ire and tension as well. Her husband, Henri d'Albret, proved himself to be highly intolerant of her engagement in theological affairs. In a 1555 letter to the Vicomte de Gourdon, Marguerite's daughter, Jeanne d'Albret, recounts a troubling memory from her youth. She describes an evening when her mother was with Gérard Roussel and Guillaume Farel, two prominent evangelical reformers. Her father stormed into the room, proceeded to slap Marguerite in the face, and warned her not to concern herself with matters of doctrine.[11] King Francis also expressed his resistance to Marguerite's engagement in theology. In the same letter, Jeanne wrote that King Francis I confronted his sister and insisted that she not "mettre en cervelle dogmes nouveaux" (get new doctrines in her head).[12] Jeanne's letter also refers to her mother's hesitation between two religions, an intriguing observation in that it demonstrates Marguerite's commitment to reformist ideas as well as her respect for Catholicism.[13] Jeanne explains that following her mother's contentious encounters with her husband and the king, Marguerite limited herself to writing *romans jovials* (amusing stories).[14] Although societal and familial pressures may have forced Marguerite to avoid traditional theological genres, Carol Thysell has demonstrated that she nonetheless persisted in addressing important religious issues in her literary works.[15] Adopting a seemingly less controversial form of expression like novellas did not prevent Marguerite from writing about religion and tackling controversial theological matters. In fact, she creatively adapted the genre to serve her purposes. A closer examination of the novella tradition and how Marguerite diverges from it, particularly with her representation of religion, women, and societal debates, is revealing in this regard.

Medieval and early modern novella collections were typically designed to amuse and divert the reader; their subject matter was rarely serious. Moreover, the genre was associated with a long tradition of misogyny, as the humor was frequently at the expense of women. The Prologue's allusions to Giovanni Boccaccio's *Decameron* have led scholars to focus extensively on comparisons between his work and the *Heptaméron*; Marguerite's reference to Boccaccio has received significant critical attention.[16] While Marguerite explicitly acknowledges the *Decameron* as a model, she also distances her work from her Italian predecessor by insisting on the truth of her tales. Moreover, the *Heptaméron* diverges from Boccaccio's text in several other important respects. Along with the gender parity of the storytellers, one of the most striking differences is the consistent focus on religion throughout the tales and the frame narrative.[17]

The storytellers temporarily reside in an abbey. Thus, apart from their time spinning tales in the meadow, they take refuge in a quintessential Catholic environment. While Marguerite clearly diverges from the norms of the Roman Church in that Oisille, a female lay person, offers lessons on Scripture each morning, her *devisants* do hold fast to Catholicism's traditional devotional practices by attending Mass and participating in the Eucharist daily.[18] Moreover, Marguerite repeatedly insists on their sincere devotion to the Catholic Mass. She writes, "le matin ouyrent la messe bien devotement" (1.6; in the morning they devoutly heard Mass); "quand ils eurent ouy une bonne heure sa leçon, et puis devotement la messe" (1.17; when they had heard her reading from the

Scriptures for a good hour and had devoutly heard Mass); "ils ouyrent la messe devotement" (2.434; they devoutly heard Mass); and "on commençoit la messe du Sainct Esprit, qui leur sembloit chose venir à leur propos, qui leur feit ouyr le service en grande devotion" (2.681; the Mass of the Holy Spirit was beginning, which seemed appropriate given their discussion and led them to listen to the service with great devotion).[19] Jourda and Betty J. Davis both contend that the *devisants* find an equilibrium between Catholic traditions and reformist principles.[20] In light of the work's setting at Notre-Dame de Serrance and the favorable representation of some, albeit not all, elements of Catholic devotion in the frame narrative, an investigation of the *Heptaméron*'s association with hagiographic tradition and the cult of the saints is useful.

An examination of Marguerite's participation in devotional practices sheds some light on her personal beliefs concerning the communion of saints. A traditional devotion to the saints was something that she consistently encountered within her own family. Numerous saints are featured in Charles d'Angoulême's book of hours, Queen Claude's prayer book, the Hours of Francis I, and Louise de Savoie's book of hours.[21] More importantly, the saints also figure prominently in the orthodox book of hours that Marguerite de Navarre requested around 1520.[22] Marguerite's mother, Louise de Savoie, was especially pious and she was particularly attached to the cult of saints. In fact, she was known to give relics to her children and to ask for intercession from various saints.[23] In response to Renaissance controversy over the cult of saints and following family pilgrimages to Apt and Sainte-Baume, Louise requested new narratives of the lives of Saint Mary Magdalene and Saint Anne.[24] As was customary for the kings of France, Francis I also undertook a well-publicized pilgrimage to Saint-Marcoul to venerate the saint's relics.[25] It was believed that this endowed the king with the power to heal scrofula, also known as the "king's evil," a tuberculosis infection that affected the lymph nodes in the neck.[26] With the intention of praying for a male heir, Francis made a pilgrimage to the shrine of Saint Martin at Tours.[27] In addition to his pilgrimages, the king regularly presented his sister with statuettes of the saints as gifts.[28]

Marguerite was known to be particularly devoted to her own patron saint, Saint Margaret, as well as to Saint Francis and Saint Anne. In her book of hours, the *Heures de Marguerite de Valois, sœur de François Ier,* Marguerite is prominently pictured in images featuring Saints Joachim, Anne, Jerome, and Martin.[29] Along with the typical suffrages to the saints, the manuscript also includes a lengthy Mass to Saint Martin. Not only did Marguerite possess several manuscripts and objects associated with the cult of saints, but her attachment to these devotional articles was such that she regularly carried them with her, even when she traveled. She also provided financial support to churches for the purchase of reliquaries.[30] Thus, even though Marguerite harbored persecuted reformers and cultivated close relationships to prominent *évangéliques* such as Guillaume Briçonnet and Jacques Lefèvre d'Étaples, she did not abandon the traditional Catholic devotional rituals that had marked her childhood. While she certainly did not approve of the excesses or abuses that were sometimes associated with the cult of saints, her request for a traditional book of hours, her regular participation in pilgrimages, and her fondness for Catholic devotional objects suggest that she held an enduring and sincere attachment to the communion of the saints. Despite this devotion to saints, the influence of hagiography on her writings has been underexplored. Scott Francis argues that the influence of saints' lives on Marguerite's work has been ignored "due to a long-standing historiographic tradition that has seen Marguerite as essentially crypto-Protestant."[31] Analyzing the connections between hagiography and Marguerite's texts reveals fresh perspectives on her religious thought and her novella collection.

Marguerite frequently represents a more traditional devotion to the saints in her writings. In her 1547–1548 *Chansons spirituelles* (Spiritual songs), she refers to "tous les saintz parfaitz" (all the perfect saints) and in the *Petit Œuvre dévot* (Brief devout work), a text that she wrote prior to 1528, she refers to the devotion and merits of several saints.[32] In a poem she composed about the period when her brother was on the brink of death, Marguerite unequivocally manifests her belief in the intercession of the saints, saying, "J'appelle chacun Saint et Sainte / Pour se joindre à mon oraison" (I call on each saint / To join in my prayer).[33] Likewise, in her 1524 *Dialogue en forme de vision nocturne* (Dialogue in the form of a nocturnal vision), she evokes the intercession of the saints when she refers to "tous ses saints, priantz tousjours pour nous" (all his saints, always praying for us).[34] Although there are numerous positive references to saints incorporated throughout Marguerite's writings, scholars have certainly not reached any consensus regarding her position on the issue.

Scholarly opinions on Marguerite's beliefs about the cult of saints prove to be as diverse as the opinions of her storytellers in the *Heptaméron*. Certain critics claim that she never took a clear stance in the debate, some argue that she rejected this Catholic tradition in various ways, and still other scholars highlight her profound attachment to devotional practices involving the communion of saints. For instance, Abel Lefranc repeatedly insists on Marguerite's rejection of the cult of saints.[35] He dismisses the importance of several favorable references to the saints in her poetry.[36] In his 1960 edition of Marguerite's *Théâtre profane,* Verdun Saulnier presents a more divided view on the subject. He initially recognizes Marguerite's attachment to traditional devotions.[37] Yet Saulnier also suggests that her position on the saints was somewhat ambiguous.[38] Jourda offers a more nuanced and somewhat less contradictory stance when he argues that Marguerite preferred to implore Christ directly, but that this did not prevent her from asking for intercession from the Virgin Mary and the saints.[39] Following an examination of the representation of saints in Marguerite's devotional poetry, Gary Ferguson concludes, "Marguerite seems to have followed in her own devotional life the ideas she outlines in the *Dialogue* and elsewhere: the saints are to be honoured, but never without reference to the Lord they served and with whom they are united."[40] In the introduction to his study of Marguerite's poetry, Georges Dottin comes to a similar conclusion when he notes that for Marguerite, the goodness of the saints comes directly from God.[41] While these scholars have examined Marguerite's religious practices and explored the representation of saints in her poetry and theatre, the present volume seeks to illustrate the importance of the multiple references to hagiography that are consistently woven throughout the pages of the *Heptaméron.*

Just as Marguerite found inspiration in medieval mystery plays when she composed her *Comédies bibliques,* traces of this genre are also reflected in the pages of the *Heptaméron.* Like Marguerite's collection of tales, medieval miracle plays also had a prologue, they were divided into performances over different days, and they typically incorporated an eclectic mix of comic, tragic, and violent scenes. Just as these plays were performed outside of the confines of the church in public squares or other outdoor settings in the later medieval period, the *devisants* also leave the walls of the monastery daily and their storytelling venture takes place in a verdant meadow. Akin to the medieval mystery plays that often had a church as a backdrop, the abbey serves as the background for the storytelling. Moreover, like the hagiographic works that sought to inspire devotion and edify the spectators, Marguerite underscores the spiritual nature of the storytelling enterprise early in the text. Much like the writers of saints' vitae who frequently began their works by emphasizing the authenticity of their stories, Marguerite also insists on the "truth" of her tales in the *Heptaméron*'s

Prologue as well as intermittently throughout the text.[42] Marguerite's emphasis on the veracity of her stories as well as other dramatic characteristics of the text point to the influence of hagiographic narratives on her novella collection.

The *Heptaméron*'s frame story is characterized by theatrical aspects that are reminiscent of medieval miracle plays on several levels. Marguerite clarifies that her *devisants* rehearse their stories before they present them to the group. Before recounting their stories, the storytellers tend to "estudier leur roole" (2.435; go over the story they were going to tell) and "visiter leurs registres" (2.297; review their story). The theatrical lexicon in these references underscores the dramatic character of the frame story. Nancy Frelick contends that the frame narrative's conversations are theatrical in nature.[43] Moreover, similar to common practices of hagiographers, the storytellers are depicted as asking for divine help to make their tales pleasing to their audience. Marguerite writes, "chacun recommanda son esprit à Dieu, à fin qu'il leur donnast parolle et grace de continuer l'assemblée" (1.155; they all commended their souls to God so that he would give them the words and grace necessary to sustain their congregation). Each storyteller also "se recommanda au Sainct Esprit, pour satisfaire ce jour là à leur plaisante audience" (2.606; commended themselves to the Holy Spirit in hopes that on that day they would satisfy the members of their amiable group). Aside from the performative nature of the storytelling for the *devisants* among themselves, it is important to remember that they also have another group of spectators. After the second day, the storytellers have a captive audience of monks, or canons regular, who eagerly listen to their tales from behind a hedge: "Parquoy voyant leur bonne volonté, leur fut permis que tous les jours ils assisteroient derriere la haye, assis à leur aise" (1.295; And given their good disposition, they were allowed to listen to the stories everyday sitting comfortably behind the hedge). Various references in the text underscore the enthusiasm of these spectators by noting that the monks are eager to take their places to listen to the stories, while at other times they become so engaged in hearing the tales that they neglect their monastic duties. These examples are not the only elements of the text that recall characteristics of theater; Marguerite's lexical choices also serve to recall this genre.

In this respect, Marguerite's use of the word *jeu* in the *Heptaméron*'s Prologue to refer to the storytelling enterprise merits examination. The term can certainly refer to a ludic activity like spinning tales, but for the Renaissance reader the word *jeu* would have also inevitably recalled a genre that Marguerite knew well, namely the popular mystery and miracle plays that were consistently performed in medieval and sixteenth-century France. Elizabeth Chesney Zegura notes, "the term 'jeu' that she uses to describe her storytelling is itself ambiguous, after all: it refers not only to a 'game,' which, despite its frivolous connotations, figures as an education device in Renaissance pedagogical treatises, but also to a medieval theatrical genre—*Le jeu d'Adam*, for example—that was often didactic and religious in nature."[44] Along with the thematic, dramatic, and lexical commonalities, other elements of hagiography that are incorporated throughout Marguerite's collection of tales also merit more extensive exploration.

The storytellers explicitly refer to Saints Paul, Luke, Peter, Lawrence, John, Benedict, Jerome, Anthony, and Mary Magdalene, among others. Moreover, at times, Marguerite and her *devisants* evoke the legends and attributes of the saints in a detailed manner. In the discussion of the thirtieth tale, Saffredent refers to Saint Jerome's temptations, saying, "Le bon sainct Hierosme, après s'estre fouëtté, et caché dans les deserts, confessa ne pouvoir eviter le feu qui brusloit dedans ses mouëlles" (2.432; The good Saint Jerome, who had flagellated himself and hidden in the wilderness, confessed that he could not escape the fire that burned in the marrow of his bones). In the sixty-first tale, Marguerite mentions "les chaisnes de Sainct Pierre" (2.690; the chains of Saint Peter). Geburon subtly alludes to Saint Lawrence's death by flame in the discussion of the sixty-third tale: "Il me semble, dist Guebron, que le diable, dont il estoit martyré, en devoit faire un sainct Laurens : car il y en a peu, de qui le feu d'amour soit si grand, qu'il ne craigne celuy de la moindre bougie" (2.702; "It seems to me that the devil, who was treating him like a martyr, should have turned him into another Saint Lawrence," said Geburon, "since there aren't many whose burning love is so great that they don't fear the flames of the smallest candle"). These examples illustrate how references to the saints, their iconography, and their attributes are interspersed throughout Marguerite's text. The next section explores various religious, literary, and rhetorical reasons that may have compelled Marguerite to draw on hagiographical sources.

Saints' Lives and the *Heptaméron*: Why Hagiography?

The arguments about the influence of pilgrimage narrative and saints' lives on the *Heptaméron* lead readers to ask a simple question: Why hagiography? Louise de Savoie's fervent Catholic piety and devotion to the saints were modeled to her children throughout their childhood; this strong family tradition undoubtedly left its mark. As an adult, Marguerite continued to engage regularly in the Catholic rituals and devotional practices that had marked her youth.[45] Marguerite's personal attachment to pilgrimage and the cult of saints unquestionably fueled her desire to incorporate Catholic devotional practices into her text, but there were also numerous other literary, theological, and sociopolitical reasons that impelled her to draw on these rich narratives. As Marguerite composed her collection of tales and dialogues, hagiography offered her countless unique benefits.

Marguerite chose to write *nouvelles*; the fact that the genre was often comical and traditionally misogynistic makes it an intriguing choice for a sixteenth-century woman writer with keen interests in theology, morality, and women's status in society.[46] Although the novella form was clearly in vogue in the first half of the sixteenth century, and the enthusiasm of Marguerite's contemporaries for this genre certainly influenced her decision, her choice is nonetheless surprising. Like Boccaccio, Marguerite's predecessors published comical novellas. While there is an abundance of amusing tales interspersed throughout the collection, the *Heptaméron* also includes a multiplicity of troubling anecdotes and contentious conversations that serve to emphasize the injustices, violence, and inequalities that women regularly experienced in the highly patriarchal society of Renaissance France. Drawing on the positive depictions of women's strength and virtue in hagiography allowed Marguerite to adapt novellas and challenge the form's tradition of disparaging women, but it also gave her an authoritative means to impel readers to reflect on women's social realities in sixteenth-century France and to question the existing representations of the female sex in the literary canon and in different Renaissance debates.

Another defining characteristic of *nouvelles* is their brevity; with a few exceptions, the stories are generally concise and thereby demand an economy of words. Marguerite's choice to compose brief narratives may relate to the *querelle des femmes*, where women were often vilified for their garrulous nature and criticized for being overly loquacious.[47] To compose succinct narratives as a female writer was an effective means to disprove unflattering generalizations about woman's so-called natural tendency to verbosity. The necessity for brevity may have been an important factor that led Marguerite to use hagiography as a source. She could depend on her readers' familiarity with the vitae and iconographies of the saints. Hagiography offered her a model for didactic short stories, but also an incomparably rich source. By alluding to the attributes and legends of the saints in her tales, she was able to use limited words to draw effectively on the widespread knowledge of hagiographic legends that her Renaissance readers undoubtedly possessed. Through these brief references, she could compel readers to establish connections between her tales and the lives of the saints. By weaving into her work a few carefully selected words, succinct references to a saint's attributes, or allusions to pilgrimage sites, Marguerite could direct her readers' thoughts to countless theological references and myriad stories. Hagiography was so omnipresent in sixteenth-century culture that it offered Marguerite an almost inexhaustible resource to address concisely the topics that mattered most to her, such as faith, gender-based violence, and women's status in society.[48]

Along with allowing her to incorporate brief, albeit powerful references into her text, the sheer number of saints' vitae may have been another important factor that drew the queen of Navarre to the genre. The encyclopedic *Golden Legend* recounts the lives of hundreds of saints. Christine de Pizan incorporates additional female saints who were absent from Voragine's work into *Le livre de la Cité des dames*. In addition, as we see in references throughout Marguerite's writings, she was also familiar with several regional saints. Given her extensive travels for political engagements, family pilgrimages, and her personal penchant for withdrawing to convents and initiating religious reforms, Marguerite possessed detailed knowledge about the local saints venerated in small villages and religious institutions throughout sixteenth-century France. She could take advantage of her familiarity with regional saints as well as her knowledge of hagiographic literature and use this wealth of material to pique the interest of diverse readers and heighten the appeal and didacticism of her own stories.

In addition to engaging with regional legends, hagiographical sources also offered Marguerite a means to respond to different debates in Renaissance France. While many texts in the *querelle des femmes* disparage women and justify their preclusion from positions of religious authority, hagiography features exemplary models of women who preached (Saint Mary Magdalene), read and taught sacred text (Saint Anne), had the gift of prophecy (Saint Anna the Prophetess), and surpassed learned men in theological debates (Saint Catherine of Alexandria). As we will see, Marguerite's allusions to these saints in her frame narrative and stories reinforce her response to controversy over the laity having access to the Bible, disputes about confession, and conflict over the limitations on women's roles in the Renaissance church. Marguerite draws on and adapts hagiographic sources to intervene on behalf of women in various sixteenth-century controversies. The genre also furnished her with important resources to strengthen her response to debates over gender equality.

From early in the text with Hircan's declaration "au jeu nous sommes tous esgaulx" (1.18; in games we are all equal), readers are acutely aware of Marguerite's commitment to greater equality in her frame narrative. Although Hircan's words are intended for Simontault, a man of lower social rank within the group, Marguerite's text offers a model of equality to her readers with the equal number of male and female discussants and the rules that demand gender parity in the spinning of the tales. The frame narrative's reference to all of the *devisants* having read the Bible offers a similar model of gender parity. The queen of Navarre's desire to offer her readers a model of increased gender equality provides yet another explanation for Marguerite's use of hagiographical source materials. While the sixteenth-century Catholic hierarchy precluded women from preaching and other authoritative positions, hagiographic tradition offered a greater, albeit far from perfect, gender equality than the existing structures of the Renaissance Church. At a time when many clerics and myriad texts in the *querelle des femmes* argued for women's spiritual inferiority, saints' lives provided powerful models of women's exemplary spirituality, undaunted courage, and unwavering faith in God.

Numerous tales of the *Heptaméron* illustrate that the widespread controversy about women's place in the church, conflicts about the cult of saints, and debates over devotional practices like pilgrimage and confession were of utmost concern to Marguerite. Although Michel de Montaigne might have praised certain aspects of the *Heptaméron,* on issues involving women and religion, his opinion was certainly not nuanced. He refers specifically to Marguerite's work as proof that "les femmes ne sont guère propres à traiter les matières de la Théologie" (women are hardly suited to dealing with matters of theology).[49] Much like Montaigne, Pierre de Ronsard declared, "Je suis plain de despit, quand les femmes fragilles / Interpretent en vain le sens des Evangilles" (I am full of despair, when fragile women / Interpret in vain the meaning of the Gospels).[50] Faced with such unfettered resistance to women's involvement in theology and biblical exegesis, Marguerite needed authoritative sources to bolster her authority as a woman writer. The necessity to shore up her authority offers yet another reason that explains why she drew on hagiography. The many clerics who wrote works disparaging women as well as the readers of the texts associated with the *querelle des femmes* could not ignore the fact that the rich narrative tradition of female saints' lives contradicted their multitude of unfavorable arguments about women's nature. Hagiographic narratives strengthened Marguerite's literary response to denigrating remarks about the female sex; they also offered her an abundance of persuasive materials to incorporate into her responses to the most contentious debates of Renaissance France. Allusions to the saints allowed Marguerite to direct her readership to reflect on issues such as religion, women's role in the church, and marriage. Consequently, she included hagiographical references in her stories as well as in the lively discussions that follow each tale.

The elaborate frame with its extensive dialogues is another unique aspect of Marguerite's work as compared to other early modern novella collections. As Nancy Frelick has shown, it is the polyphonic nature of these discussions following the tales that allows Marguerite to present her readers with myriad conflicting opinions on women that were present in Renaissance society.[51] The very issues at the core of sixteenth-century conflicts over religion, women, and sanctity are frequently incorporated into the discussions of the *devisants* and their conflicting interpretations of the stories. Hagiographic references are woven throughout the tales, but they also regularly appear in the arguments of the storytellers. These expansive discussions where the storytellers voice their contradictory opinions incite readers to question the commonplace misogynistic discourses of the *querelle des femmes* as well as received ideas from traditional hagiographies and the literary canon.

Along with narratives that extolled faith and virtue in both genders, common topoi of hagiography such as sufferings and death may have also motivated Marguerite to draw on these narratives. Physical sufferings are an omnipresent theme in saints' lives; these torments take on a deeply spiritual value when they are identified with the passion of Christ. Hagiographic narratives typically present the tribulations of the saints as imitations of Christ's ultimate sacrifice. Related to this topos of suffering, death is also a ubiquitous theme in saints' lives as the legends feature detailed accounts of cruel tortures and graphic martyrdoms. It is not surprising that suffering and death are also frequent themes in sixteenth-century literature given that France was perpetually at war, the plague continued to spread throughout Europe, and maternal and infant mortality rates soared. Marguerite had multiple personal experiences with loss in her own life. Her father died during her childhood, then she had to confront the deaths of her first husband, her infant son, and her young niece. Later, she mourned her beloved brother and mother. In fact, she sought solace from mourning both in her faith and in her writing. Not only does Marguerite make multiple references to death in her devotional poetry, but she also composed *Le Dialogue en forme de vision nocturne* after her niece's death, as well as *La Navire* after losing her brother. Given the queen of Navarre's own experiences with suffering and loss, it is not surprising that several novellas in the *Heptaméron* involve these very themes. The precarity of life in Renaissance France may have been yet another factor that led Marguerite to use saints' vitae as a literary source. The patience that the saints manifested amid sufferings and their exemplary, and even joyous, deaths could be easily adapted to a sixteenth-century context and ultimately serve as a model of faith as well as a source of comfort and strength for Marguerite and her readers.

The next chapter's examination of saints, feast days, and pilgrimage in the *Heptaméron*'s Prologue is particularly revealing in that one can see how the introductory section of Marguerite's text prepares readers to be mindful of the multiple allusions to hagiography and pilgrimage that one finds throughout her collection of tales.

CHAPTER TWO

The Prologue, Pilgrimage, and Prophetesses in the *Heptaméron*

> Le temps de pelerinage cest le temps de ceste
> presente vie, auquel nous pelerinons et y sommes
> tousjours en batailles.
>
> [The time of pilgrimage is that of our present life,
> For we are on pilgrimage and constantly engaged in warfare.]
>
> —Jacques de Voragine, *La légende dorée*

The *Heptaméron* is a collection of seventy-two novellas within a frame story, but it is also a travel text in many respects.[1] Marguerite de Navarre's contemporary Pierre de Bourdeille, seigneur de Brantôme, noted that the queen of Navarre composed her tales as she traveled throughout France in her litter.[2] Not surprisingly, Marguerite's novella collection includes stories from diverse regions in France. Corinne Wilson has demonstrated that the geographical locations referenced in the tales more or less represent the circumference of the French borders in the sixteenth century.[3] However, Marguerite's tales extend well beyond French lands. Certain tales take place in Italy, the thirteenth novella involves preparations for a pilgrimage to the Holy Land, and the collection ends with the story of a nun who begins a pilgrimage to Rome. Floride's and Amadour's turbulent story is set in Spain. The haunting circumstances of tale 32 take place in a German castle. The sixty-seventh tale is the first literary text situated in Canada. While travel and distant lands play a role throughout the *Heptaméron*, this chapter examines how Marguerite incorporates elements of pilgrimage and the interrelated concepts of feast days and hagiography into the journey of her *devisants*. It also demonstrates how the interconnected nature of these references and the portrayal of Oisille in the *Heptaméron*'s Prologue prepare readers for the pilgrimage narrative traditions and hagiographic references that are present throughout the work.

Pilgrimage and the Prologue

Throughout her life, Marguerite participated in several pilgrimages, both publicly and privately. She made numerous journeys to sites devoted to the Virgin Mary such as Notre-Dame des Fontaines, Notre-Dame de Cléry, and Notre-Dame de la Garde with specific intentions in mind.[4] Marguerite and her family traveled to the South of France and saw the relics of Saint Mary Magdalene at Saint-Maximim-la-Sainte-Baume. They subsequently offered financial support for the restoration of this holy site.[5] On that same trip, they visited the relics of Saint Martha, the Marys of the Sea, and Saint Anthony. They also made pilgrimages to La Roche de la Balme in Dauphiné and Saint-Suaire in Chambéry.[6] In light of Marguerite's consistent participation in pilgrimages, it is important to recognize that this devotional practice was a matter of controversy between Catholics and Protestants in sixteenth-century France.[7] Theresa Brock remarks, "Marguerite was aware of Protestant ideology and was even in contact with some of its key disseminators, yet she chose not to renounce pilgrimage as a practice."[8] Marguerite's pilgrimages are not insignificant, for they demonstrate that the queen of Navarre maintained a strong attachment to Catholic rituals and devotional sites throughout the polemics. Furthermore, she also portrays the characters in the *Heptaméron* who participate in pilgrimages in a favorable light. In the tenth tale Marguerite writes, "Je laisseray à dire les *voyages*, prieres, oraisons, et jeusnes que faisoit ordinairement Florinde pour le salut de Amadour" (1.127, emphasis added; I won't speak of the pilgrimages, prayers, invocations, and fasts that Floride regularly engaged in to bring about Amadour's salvation). In tale 21, Rolandine "ne cessoit de prier Dieu, et d'aller en *voyages*, et faire abstinences" (2.302, emphasis added; continually prayed to God, went on pilgrimages, . . . , and observed abstinence). An analysis of references to pilgrimage in the *Heptaméron* in light of early modern pilgrimage practices provides unique insights into this facet of Marguerite's work.

Ruth Barnes notes that pilgrimage was frequently undertaken to "bring well-being to the sick."[9] Throughout the sixteenth century, countless pilgrims embarked on a quest for physical healing by means of a pilgrim's journey. Significantly, Marguerite emphasizes her characters' poor health as she introduces them to the reader, describing them as "malades" (1.1; sick). The text clarifies that the group had gone to the spa town of Cauterets for healing waters and muds. Judy Kem notes, "The devisants have all traveled to the waters of Cauterets to cure various maladies. Before their arrival there, many, we are told, had been 'abandoned by doctors' but are on the point of returning home completely healed."[10] Once their bodily ailments have been cured, God intervenes by bringing torrential rains and flooding. The extreme weather forces the group to flee and make an arduous trek through the Pyrenees. While the storytellers do not intentionally partake in a spiritual journey, they nevertheless set out on what can be interpreted as an involuntary pilgrimage. In her work on medieval pilgrimage, Diana Webb refers to "involuntary pilgrimage" as an identifiable category; these pilgrimages were typically associated with penance or purification.[11] In her insightful analysis of the *Heptaméron*'s Prologue and pilgrimage, Brock refers to the discussants as "accidental pilgrims,"[12] though the expression "involuntary pilgrims" may be more fitting given that Marguerite presents the events of the Prologue not as accidental but rather as carefully orchestrated by God.

Along with the aforementioned elements of pilgrimage in the text, references to specific feast days of the church also point to the Prologue's connection to this devotional practice. The first sentence of the Prologue begins with a reference to a specific date, the first of September: "Le premier jour de septembre, que les baings des monts Pyrenées commencent d'entrer en vertu, se trouverent à ceux de Caulderets, plusieurs personnes tant de France, Espaigne, que d'autres lieux : les uns pour boire de l'eau, les autres pour s'y baigner, et les autres pour prendre de la fange: qui sont choses si merveilleuses, que les malades abandonnez des medecins, s'en retournent tous gueriz" (1.1; On the first day of September, when the springs of the Pyrenees Mountains start to approach the peak of their powers, there were several people from France and Spain in Cauterets, some there to drink the waters, others to bathe, and still others for the mud baths, which are so marvelous that the sick on whom doctors have given up return completely cured). While early September coincides with the rainy season in the Pyrenees, the importance of this date may also relate to the liturgical calendar.

The first sentence in the work refers to a date, and in certain manuscripts it includes a reference to the "miraculous."[13] While it is not the case for modern readers, a Renaissance reader confronted with a date and a reference to miracles would have made a connection to the feast days of the church. While September 1 was widely known as the feast of Saint Giles, according to a 1515 manuscript of Usuard's Martyrology, it is also the feast day of Saint Anna the Prophetess.[14] Molanus's 1568 edition also mentions her on this date, referring to "Annae prophetessae, cuius sanctitatem evagelicus fermo prodit" (Anna, prophetess, whose sanctity the holy Gospel relates).[15] Saint Anna the Prophetess is presented in the New Testament in the Gospel of Luke. The second chapter of Luke's Gospel clarifies that she was of advanced age, and after spending most of her life as a widow, at the age of eighty-four she chose to serve God both day and night by never leaving the temple. She is designated as a prophetess, a term that underscores both her spiritual and her rhetorical gifts.

This reference to the feast day of Saint Anna the Prophetess in the first paragraph of the work foreshadows the introduction of Oisille, the *Heptaméron*'s most prominent storyteller. In the second paragraph of the text, Marguerite introduces Oisille, an elderly widow with much experience of life. Like Saint Anna the Prophetess, she is presented to readers with emphasis on her age, her status as a widow, and her religious fervor. When Oisille makes her way to Notre-Dame de Serrance, Marguerite emphasizes her strong determination throughout the arduous journey (1.3). However, Marguerite also notes that Oisille was not "si supersticieuse qu'elle pensast que la glorieuse Vierge laissat la dextre de son filz où elle est assize pour venir demourer en terre deserte" (1.2–3; so superstitious as to believe that the glorious Virgin had left her son's right hand, where she sits, to go dwell in such a desolate place). Although this can be interpreted as Marguerite's personal skepticism vis-à-vis traditional Catholic beliefs, it is more accurate to say that Oisille questions a single facet of Marian devotion. The reference serves to cast doubt on the actual presence of the Virgin Mary at the pilgrimage site, but it does not dismiss the practice of Marian devotion. Moreover, despite the morally questionable abbot, Oisille nonetheless classifies the monastery as a holy place, a "devot lieu" (1.3). She also describes the Virgin as "glorieuse" (1.2; glorious). In addition, Ferguson and McKinley remark, "There is no questioning of the belief that the Virgin Mary is in heaven, seated at her Son's right hand, no questioning that is, of the Catholic doctrine of the assumption."[16]

Later in the Prologue, Oisille is unanimously chosen among all the storytellers to give a biblical lesson each day; this is noteworthy, given that Marguerite characterizes the group on more than one occasion as having "diverses opinions" (1.2; disagreements). Moreover, in the daily prologues, Marguerite consistently portrays Oisille's teachings in a highly positive light (2.297, 2.434, 2.517, 2.681, 2.768). Thus, similar to the Gospel's emphasis on the divinely inspired words of Saint Anna the Prophetess, Marguerite repeatedly underscores Oisille's oratory and spiritual gifts. Interestingly, the indirect reference to the feast day of Saint Anna the Prophetess is not alone. In fact, the only other date that is explicitly evoked in the Prologue is a feast day of the Church.

Marguerite writes, "arriva un vieil moyne, qui toutes les années ne failloit point à la Nostre Dame de Septembre d'aller à Serrance : et, en luy demandant des nouvelles de son voyage, dit qu'à cause des grandes eaux, estoit venu par les montaignes, et par les plus mauvais chemins qu'il avoit jamais faicts" (1.7; an old monk—who never failed to go to Sarrance every year in September for the Nativity of the Blessed Virgin Mary—arrived at the abbey. They asked him about his trip, and he said that he had come through the mountains because of the flooding and had never taken trails in worse condition). This monk has typically been overlooked and viewed as a minor character, yet for various reasons his role merits more extensive examination. Despite his advanced age, the text emphasizes that he is a repetitive, or recurrent, pilgrim.[17] Marguerite clarifies that he commits to an annual pilgrimage for the feast of Mary's nativity (the Virgin's birth is celebrated on September 8). This reference establishes an explicit connection between Marguerite's text, pilgrimage, and the liturgical calendar. In contrast to the many depraved clerics depicted in the tales of the *Heptaméron*, Marguerite's portrayal of this monk underscores his faith and spiritual commitment. She also specifies that God placed the monk on this particular path (1.8). This positive depiction of a recurrent pilgrim doing God's work is not insignificant; Marguerite represents this dedicated monk in unambiguous terms as an instrument of God. During his pilgrimage, he directs Simontault to Notre-Dame de Serrance by showing him the way. In fact, this monk plays a role in helping to bring about the "miracle" of the group's safe arrival at the abbey.[18] Along with the references to feast days and pilgrims, Marguerite's lexical and geographic choices also encourage readers to view the journey of her *devisants* in connection with pilgrimage tradition.

Marguerite chose to write in a genre that is typically characterized by an economy of words. For this reason, terms that are repeatedly emphasized in the text merit attention. Within the first seven paragraphs of the Prologue, the word "chemin" (path, or way) is repeated eight times. Marguerite's repeated use of the term is striking, especially since it is frequently combined with unambiguous references to God intervening and guiding the characters on their way.[19] Indeed, Marguerite consistently uses the word to evoke the journey of her characters through the Pyrenees to Notre-Dame de Serrance either directly or by way of the abbey of Saint-Savin. Throughout the sixteenth century Saint-Savin was a renowned pilgrimage site for those seeking healing as well as a frequent stop for pilgrims on the Chemin de Saint-Jacques-de-Compostelle, or Way of Saint James. Notre-Dame de Serrance was also widely recognized as part of the celebrated pilgrimage route to Santiago de Compostela.[20] In fact, the text alludes to this when the greedy abbot of Notre-Dame de Serrance delights in the construction of a new bridge simply because it will increase the "pelerins et passans" (1.10; pilgrims and travelers).[21] Some manuscripts of the *Heptaméron* (BnF Français 1511, 1512, and 1515) even mention "pelerins and pelerines" (pilgrims, both men and women), suggesting that the abbot was not only greedy, but also corrupt in his desire to attract female pilgrims to the site. Marguerite's lexical and geographical choices establish a solid connection between the storytellers' journey in the *Heptaméron* and pilgrimage; the specific threats that they encounter during their travels serve a similar purpose.

In *The Age of Pilgrimage*, Jonathan Sumption evokes a customary twelfth-century pilgrim blessing: "O Lord, heavenly father, let the angels watch over thy servants . . . that they may reach their destination in safety . . . that no enemy may attack them on the road, nor evil overcome them. Protect them from the perils of fast rivers, thieves, or wild beasts."[22] This common medieval pilgrim's prayer highlights the typical dangers encountered on pilgrimage routes. It cannot be mere coincidence that these are the exact perils that Marguerite's frame characters confront on their different paths to Notre-Dame de Serrance. During their travels, six of the storytellers barely escape with their lives when bandits brandishing swords attack them, Longarine's husband perishes during a skirmish, and they all lose several servants. Nomerfide and Ennasuite encounter a great danger as well: an enraged bear chases them down the mountain and kills all their servants. Their horses die from exhaustion just as they pass through the abbey gates. After surviving these harrowing situations and despite knowing that the path will be very difficult, the group nonetheless persists in making their way primarily on foot to Notre-Dame de Serrance. Another nobleman, Simontault, barely escapes drowning when he attempts to cross a raging river with his horse; he is saved by a shepherd and then sent on his way by the old monk on pilgrimage.

A fifteenth-century painting in the abbey of Saint-Savin features a priest who nearly drowned while crossing a river on horseback, but he was ultimately rescued thanks to the intercessory prayers of Saint Savin (Figure 2.1). The similarities between this episode and the representation of Simontault are compelling.[23]

Figure 2.1. Photograph, *Vie de St. Savin: Primitifs du 15e siècle.* Paris: Compagnie des Arts Photomécaniques. Credit: Compagnie des Arts Photomécaniques.

Furthermore, Saint Savin's legend has another interesting parallel in Marguerite's text. Saint Savin was known to have withdrawn from the world to focus uniquely on God during his solitary life as a hermit in the Pyrenees. In scenes of his life that have been displayed in the abbey of Saint-Savin since the fifteenth century, a painting portrays five women and five men in prayer around him (Figure 2.2). The group is featured amid their devotions in the wilderness of the Pyrenees with an abbey looming in the background. Marguerite's visit to this location would have familiarized her with this very image. This depiction of five men and five women receiving spiritual instruction in the Pyrenean wilderness may have been one factor that inspired the setting for the *Heptaméron* and the gender equality of the *devisants*. The fact that the *devisants* and their adventures share clear parallels with Saint Savin's legend again points to hagiography as one of Marguerite's primary sources.

Although the text evokes various hazards that the group encounters on the trek through the mountains, Marguerite also reminds her readers that God offers His protection to the travelers every step of the way. In fact, as is customary with pilgrimage, the group intermittently praises God for His protection and mercies: "Et le matin ouyrent la messe bien devotement, loüans Dieu, des perils qu'ils avoient eschappez" (1.6; In the morning they devoutly heard Mass, praising God that they had escaped such perils). Much like a pilgrim's travels, the challenging nature of the journey serves to increase their faith in God: "La joye fut si grande en toute ceste compagnie miraculeusement assemblée, que la nuict leur sembla courte à louër Dieu, de la grace qu'il leur avoit faicte" (1.9–10; The miraculously assembled group was so joyful that the night—spent in the abbey's church praising God for the grace he had given them—seemed short). The fact that their different paths ultimately lead them to Notre-Dame de Serrance, where Marguerite describes the group as "miraculously assembled," is also significant.[24] The characterization of the group's coming together as a miracle serves to situate their story in the traditional discourse of pilgrimage and miracle narratives.[25] Furthermore, Marguerite also writes, "[ils] allerent ouïr la messe, et recevoir le sainct Sacrement d'union, auquel tous Chrestiens sont uniz en un, suppliant celuy qui les avoit assemblez par sa bonté, parfaire leur voyage à sa gloire" (1.10; they went to hear Mass and all received the holy sacrament of unity, which unifies all Christians into one body, imploring Him, who had assembled them in his benevolence, to complete the journey to his glory). It is particularly telling that when the storytellers attend Mass and receive the

Figure 2.2. Photograph, *Vie de St. Savin: Primitifs du 15e siècle.* Paris: Compagnie des Arts Photomécaniques. Credit: Compagnie des Arts Photomécaniques.

Eucharist at the celebrated pilgrimage site, they also evoke a common motif of pilgrimage when they pray that their journey could ultimately bring God glory. The unambiguous representation of God's intervention in bringing the travelers together at a religious site where they devoutly attend Mass and take Holy Communion also aligns with the norms of pilgrimage.

Scholars have frequently remarked on the fact that while some pilgrims preferred to undertake a solitary journey, early modern pilgrimage was often very social in nature.[26] One of the outcomes of this social aspect of pilgrimage was an emphasis on diversion during the journey.[27] It would be erroneous to view early modern pilgrimages as purely ascetic experiences. Significantly, Marguerite's Prologue presents the group as eagerly engaging in biblical lessons and devotedly participating in daily Mass, but as also needing entertainment, namely "quelque passetemps, qui ne soit point dommageable à l'ame, et soit plaisant au corps" (1.14; some pastime that is not damaging to the soul and yet is pleasing to the body); thus the text reflects the balance between devotion and pleasure that characterized sixteenth-century pilgrimage practices. While there were various forms of diversion available to pilgrims, the fact that Marguerite's group opts for storytelling to accompany their exploration of Scripture establishes an important commonality with pilgrimage narrative. Wes Williams refers to "the central assertion of early modern pilgrimage writing: that travelling, listening to others' stories, writing one's own, and then reading still more, are part of one and the same collective continuum."[28]

The group's storytelling venture is yet another facet of the *Heptaméron*'s Prologue that can be viewed in close connection with pilgrimage narrative, especially when Marguerite characterizes the stories as an offering, or gift. Parlamente states, "si Dieu faict que nostre labeur soit trouvé digne des yeux des seigneurs et dames dessus nommées, nous leur en ferons present au retour de ce voyage, *en lieu d'images ou de paternostres*, vous asseurant qu'ils auront ce present ici plus agreable" (1.16–17; if, God willing, our labor is worthy of the eyes of the lords and ladies mentioned above, we will offer it to them on our return from this journey instead of offering holy images or rosaries. I am sure that they will find this gift more pleasant).[29] While this has been interpreted as a rejection of the images, rosaries, or similar devotional objects that pilgrims acquired during their travels, Parlamente's statement can also be interpreted in a more positive sense, especially when viewed in relation to pilgrimage and miracle narrative.[30] Robert Maniura argues that miracle narratives can be viewed as gifts, much like the material offerings of pilgrims.[31] Parlamente's reference to the worthiness of their stories in the eyes of God, together with the suggestion that their tales have commonalities with devotional gifts, places the work in the discourse of pilgrimage narrative. When Parlamente suggests that the stories will be enjoyed more than other religious objects, this should be interpreted more as an expression of Marguerite's appreciation for literature and belief in the power of the written word, rather than as a dismissal of Catholic devotional objects, especially given that there is ample evidence that she remained attached to images and relics throughout her life.

At the beginning of the work, Marguerite's *devisants* suffer from physical afflictions that lead them to partake in the healing waters of Cauterets, but rains from heaven force them to set out on another physical journey. The fact that they travel for the most part on foot, triumphing over multiple dangers, passing by one abbey, and ultimately arriving for a long sojourn at another abbey that was part of a celebrated pilgrimage route, encourages readers to view their journey in the pilgrimage tradition. In a certain sense, the representation of the interrelated concepts of pilgrimage, feast days, and hagiography in the Prologue prepares the reader to be mindful of the presence of these very elements throughout the entire collection of tales. Marguerite draws on pilgrimage narrative structures by having her characters spend their days hearing biblical lessons and attending Mass, but also by asking for God's blessings on their stories before sharing them. Moreover, she depicts her characters as slowly moving toward the transformative objective of pilgrimage.[32] Despite continued disagreements and tensions between the *devisants*, Marguerite's daily prologues nonetheless serve to highlight the spiritual evolution of the group.[33] On the sixth day she evokes their "cueur" (2.606; fervor) and on the seventh day she refers to their "grande devotion" (2.681; great devotion). Thus, the daily prologues underscore the increasing faith and devotion of the *devisants* on their journey. By constructing her text in such a way, Marguerite beckons her readers to join the pilgrimage of her storytellers, thereby inviting them to reflect on their own beliefs and be transformed as they journey through the pages of the *Heptaméron*. Taken together, these various elements from the Prologue and the introductions to each day of storytelling point the reader to miracle and hagiographic narratives as one of the primary sources for the *Heptaméron*. The next section explores how different facets of the representation of Oisille, the group's spiritual leader, reveal yet another influence of hagiography on Marguerite's text.

The *Heptaméron*'s Mothers: Oisille and Saint Anne

Devotion to Saint Anne, the Virgin Mary's mother, increased dramatically from the late fifteenth to the mid-sixteenth century throughout Europe.[34] Anne's various roles as wife, mother, teacher, and widow appealed to a vast range of women.[35] Representations of Saint Anne were ubiquitous in the early Renaissance; she was prominently featured in the visual arts, and altars and chapels of churches were dedicated to her.[36] The popularity of pilgrimages to her relics in Apt and Chartres also increased her celebrated status within France's borders. The publication of Saint Anne's life in the account of the Birth of the Blessed Virgin Mary in the *Golden Legend* resulted in her becoming one of the most popular saints in medieval and early modern Europe. Along with the ongoing controversy over the saints in general, a 1518 debate involving the number of Saint Anne's husbands and daughters also fueled the explosive growth of the cult of Mary's mother in Renaissance France.[37]

Like the depiction of Saint Anne in the *Golden Legend*, Catholic traditionalists such as the Sorbonne theologian Noël Beda argued that Saint Anne remarried twice after the death of Saint Joachim and that she had two more daughters named Mary.[38] Reformers like Jacques Lefèvre d'Étaples and François Demoulins de Rochefort saw these claims as an affront to the saint's virtue and insisted that she had married only once and that her sole child was the Virgin Mary. Lefèvre presented his arguments about Saint Anne in Latin in the appendix of his 1518 *De Maria Magdalena, triduo Christi, et ex tribus una Maria disceptatio*.[39] At first glance, a debate over Saint Anne may not appear far-reaching in its consequences, but Ann Moss highlights the importance of this controversy, arguing that Beda viewed Lefèvre and his tract as "a general threat of major proportions to the stability of Church order, faith, and morals."[40] Soon after Lefèvre's text appeared, Demoulins paraphrased Lefèvre's ideas in his *Petit livret faict à l'honneur de madame saincte Anne et de la royne, sa fille, vierge pure, mere de Jesus-Christ*.[41] Significantly, Demoulins dedicated his text to Louise de Savoie.[42] Moreover, he refers directly to Louise, François, and Marguerite within the text, thereby embroiling the royal family in the controversy over Saint Anne.[43]

Scholars have frequently argued that Marguerite's mother, Louise de Savoie, was the inspiration for Oisille.[44] While the *Heptaméron*'s portrayal of Oisille shares parallels with Louise and with Saint Anna the Prophetess, it also incorporates several important elements of Saint Anne's iconography. This is hardly surprising as these two saints were undoubtedly linked in Marguerite's mind, especially since Saint Anna the Prophetess is explicitly referred to in connection with Saint Anne in Demoulins's text.[45] An examination of Louise's and Marguerite's devotion to the Virgin Mary's mother and a close reading of the *Heptaméron*'s frame story together with hagiographic narratives and texts associated with the debate over Anne's life highlight the connections between Oisille, Saint Anne, and Louise. This section demonstrates that Marguerite formed a strong association between Saint Anne and her own mother's spirituality while it also establishes another important influence of hagiographic tradition on the *Heptaméron*.

The French royal family publicly displayed reverence to Saint Anne in several respects. In 1537, King Francis made a well-publicized pilgrimage to Apt to honor Saint Anne. Around 1518, *L'Office de sainte Anne* (The Mass for Saint Anne), an anonymous Mass for the saint, was written for Marguerite.[46] Michael Alan Anderson suggests that it was Louise de Savoie who requested this work for her daughter.[47] Queen Claude's prayer book also features numerous depictions of Saint Anne's life.[48] Marguerite's own book of hours includes a compelling image of the queen of Navarre kneeling next to Saints Anne and Joachim (as depicted in the cover image of this book). Marguerite was known to carry devotional objects depicting the saints, especially Saint Michael, Saint Francis, and her own patron saint, Marguerite. However, Raymond Ritter also notes that she typically carried a figure of a female saint with a small child.[49] This was most likely Saint Anne, given that she was commonly depicted in the Renaissance with a young Mary in her arms.[50] It was when Marguerite and Louise made a pilgrimage to the South of France to visit the shrines of Saint Mary Magdalene and Saint Anne that Louise requested from Demoulins the new written version of Saint Anne's life. In yet another example of Marguerite's and Louise's attachment to these saints, Marguerite and her mother offered financial support for the shrines of Saint Anne and Saint Mary Magdalene.[51] Louise and Marguerite also sought this saint's intercession for Claude's repeated pregnancies and Marguerite's ongoing struggles with infertility.

Along with personal reasons, there were political motivations for the French royal family's affinity for Saint Anne. The explosion of images of the "Trinité mariale," or Saint Anne Trinitarian, such as Leonardo da Vinci's *Virgin and Child with Saint Anne*, were also of particular interest to France's royal family. In fact, François, Louise, and Marguerite were widely referred to as "La Trinité" in sixteenth-century France. Anderson asserts, "It was no accident that this dynamic, ambitious trio was dubbed the 'Royal Trinity' by their contemporaries, and it is in this symbolic threefold entity that St. Anne begins to resurface at the French court."[52] Virginia Nixon argues that the royal family intentionally promoted the parallels that they shared with the Anne, Mary, and Jesus trio to strengthen their own political authority.[53] However, Saint Anne appealed to their family for other reasons, as well.

Among Saint Anne's multifaceted roles in the sixteenth century, she was associated with protection and intercession during storms and travels.[54] The royal family's extensive journeys for political reasons may have motivated them to implore Saint Anne's intercession for their well-being as they traveled. Her assistance to those confronting tempestuous weather explains why Martin Luther cried out to Saint Anne when he was caught in a severe thunderstorm in June of 1515. He vowed to become a monk if his life was spared and, true to his word, he abandoned his studies of law and entered a monastery the following month.[55] Among the different adages that connect Saint Anne with storms, the saying "S'il pleut pour la Sainte-Anne, il pleut un mois et une semaine" (If it rains on the feast of Saint Anne, it rains for one month and one week) is particularly intriguing since Saint Anne's feast day falls on July 26; five weeks after that would be the exact date that Marguerite mentions in the first phrase of the *Heptaméron*.[56] Given Saint Anne's association with storms and voyages, the torrential rains in the Prologue that result in Oisille's harrowing trek to a celebrated site of devotion to the Virgin Mary can be interpreted in connection with Saint Anne's iconography.

After arriving at Notre-Dame de Serrance, Oisille also suggests that their biblical readings will make the "desert" where they are stranded more beautiful (1.13). Oisille refers to the group's surroundings as a desert on two different occasions in the Prologue. This lexicon has compelling spiritual connotations; her words establish parallels between the group of storytellers and the saints who withdrew to the wilderness to focus solely on God. Marguerite would have been cognizant of the narrative tradition of depicting Saint Anne as a holy woman in the desert, thus the fact that she represents Oisille in a similar light also points to Saint Anne's legend as one source of inspiration for the *Heptaméron*'s spiritual leader.

Another intriguing element of Saint Anne's iconography that has parallels with Oisille involves references to birds. Scholars often view Oisille as an anagram for Louise, but they have also commented on the arrangement of letters and the closeness of the name with the word *oiseau* (bird) or *oiselle* (a female bird).[57] Significantly, birds are also a recurring motif in Saint Anne's legend. In their research on representations of Saint Anne during the Middle Ages, Kathleen Ashley and Pamela Sheingorn evoke "the noncanonical legend of Anne as a child abandoned in an eagle's nest."[58] Medieval accounts of Saint Anne's life relate how a nest of singing birds led to her lamentation about her own sterility.[59] For these reasons, Saint Anne is sometimes depicted in a nest of birds in the visual arts. Moreover, Myra Orth notes that wings are one of the emblems of Louise de Savoie.[60] The multiple references to birds in Saint Anne's iconography together with the fact that Louise de Savoie chose wings as her personal emblem suggest that Marguerite selected this specific anagram to establish connections between Oisille, Louise, and Saint Anne.

Marguerite would have known that in religious iconography Saint Anne was widely recognized as the patron saint of widows, especially given that Saint Anne's status as a widow received extensive attention in the sixteenth-century debate over the number of her marriages. Reformers vehemently disagreed with the concept of the *trinubium* (her three marriages), arguing that Saint Anne had only one husband, Saint Joachim, and that she avoided remarriage after Joachim's death. For instance, in Demoulins's text on Saint Anne, he highlights her sole marriage and virtuous widowhood, saying, "Car saincte Anne, bonne et pudicque vefve fut contante dung seul mari" (Because Saint Anne, a good and chaste widow, was content with only one husband).[61] In connection with promoting the idea of her single marriage, he also insists that she gave birth to only one child: "Donc est ce choze certaine que Anne ne conceut de Joachim que une seule fille nommee Marie" (Thus, one thing is certain that Anne conceived from Joachim only one daughter named Mary).[62] Much like the reformers' emphasis on Saint Anne's widowhood, historians have often emphasized that Louise de Savoie lost her first husband at a young age.

Even though Louise was only nineteen when she was widowed, she successfully fought for the right to maintain guardianship of her children. Like Saint Anne, she never remarried after the death of her husband. Saint Anne's role as patron saint of widows may explain in part Louise's deep attachment to her. Marguerite would have been familiar with Louise's devotion to Saint Anne, the details of Lefèvre's and Demoulins's texts, and the ongoing controversy over Anne's marriages and daughters. In fact, Marguerite personally intervened to protect Lefèvre when he was threatened by the Sorbonne after voicing his opinions on the matter. Significantly, the disputes over Anne's marriages in no way diminished the reformers' fervor for Saint Anne, the patron saint of widows.[63] In fact, Demoulins even concludes his work with an affirmation of his belief in the intercession of the Virgin and saints by declaring that he will ask the Virgin Mary, Saint Anne, and Saint Joachim to intercede and pray for the members of the French royal family.[64] In light of Louise's and Marguerite's close ties to the writers and texts associated with the debates over Saint Anne's marriage(s), the emphasis on widowhood in the *Heptaméron*'s depiction of Oisille is noteworthy.

From her very first mention, Oisille is portrayed as an elderly widow (1.2). Marguerite insists on this aspect of Oisille's life by referring to her status as a widow once again in the text's second reference to her as "une ancienne vefve" (1.8; an elderly widow). Marguerite's choice of the word "ancienne" is also compelling. She could have opted for the word "vieille" to describe Oisille's advanced age, as she does when describing an older woman in tale 65. However, by using "ancienne," Marguerite bestows a certain authority on Oisille, while she may also hint at the possibility of an older model for Oisille, namely Saint Anne. In fact, Demoulins refers to "madame Saincte Anne antique" (Old Madame Saint Anne) in his text.[65] Scholars have frequently drawn attention to the importance of widowhood in the representation of Oisille's character.[66] The *Heptaméron*'s insistence on Oisille's status as a widow who did not remarry can be interpreted as an expression of Marguerite's agreement with Lefèvre and Demoulins in the ongoing controversy over the number of Saint Anne's marriages.

Saint Anne's prominent role as patron saint of widows was frequently accompanied by emphasis on her maternal exemplarity; her privileged role as Mary's mother was strongly emphasized in Renaissance texts and the visual arts. Medieval and early modern hagiographies highlight her sterility until an advanced age and underscore the miraculous nature of her conceiving a child so late in life. The close connection between Saint Anne and motherhood is apparent in that she was frequently referred to as "Mother Anne" during the sixteenth century.[67] Saint Anne's privileged position as Mary's mother was a central component of her iconography.

Louise's prominent role as mother and sole living parent also garnered substantial attention during her lifetime. For Marguerite and François, Louise was their only living parent for most of their existence. As a widowed mother, Louise played a highly influential role in her children's lives. The close relationship that she shared with her children throughout their lives is evidence of the strong maternal bond that Louise had with François and Marguerite. In connection with Saint Anne's unique role as mother of Mary, she was designated as the patron saint of pregnancy, infertility, and those trying to conceive. This aspect of her cult undoubtedly piqued the French royal family's interest in her, especially given Marguerite's long, personal struggles with infertility and Queen Claude's repeated pregnancies. Saint Anne gave birth to Mary after an extensive period of infertility. On the church calendar, Mary's nativity is celebrated on September 8. Marguerite refers to this specific feast day in the Prologue (1.7). Like Saint Anne, the *Heptaméron* portrays Oisille as an older woman who becomes a mother figure to the storytellers in the early days of September. Parlamente designates Oisille as a mother for the group, saying, "vous qui avez tant d'experience, et qui maintenant aux femmes tenez lieu de mere" (1.10–11; you, who have so much experience and who are now playing the role of mother to us women). The *Heptaméron*'s spiritual leader embraces her maternal role wholeheartedly. In fact, immediately after Parlamente's declaration, Oisille addresses the group as her "children" twice (1.11–13). In this same monologue, she also emphasizes the essential role of reading Scripture daily (1.11–13). Oisille's role as mother figure to the group can be viewed in connection with Saint Anne and so can the representation of her as an older woman teaching sacred text to her children.

Along with her unique status as mother to the Virgin Mary, Saint Anne was also celebrated as a model of female literacy and a spiritual teacher to her daughter.[68] In medieval and Renaissance iconography, Saint Anne is most frequently featured holding a book and instructing Mary. In Marguerite's own circle, this feature of Saint Anne's life is clearly depicted in Queen Claude's prayer book (Figure 2.3). Karin Tilmans emphasizes the important connections between Saint Anne's role as teacher and the depiction of mothers in early modern humanism.[69] The important link between Saint Anne, the Virgin Mary, and spiritual literacy is also depicted in an illustration in the *Office de sainte Anne* that was presented to Marguerite.[70] The image features several men, but only Saint Anne, the Virgin Mary, and two other women are portrayed holding books on their laps (Figure 2.4). This illustration is striking in that it makes an unequivocal statement about women's literacy and their having unfettered access to sacred texts.

Louise de Savoie was also well known for her commitment to reading. Her personal motto, "libris et liberis" (my books and my children), underscores the importance she placed on reading and motherhood.[71] Like Saint Anne and Louise, Oisille is designated from the Prologue as the group's spiritual teacher and a wise authority for interpreting Scripture. She emphasizes her daily commitment to reading the Bible and she also instructs the group on how to find

Figure 2.3. *St. Anne Teaching the Virgin Mary* and *The Annunciation to St. Anne*, illuminated by the Master of Claude de France, 2¾ × 2 inches. From *Prayer Book of Claude de France* (Tours, France, ca. 1517), MS M.1166, fol. 42r., The Morgan Library and Museum, New York. Gift of Mrs. Alexandre P. Rosenberg in memory of her husband, Alexandre Paul Rosenberg, 2008. Courtesy of The Morgan Library and Museum.

Figure 2.3a. Detail of *St. Anne Teaching the Virgin Mary.*

true joy in this activity. Even Hircan, the most misogynistic of the male storytellers, states, "vous qui estes la plus ancienne, nous lisiez au matin de la vie que tenoit Nostre Seigneur Jesus Christ, et les grandes et admirables œuvres qu'il a faictes pour nous" (1.13–14; you, who are the oldest, should read to us in the morning from the life of our Lord Jesus Christ and the great and admirable works that he did for us). Oisille's age and spiritual wisdom distinguish her from the other *devisants,* thus she reads from the Scriptures and offers the group religious instruction in the form of a biblical lesson each day during their sojourn in the Pyrenean abbey.

While emphasis on Oisille's role as spiritual leader and teacher is present in the Prologue, her pedagogical skills are underscored regularly throughout the entire frame narrative. Marguerite repeatedly highlights Oisille's invaluable religious lessons in the introductions to the individual days (2.434, 2.606). The

Figure 2.4. [The Virgin Mary, Saint Anne, and other female saints reading]. From *L'Office de sainte Anne* (ca. 1501–1600), Français 1035, fol. 4v., Bibliothèque nationale de France, Département de Manuscrits. Courtesy of the Bibliothèque nationale de France.

text also emphasizes the exceptional efficacy of Oisille's teaching, saying, "il leur sembloit bien n'avoir jamais oy sermon, qui leur profitast tant" (2.517; it seemed to them that that they had never heard a more edifying sermon). Oisille's lessons are unequivocally presented as superior to any other sermons the *devisants* had heard. The representation of Oisille as a highly effective spiritual teacher responds to ongoing controversy over women and preaching, while it also establishes important parallels between Oisille's role as spiritual teacher, Louise's commitment to her children's religious education, and Saint Anne, the pedagogical saint.

Reflections between Saint Anne's iconography and the representation of Oisille such as references to pilgrimages, storms, and birds encourage an intertextual reading. Marguerite's emphasis on Oisille's position as mother figure, spiritual teacher, and Christian widow serves to recall these roles in Saint Anne's hagiographies and in Louise's lived experiences. The French royal family's multifaceted devotion to Saint Anne explains in large part why Marguerite would have formed such a strong association between this saint and her own mother. Louise's and Marguerite's direct involvement with controversy over Saint Anne, and Marguerite's active support for reformers like Lefèvre and Demoulins who wrote accounts of Saint Anne's life, also point to their family's personal engagement in the debate. The fact that Marguerite integrated numerous elements of Saint Anne's legend into her representation of Oisille serves a triple purpose; it honors a saint who was dear to Marguerite personally, it serves as a tribute to her own mother's piety, and it suggests that Marguerite espoused the evangelical reformers' perspectives on the sixteenth-century debate over Saint Anne's life.

Various facets of the Prologue equate the journey of the *devisants* with pilgrimage. This introductory section of Marguerite's text also depicts Oisille as an exemplary maternal figure and spiritual teacher. Significantly, the first tale that Oisille recounts presents a sixteenth-century heroine as a saint-like figure. The next chapter demonstrates how Oisille's story about the martyrdom of the mule-driver's wife and Marguerite's other tales of saintly women who suffer physical violence can also be interpreted in connection with saints' vitae.

CHAPTER THREE

Violence, Sufferings, and Women of Faith

Sy cruel n'est le lieu
Ne sy fort le Martyre,
Que la bonté de Dieu
Soudain ne nous en tire.

[Neither so cruel is the place
Nor so strong the martyrdom,
That the goodness of God,
Does not suddenly draw us out of it.]

—Marguerite de Navarre, *Chansons spirituelles*

The world as portrayed in the *Heptaméron* is frequently dangerous, violent, and unjust, but particularly so for women. Marguerite repeatedly illustrates the unfortunate consequences of the highly patriarchal society of Renaissance France for the female sex. Physical assault and rape or attempted rape are central themes, and they are depicted on several occasions throughout the work. Patricia Francis Cholakian's *Rape and Writing in the Heptaméron of Marguerite de Navarre* (1991) provides a persuasive analysis of rape in the text in connection with the queen of Navarre's own alleged traumatic experience with sexual assault.[1] Physical sufferings are also prominently featured in female saints' vitae. Graphic tortures and the threat of sexual assault are recurrent topoi in hagiography. While the representation of rape and physical assault in the *Heptaméron* has been widely discussed in literary criticism, an analysis of the theme in connection with saints' lives provides fresh insights into Marguerite's text. A close reading of the physical sufferings of the heroines in tales 2, 10, and 22 alongside analysis of hagiographic writings and visual images of saints from early modern devotional books illustrates how Marguerite draws on saints' lives to represent these women as saint-like figures whose exemplary faith in God allows them to persevere throughout their tribulations. Although Marguerite borrows from hagiography, the representation of her heroines also serves to question certain gender biases that were prevalent in the genre. Thus, through her saintly heroines, she engages in Renaissance debates about women and religion and makes a powerful statement about saints, male violence, and female heroic virtue in Renaissance France.

Saint Sebastian and the Mule-Driver's Wife: Marguerite de Navarre's Renaissance Martyr

The second tale has a privileged position in the *Heptaméron*; it is the first tale told by a female narrator and it is recounted by Oisille, the spiritual leader and oldest member of the group.[2] Moreover, the exceedingly violent nature of the crimes depicted makes it among the most memorable of the entire collection. In response to Simontault's unflattering portrayal of women in the first tale, Oisille introduces the tragic story of the mule-driver's wife, noting, "celuy qui m'a donné sa voix, a tant dict de mal des femmes par une histoire veritable d'une malheureuse, que je doibs rememorer tous mes vieux ans pour en trouver une, dont la vertu puisse desmentir sa mauvaise opinion" (1.31; he who gave me the floor spoke so ill of women by telling a true story of a wretched woman that I have to recall all my many years of life to find one whose virtue could refute his poor opinion of them). Oisille then relates how this virtuous woman is viciously attacked with a sword, raped, and murdered. Scholars have noted that the extreme violence of the assault and the heroine's spiritual response to physical brutality recall various aspects of saints' lives.[3] While the similarities between this tale and hagiographical narratives have been recognized, the multiple parallels between the heroine and Saint Sebastian merit examination. Like Sebastian, the mule-driver's wife is depicted as a soldier, she suffers from an excessive number of piercing wounds, and she joyously embraces a martyr's death while recalling Christ's blood and sacrifice. By exploring different literary and visual portrayals of Saint Sebastian it becomes clear that Marguerite's heroine manifests exemplary spiritual fortitude when confronted with extreme brutality, just as the revered martyr did. This section demonstrates that Marguerite's second tale borrows from saints' vitae to engage in Renaissance religious controversy while it also makes a novel statement about the cult of saints, violence, and female heroic virtue through its revision of hagiography.

Marguerite's mention of the church of Saint Florentin at the beginning and the end of the tale serves to emphasize the veracity of the narrative by situating it geographically, but it also evokes a martyred saint.[4] Saint Florentin, frequently depicted as a Roman soldier, was a martyr who had his tongue cut out and then was killed with a sword. Like Saint Florentin, Saint Sebastian was also depicted as a soldier who had his body pierced, albeit with multiple arrows rather than with a sword. The sixteenth-century readers of the *Heptaméron* would have been highly familiar with Saint Sebastian's legend and iconography. He was among the most revered saints of Renaissance France, and there were numerous depictions of his martyrdom in sixteenth-century art. Representations of multiple arrows piercing the saint's body were common in the visual arts. Like her readers, a woman as religious and educated as Marguerite would have been cognizant of various details of Saint Sebastian's story. In fact, she encountered different representations of this saint within her close-knit circles. Saint Sebastian is one of the saints featured in both Queen Claude's prayer book and Louise de Savoie's book of hours. The two pages of images in Queen Claude's prayer book that are dedicated to Saint Sebastian portray both of the violent episodes from his life, the arrow attack as well as his death by clubbing (Figures 3.1 and 3.2).[5] In Louise de Savoie's book of hours, Saint Sebastian is portrayed as stoic and peaceful while multiple arrows puncture his body, producing bleeding wounds (Figure 3.3).[6] Different elements of visual and written representations of Saint Sebastian that Marguerite encountered throughout her life are reflected in her account of the mule-driver's wife.

While Saint Sebastian's role as intercessor for plague sufferers was often evoked during the sixteenth century, he was also venerated as the patron saint of soldiers. He was an esteemed officer in the Roman military, and some scholars claim that he entered Diocletian's army to help defend Christians who were being martyred for their faith. Significantly, Saint Sebastian's portrayal as a soldier with remarkable physical strength has parallels with Marguerite's representation of this humble woman. When the mule-driver's wife is accosted in her bed, she attempts to use virtuous appeals as well as her physical strength to fight off her attacker. In fact, she is portrayed as so fast and strong that she manages to free herself twice from his clutches. The text then clarifies that the assailant resorts to stabbing her violently in the small of the back, thinking that the pain will make her surrender: "desesperé de jamais ne la pouvoir avoir vive, luy donna un grand coup d'espée par les rains, pensant que si la peur et la force ne l'avoient peu faire rendre, la douleur le feroit" (1.33–34; he lost hope of ever

Figure 3.1. *St. Sebastian Shot with Arrows,* illuminated by the Master of Claude de France, 2¾ × 2 inches. From *Prayer Book of Claude de France* (Tours, France, ca. 1517), MS M.1166, fol. 33v., The Morgan Library and Museum, New York. Gift of Mrs. Alexandre P. Rosenberg in memory of her husband, Alexandre Paul Rosenberg, 2008. Courtesy of The Morgan Library and Museum.

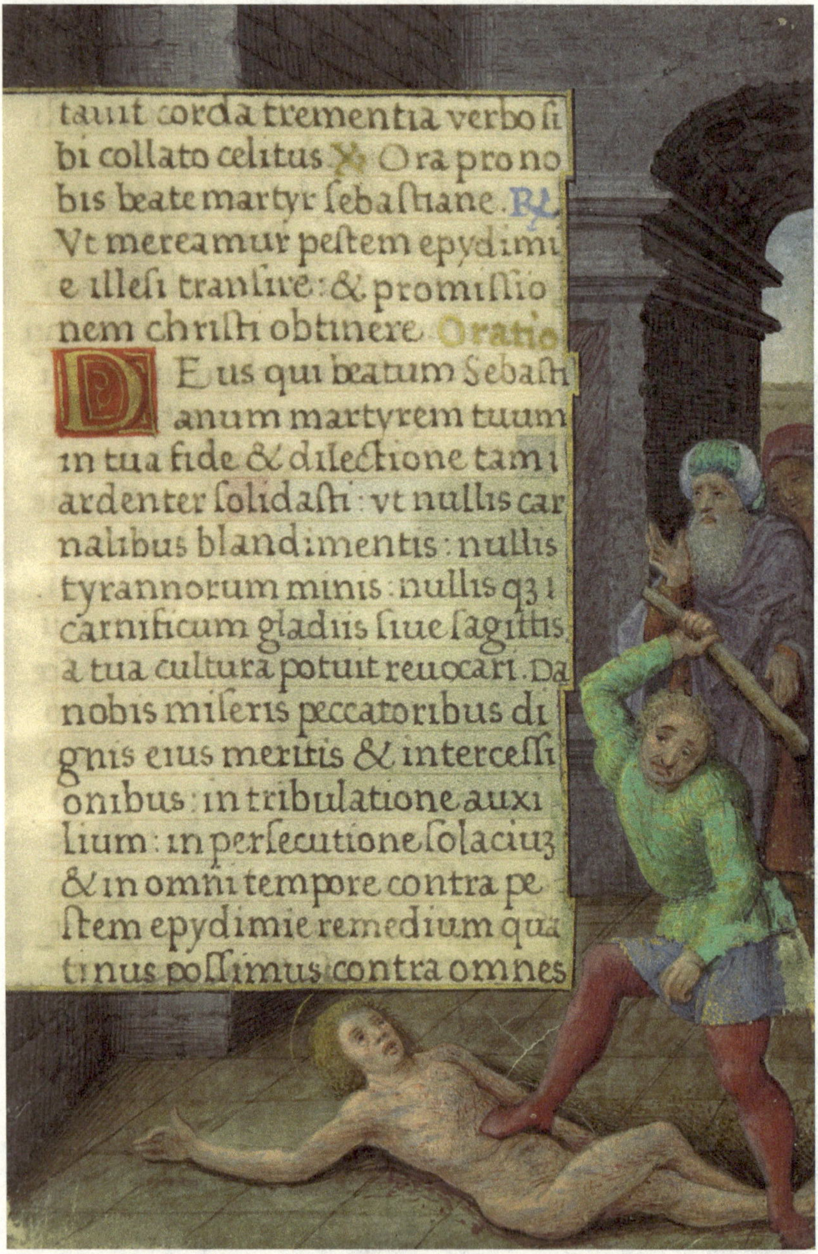

Figure 3.2. *St. Sebastian Clubbed to Death*, illuminated by the Master of Claude de France, 2 ¾ × 2 in. From *Prayer Book of Claude de France* (Tours, France, ca. 1517), MS M.166, fol. 34r., The Morgan Library and Museum, New York. Gift of Mrs. Alexandre P. Rosenberg in memory of her husband, Alexandre Paul Rosenberg, 2008. Courtesy of The Morgan Library and Museum.

Figure 3.3. "Martyrdom of St. Sebastian," 192 × 123 mm. From *Hours, use of Rome* (France, ca. 1500–1515), MS 411, fol. 137r., General Collection, Beinecke Rare Book and Manuscript Library, Yale University, New Haven, CT. Courtesy of Beinecke Rare Book and Manuscript Library.

taking her alive. So he thrust his sword into the small of her back, thinking that if fear and brute force had not made her surrender, then pain would). The term "rendre" (to yield) can have a military connotation and so does the metaphor that Marguerite uses to describe the woman's resistance and force. The narrative specifies, "tout ainsi, qu'un bon *gendarme* voyant son sang, est plus eschauffé à se venger de ses ennemis, et à acquerir honneur : ainsi son chaste cueur se renforça doublement à courir et fuir" (1.34, emphasis added; since just as a good soldier is all the more driven to take revenge on his enemies and to seek honor when he sees his own blood, her chaste heart redoubled its efforts to run and flee). Cholakian argues that the tale "equates her honor with that won by men on the field of battle."[7] Moreover, the use of the word "gendarme" shares another association with Saint Sebastian, who was also well known as the patron saint of archers. According to Cotgrave, a gendarme "must have beene, at least one yeare, an archer."[8] The tale underscores the heroine's moral resolve and physical strength while it also establishes a parallel with Saint Sebastian's role as the patron saint of soldiers and archers.

Along with Saint Sebastian's association with soldiers, he was frequently evoked in the Renaissance as a model of Christian death. In early modern paintings and prayer books, he is typically depicted as uncannily serene while multiple arrows inflict deep wounds in his flesh. Other portrayals of his brutal death from clubbing represent him as stoic while enduring extreme physical suffering. A similar phenomenon is seen in this novella in Marguerite's portrayal of the mule-driver's wife's spiritual response to her brutal injuries and impending death. Throughout the violent attack, Marguerite's heroine repeatedly attempts to stop her attacker with words of wisdom and reason. However, she eventually loses so much blood that she realizes that death is inevitable. Akin to the early Christian martyrs, the heroine's blood is portrayed as a sacrifice to honor Christ's own blood that was shed for humanity. Marguerite writes, "Et quand à force de perdre son sang, elle sentit qu'elle aprochoit de la mort, levant les yeux au ciel, et joignant les mains, rendit graces à son Dieu, lequel elle nommoit sa force, sa vertu, sa patience et chasteté, luy suppliant prendre en gré le sang, qui pour son commandement estoit respandu en la reverence de celuy de son fils" (1.34–35; And when, having lost a great deal of blood, she felt that death was near, raising her eyes toward the heavens and joining her hands, she gave thanks to her God, whom she called her strength, her virtue, her patience, and her chastity. She implored him to receive the blood that was shed to keep his commandments, in reverence for the blood of his Son). Significantly, this passage has commonalities with the *Golden Legend*'s account of Saint Sebastian's life. Voragine concludes by referring to "Le sang du benoit martir Sebastien espandu . . . pour la confession de ton nom" (The shedding of the blood of the blessed martyr Sebastian for the confession of your name).[9]

The excessive number of injuries and extreme violence that the mule-driver's wife endures also recall the torture and agony of Saint Sebastian. Marguerite's text specifically notes that when surgeons eventually come to assist the heroine, they discover that she has endured twenty-five mortal injuries. A sixteenth-century reader would have made a connection between her excessive number of stab wounds and the multiple arrows that pierced Saint Sebastian's body. The heroine's spiritual response to intense pain and suffering also recalls his legend. In Marguerite's text, the virtuous woman involuntarily elicits her attacker's desire. When confronted by her tenacious resistance, he proceeds to repeatedly penetrate her body with a knife, a substitution for the penetration of rape. The mule-driver's wife ultimately succumbs to her injuries, but not with the extreme anguish and torment that one might expect. The mule-driver's wife is portrayed as approaching death by expressing gratitude as she looks toward heaven with a joyous expression: "Et ainsi avec un visage joyeux, les yeux eslevez au ciel, rendit ce chaste corps à la terre, et l'ame à son createur" (1.36; And so with a joyous face, her eyes raised to the heavens, this chaste body returned her soul to its Creator). Zegura asserts that "she renders her soul to God in a posture of Christian martyrdom that permeates medieval and early modern religious texts and iconography."[10] In many ways, this heroine exemplifies the notion of a glorious Christian death that Marguerite frequently evokes in her *Chansons spirituelles*.[11]

Along with the representation of her death as prayerful and joyous, another term that solidifies the association of the mule-driver's wife with hagiography is Marguerite's choice of the word "martire" to describe her heroine, specifically calling her a "martire de chasteté" (1.36; martyr for chastity). While countless religious terms appear consistently throughout Marguerite's novella collection, the word "martyr" is rare in the pages of the *Heptaméron*. Not only does the term confer upon the mule-driver's wife the status of a martyr, but the lasting impact of her example and the conversions that follow her death encourage this interpretation as well. Accounts of the lives of saints were written to provide the faithful with exemplary behaviors to emulate and to remind them of God's ability to manifest holiness in ordinary human lives. Marguerite's representation of the response to the mule-driver's wife's torturous death evokes this phenomenon. Just as visual portrayals of Saint Sebastian frequently show onlookers witnessing his suffering (see Figure 3.1), the tale also has various people observing her heroic acts. The young girl who was hiding in the room during the attack and the townspeople who arrive at the window soon after it serve as eyewitnesses to her saint-like behavior. In addition, at the close of the narrative Marguerite notes that even "les folles et legeres" (1.36; the immodest and frivolous women) in the town are so moved by the actions of the mule-driver's wife that they resolve to amend their own lives. Cholakian remarks on this phenomenon, saying, "her tomb becomes a local shrine venerated by the local townswomen."[12] Furthermore, the fact that Marguerite evokes "l'honneur que l'on faisoit à ce corps" (1.36; how this body was honored) after her death recalls the long-standing tradition of honoring the relics of the saints. The terms that Marguerite chooses to describe the mule-driver's wife's death are commonly used in the depiction of the deaths of saints in hagiography.

Just as the saints' lives were meant to provide the faithful with models to imitate, the story of Marguerite's heroine is presented as offering a model for the townswomen in the tale as well as for the *devisantes*. In the frame narrative, the women in the group are moved to tears by the death of the mule-driver's wife. The emotional response to the narrative is so strong that Hircan mentions the group's tearful response again after the seventh tale (1.80); this is exceptional in the *Heptaméron*. While Marguerite's repeated emphasis on the women's grief underscores the unsettling violence that the mule-driver's wife experienced, these references may also serve to question the excessive emphasis on female chastity both in the teachings of the Renaissance Catholic Church and in saints' lives.[13] Marguerite writes, "Chacune pensoit en elle mesme, que si la fortune leur advenoit pareille, elle mettroit peine de l'ensuivre en son martyre" (1.37–38; Each of them thought to themselves that, if they were to encounter such a misfortune, they would struggle to follow her into martyrdom). The fact that Marguerite specifies that the *devisantes* would have trouble following the mule-driver's wife's example can be interpreted as a critique of early modern society's view that women's chastity is more important than their survival. In contrast to the conversations following other stories, the male storytellers remain silent after the tale. While the *Heptaméron*'s novellas consistently elicit conflicting opinions, this tale stands out as a rare exception. The lack of controversy over this bloody murder and violent rape provides readers with a powerful message. It suggests that from Marguerite's perspective, there was only one appropriate response to the brutality and exemplarity of the mule-driver's wife's story.

Marguerite also responds to the *querelle des femmes* by emphasizing the morality, strength, and faith of this woman. The positive representation of her heroine contrasts sharply with that of the attacker, a cruel, irrational, and immoral man.[14] The narrative contests the traditional gender stereotypes of the misogynistic texts of the *querelle des femmes*. Oisille's argument at the end of the narrative (a rhetorical position that frequently appears throughout the *Heptaméron*) that God uses what is lowly to confound that which men find most honorable also serves to challenge the claims of the misogynists. However, by emphasizing that God works through those whom society perceives as lowly or weak, not only does Marguerite make a statement about gender, but her words also relate to class. This connection is especially significant since the novella emphasizes the heroine's humble social position.

In contrast to traditional hagiography where female saints are frequently depicted as members of the nobility, Marguerite presents a revisionist hagiography by emphasizing the humble origins of this saintly woman. She is referred to as a "pauvre femme" (1.33; poor woman), yet her exemplary behavior clearly allows her to transcend her low social position. The tale specifies that the townspeople honored and esteemed her as if she were a "femme de la ville" (1.35; woman in the city). The reader must also remember that in the stories of the first day, there are three unsuccessful rape attempts. In the fifth tale, a simple ferrywoman must rely solely on her wit to escape from her assailants. However, in tales 4 and 10, the noblewomen avoid rape in large part due to the resources and safeguards that their elevated position in society furnish them. Without recourse to the same protections, the mule-driver's wife's only choice is to courageously defend herself until death and then offer herself up as a sacrifice to God. This tale contributes to debates about women and social class, but Marguerite also engages in theological arguments that were matters of intense controversy in sixteenth-century France.

The second tale offers compelling insights into Marguerite's position on the communion of saints. While there are numerous parallels between the heroine and Saint Sebastian, Marguerite repeatedly insists on the mule-driver's wife's belief that her salvation is in Jesus Christ alone. She emphasizes her heroine's confidence in Christ's sacrifice and her hope for salvation solely through Him (1.35–36). In addition to these examples, it is noteworthy that the only example of direct discourse in the narrative highlights Christ's all-powerful role in the heroine's salvation. When she is on the brink of death, the mule-driver's wife cries out, "Seigneur recevez l'ame qui par vostre bonté a esté racheptée!" (1.35; Lord, receive this soul that by your goodness has been redeemed!). Mary McKinley remarks, "Her sins have been effaced, not by any effort on her part, not by works, but by the blood that Christ shed through his crucifixion, his redeeming death."[15] Marguerite's tale recalls Saint Sebastian's story while it clearly emphasizes Jesus Christ's unique and all-encompassing role in her heroine's salvation. In this way, Marguerite finds a compromise between the reformers who rejected the excesses associated with the cult of saints and respect for this important tradition of the Catholic Church.[16]

While the second tale borrows from Saint Sebastian's iconography, Marguerite does opt for a gender reversal. This gender reversal serves a dual purpose. On one hand, Marguerite's determined heroine serves to question the representation of female passivity that is prevalent in traditional saints' vitae.[17] The courage and the resolve of the mule-driver's wife firmly dispel the idea of women as passive since she literally fights to the death to protect her chastity. On the other hand, this gender reversal allows Marguerite to demonstrate the horrors of sexual assault for women, which was a standard mechanism of torture against women that was more rarely used against men. Thus, although the heroine's pierced body recalls Saint Sebastian's wounds, she suffers even more extensively, given that she endures the additional terror of a brutal rape. In this sense, the tale also diverges from traditional female saints' vitae. Patricia Grieve has demonstrated that it is rare for female saints to experience rape in hagiographic narratives.[18] In contrast, the *Heptaméron*'s tale does not shy away from depicting the harsh realities of sexual assault. Thus, while Marguerite portrays a saintly heroine in the second tale, her narrative is distinct from earlier hagiographies in its questioning of female passivity as well as its representation of the realities of sexual violence.

The second tale describes a brutal attack against one woman by one man, but it also contains another powerful message. Oisille tells this story to disprove Simontault's misogynistic assertion that "depuis que Eve feit pecher Adam, toutes les femmes ont prins possession de tourmenter, tuer ; et damner les hommes" (1.30; ever since Eve made Adam sin, all women have taken it upon themselves to torment, kill, and damn men). Simontault's comment reflects the commonplace misogynistic arguments in the *querelle des femmes* and it emphasizes men's tendency to use sacred texts (like the Bible and the writings of the Church fathers) to denigrate women. This brief tale also skillfully evokes the violence that men have perpetrated on holy men with its references to

Saint Florentin and its parallels with Saint Sebastian. Marguerite's portrayal of this woman's heroic faith and saintly response to one man's violent acts disproves Simontault's claim about women, and it also demonstrates that typically it is men who are responsible for death and torture.

Marguerite's Renaissance martyr exemplifies unswerving courage and faith even while her body is repeatedly pierced in a fashion reminiscent of the legend of Saint Sebastian. This representation of the mule-driver's wife suggests that the heroine's story can be viewed in the same light as the narratives of saints' lives that were so widely disseminated in early modern France. This tale shows that despite Marguerite's strong conviction that salvation comes from Christ alone, she nevertheless viewed hagiographic narratives as a rich source of both spiritual and literary inspiration. The second tale draws on hagiography through its portrayal of an admirable example of one woman's heroic faith in Renaissance France while it also diverges from hagiographic tradition by highlighting the heroine's active resistance and her brutal rape and murder. Moreover, Marguerite's allusion to the difficulty that the *devisantes* experience in fully embracing a model that values their chastity more than their survival questions the excessive emphasis on female chastity in the Catholic Church and in traditional saints' vitae. The next section explores the violence depicted in the tenth tale of the *Heptaméron* and reveals another influence of hagiography on the text, namely how Marguerite weaves various elements of the lives of Saint Eusebia and Saint Amadour into her compelling narrative.

Women and Self-Mutilation: Floride and Saint Eusebia

The tenth tale is the longest and arguably the most celebrated story in the *Heptaméron*. Along with its exceptional length, it has a unique position in the text in that it concludes the first day of storytelling. Moreover, the story is also privileged given that Parlamente, the *devisante* who is often associated with Marguerite's own voice, recounts the tale. Parlamente introduces the story by noting that the friend who told it to her did so "à la louange et honneur de celuy du monde qu'il avoit le plus aimé" (1.102; in praise of the man that he had loved the most in this world). However, rather than praising the male protagonist, Parlamente's version of the events highlights Amadour's ruthless and calculating nature while it also emphasizes Floride's virtue, temperance, and faith. Although some scholars have briefly mentioned the tale in association with hagiography, numerous elements of the story vividly recall Saint Eusebia's legend.[19] The queen of Navarre would have been cognizant of Saint Eusebia's story, given her various pilgrimages with family members to religious institutions in Marseille.[20] Moreover, Saint Eusebia's tomb is at the abbey of Saint-Victor in Marseille. This detail is significant given that the abbey of Saint-Savin, one of the two holy sites included in Marguerite's Prologue, was formally associated with the abbey of Saint-Victor.[21] Saint Eusebia's story would have resonated with Marguerite given her keen interest in violence toward women and female resistance to such brutality. An analysis of the tenth tale's depiction of Floride reveals notable parallels with Saint Eusebia's legend, such as the imminent threat of sexual assault, a young woman's brutal self-mutilation in a chapel, and the bride of Christ motif. In addition to the connections with Saint Eusebia, Marguerite also draws on hagiographic legend in her depiction of Amadour. The tale's parallels with hagiography serve to highlight Floride's exemplary faith whereas they emphasize Amadour's misdeeds.

Marguerite chose to give Amadour the name of a revered saint. Saint Amadour, the husband of Saint Veronica, is depicted twice in Queen Claude's prayer book.[22] He was known for his profound devotion to the Virgin Mary. According to legend, he built a chapel in Mary's honor at Rocamadour. The etymology of the name is compelling since, along with its hagiographic connections, it also shares linguistic similarities with both "amour" (love) and "doré" (golden).[23] While the name may evoke love, recall a faithful saint, and even allude to the *Golden Legend*, the events of the tale repeatedly demonstrate that Amadour's love for Floride is neither selfless nor holy. In fact, from the start, the text unequivocally specifies that what Amadour primarily seeks is the "heureuse fin à ses labeurs" (1.105; favorable conclusion to his labors), namely his own sexual satisfaction. Later in the tale, when he eventually realizes that he is powerless to sway Floride, he instead desires to have a "victoire de son ennemie" (1.141; victory over his enemy). Marguerite utilizes a specific vocabulary associated with holiness in her description of Amadour: "On se fioit en luy de toutes choses, comme à un sainct ou un Ange" (1.114; He was trusted in all things, as if he were a saint or an angel). However, although he outwardly seems to be angelic and saintly, like the many stories depicting corrupt clerics, this tale warns readers to be skeptical of appearances.

Despite Amadour's charming public demeanor, the excessive violence of his actions, his cold calculations, and his threatening words toward Floride ultimately reveal his true nature. When he initially attempts to persuade Floride to satiate his carnal desires, he states, "Pardieu, madame, le fruict de mon labeur ne me sera point osté pour scrupules : et puis qu'*amour*, patience et humbles *prieres* n'y servent de rien, je n'espargneray point ma force pour acquerir le bien, qui sans l'avoir me la feroit perdre" (1.143, emphasis added; "By God! Floride, the fruit of my labors will not be taken from me on account of your scruples. Since love, patience, and humble requests have been of no use whatsoever, I will not spare my strength to acquire the reward without which I would be drained of all vigor"). Throughout the tale, Parlamente employs the words love, God, and prayer in a spiritual sense in reference to Floride. In sharp contrast, Amadour uses these very terms to justify his sexual aggression. The passage when Amadour passes from courtly *serviteur* (servant) to attempted rapist is particularly revealing:

> Quand Florinde veit son visage et ses yeux tant alterez, que le plus beau teinct du monde estoit rouge comme feu, et le plus doux et plaisant regard si horrible et furieux, qu'il sembloit qu'un feu tresardent estincelast dedans son cueur et visage : et qu'en ceste fureur d'une de ses fortes mains print ses deux foibles et delicates, et d'autre part voyant que toutes deffences luy failloient, et que ses pieds et mains estoient tenuz en telle captivité, qu'elle ne pouvoit fuir ne se deffendre, ne sceut quel remede trouver, sinon chercher s'il y avoit point en luy encores quelque racine de la primiere amour, pour l'honneur de laquelle il oubliast sa cruauté. (1.143)
>
> [Then Floride saw his face and his eyes so transformed that the most beautiful complexion in world had become as red as flames and the most tender and pleasant demeanor had become so horrible and enraged that it seemed that a fierce fire was crackling in his heart and his face. In this fury, one of his large and powerful hands grabbed Floride's two delicate and weak hands. Seeing that all of her defenses were failing and that her hands and feet were being held so tightly that she could not escape and even less defend herself, she did not find any better solution than to see if there wasn't still in him some seed of his first love, in honor of which he would forget his cruelty.]

Marguerite utilizes a brutally realistic vocabulary in the description of Amadour's first attempt to rape Floride. While he is initially portrayed as "beau," "doux," and "plaisant," he subsequently becomes "horrible et furieux." Moreover, the "hardiesse" that was initially lauded as a positive quality takes a much more sinister turn in this passage as he uses his physical strength and power to entrap and attack Floride. She is depicted as captive to his cruelty, unable to move her hands and feet, and helpless to defend herself. Just as Amadour's physiognomy changes radically when he tries to sexually assault her, Floride's face is subsequently transformed through a sacrificial act of self-mutilation.

Self-inflicted facial mutilation is a recurring motif in female saints' vitae.[24] Saint Ebba the Younger and the nuns in her cloister sliced off their noses and upper lips to avoid rape during a Viking invasion.[25] Saint Oda of Brabant also engaged in self-inflicted rhinotomy when she brutally disfigured her face to avoid a forced marriage and gain the freedom to enter the convent.[26] Another example of self-inflicted mutilation in hagiography is the story of Saint Eusebia. In 724, Saint Eusebia was an abbess at Saint-Sauveur in Marseille when her cloister was attacked. Knowing that she and her cloistered sisters would be brutally raped upon the entry of the enemy into the convent, she demonstrated extreme physical self-sacrifice. To protect herself from sexual assault, she went to a chapel where she mutilated her face with a knife and encouraged the other nuns to follow her example.[27] The Annals of the Order of Saint Benedict from 732 note, "Extat in sancti Victoris monasterio Eusebiae tumulus, cui imposita est eiusdem heroinae effigies, dimidià facie et naso mutila" (In the monastery of Saint Victor there is a tomb of Eusebia, on which is placed an effigy of the same heroine, with half her face and nose mutilated).[28] There are numerous important similarities between the actions of Saint Eusebia and Floride.

When Floride discovers that her mother has invited Amadour, her attempted rapist, to their home once again, the young woman's first response is religious in nature. Like Saint Eusebia, Floride goes to a chapel to pray and to commend herself to the Lord. After spending time in prayer, Floride undertakes a self-brutalizing action that bears a striking resemblance to Saint Eusebia's sacrifice. Marguerite writes, "aimant mieux faire tort à sa beauté en la diminuant, que de souffrir par elle le cueur d'un si honneste homme brusler d'un si meschant feu, prit une pierre qui estoit dedans la chappelle, et s'en donna par le visage si grand coup, que la bouche, les yeux, et le nez en estoient tous difformés" (1.142; Preferring to disfigure her face rather than allow it to make her suffer on account of such an honorable man's heart, which was burning with such a wicked desire, she took a rock that was in the chapel and struck her face with it so forcefully that her mouth, nose, and eyes were completely disfigured). Like Saint Eusebia, Floride's self-mutilation takes place in a chapel immediately after she has commended herself to God. She also chooses to violently disfigure her face to protect herself from the trauma of rape. Carla Freccero remarks, "The defacement masks her beauty; it is the shield she holds to deflect his blows."[29] Marguerite's text emphasizes the extremity of Floride's injuries, specifying that she strikes herself with a stone so forcefully that her mouth, her nose, and her eyes are all deformed. This young woman's self-sacrifice is all the more striking in contrast to Amadour's utterly selfish behavior. While Saint Amadour built a shrine to the Virgin Mary at Rocamadour (originally "la roque de Saint Amadour"), Amadour's threatening actions result in Floride literally disfiguring herself with a stone; the stark contrast between the saint and Marguerite's male protagonist is compelling.[30]

Amadour is not swayed by Floride's painful self-sacrifice. The extremity of his brutality is evident in his appalling response to Floride's severe injuries. Amadour says, "la difformité de vostre visage (que je pense estre faicte de vostre volonté) ne m'empeschera de faire la mienne : car quand je ne pourrois avoir de vous que les oz, si les voudrois-je tenir auprès de moy" (1.145; but your disfigured face, which I believe was a product of your own will, won't keep me from imposing my own will. If I could have nothing but your bones, I would still want to have them close to me). His statement is chilling for its rhetorical violence; his desire to physically possess Floride is such that he would prefer her death and literally holding her bones over respecting her desire to protect her honor. In traditional saints' vitae, once women have sacrificed their beauty through self-mutilation, rape does not take place. This commonplace of medieval hagiography suggests that rape is motivated by physical attraction. While self-disfigurement typically eliminates the threat of rape in hagiographic legends, Marguerite's narrative casts doubt on this perspective. In tale 10, even though Floride disfigures herself, Amadour doggedly persists with his threats and his obsessive desire to possess her. In contrast to her medieval sources, Marguerite demonstrates that rape, or attempted rape, is not a response to women's beauty or appearance, but instead a consequence of men's maliciousness and unregulated desires. Marguerite makes this clear when Floride refers to Amadour's "meschanceté et appetit desordonné" (1.145; evil intentions).

Although Amadour shows no reserve whatsoever in evoking Floride's death in a threatening manner, he remains highly invested in preserving his own life, at least while there is still hope for his sexual satisfaction. The text clarifies that Amadour refused to acknowledge his wrongdoing to Floride's mother since he "n'estoit pas si prest à mourir qu'il disoit" (1.145; was not as ready to die as he had said). However, once he realizes that he is powerless to sway Floride's commitment to protect her chastity, he expresses his willingness to die, saying, "combien que la mort me fuyt, si la chercheray-je tant que la trouveray" (1.149; even though death has evaded me so far, I will nonetheless pursue it to such an extent that I will find it). The text also foreshadows his death when it evokes his reckless behavior, saying his actions were "si estranges, qu'ils sembloient autant pleins de desespoir que de hardiesse" (1.149; so unusual that they seemed to come more out of desperation than from bravery). Subsequently, Amadour chooses to take his own life rather than being captured where he would either suffer a painful death or even renounce his Christian faith (1.150). The fact that Marguerite evokes the renouncement of his faith as a possibility is another element of the text that serves to distinguish his actions from those of the saints, who adamantly refuse to recant their faith even when faced with brutal tortures and death.

After Amadour acknowledges that he did not want to fail God as he had failed Floride, he kisses the cross on his sword and stabs himself forcefully in the heart. Marguerite writes, "Ainsi mourut le pauvre Amadour, autant regretté, que ses vertus le meritoient" (1.151, So died poor Amadour, who was as mourned as his virtues merited). Nora Martin Peterson offers an intriguing interpretation of this passage: "At first glance, this seems to be an endorsement of Amadour's virtue and prowess, but the formulation leaves this open to interpretation. How much grieving *does* Amadour deserve exactly? . . . It is possible to read this sentence with some degree of skepticism and irony."[31] The story does not end with Amadour's death on the battlefield, however; rather, it concludes with a compelling representation of Floride's saintly actions following his demise.

Aside from Floride's brutal self-mutilation and long-sufferings, the tale's conclusion has several characteristics of saints' lives. After losing her husband, Floride independently chooses to join a convent and become a bride of Christ. Floride "s'en alla rendre religieuse au monastere de Jesus, prenant pour *mary* et *amy* celuy qui l'avoit delivrée d'une amour si vehemente que celle d'Amadour, et de l'ennuy si grand que de la compaignie d'un tel mary" (1.151, emphasis added; left to become a nun in the convent of Jesus, taking as her husband and friend He who had freed her from a love as violent as that of Amadour, and from the great ennui of a husband such as hers). Following her forced marriage to a man that she did not love and her traumatic relationship with Amadour, Floride escapes from both the dissatisfaction of her marriage and the violent passion of her *serviteur*. Marguerite underscores how Floride eventually shuns the world to focus solely on her love of God and ultimately experiences true joy by loving

God perfectly as a bride of Christ: "Ainsi tourna toutes ses affections à aimer Dieu si perfaictement, qu'après avoir vescu longuement religieuse, luy rendit son ame en telle joye, que l'*espouse* a d'aller veoir son *espoux*" (1.151, emphasis added; She turned all of her affections toward loving God so perfectly that after having lived for a long time as a nun, she gave her soul back to him with a joy resembling that of a wife going to see her husband). The repeated emphasis on Floride as a bride of Christ, the portrayal of her "perfect" love for God, and the deep spiritual joy she experiences at death all vividly recall central elements of hagiography.

Although Parlamente highlights Floride's virtue, courage, and faith in God while she simultaneously underscores Amadour's calculating and selfish nature, the conflicting reactions of the storytellers illustrate Marguerite's intent to realistically portray the extreme tensions between societal expectations for men and women in Renaissance France. In the discussion following the tale, Parlamente asks Hircan, "Vous semble-il pas que ceste femme ait esté pressée jusques au bout, et qu'elle ait vertueusement resisté?" (1.151; Don't you think that this woman was pushed to the limit and that she resisted with great virtue?). Hircan responds by saying that Amadour was too fearful in his pursuit of Floride, thereby suggesting that he should have taken her by force. Oisille is quick to defend women, saying, "Appellez-vous faire son devoir à un serviteur, qui veult avoir par force sa maistresse, à laquelle il doit toute reverence et obeissance?" (1.152; Are you saying that a servant is doing his duty if wants to take his mistress by force, a mistress to whom he owes reverence and obedience?). Saffredent fully sides with Hircan, arguing that men control women's honor, and they are therefore deserving of sexual satisfaction. Longarine quickly intervenes on behalf of women, asserting that he is not talking about "true honor," while Geburon nonetheless insists that Amadour was noble and virtuous (1.153). The storytellers' responses reveal the extreme divisions along gender lines in sixteenth-century society, while the tale also illustrates how Marguerite skillfully draws on saints' lives to highlight women's virtue and holiness, to represent the extent of women's sufferings, and to defend the female sex in contentious societal debates.

The tenth tale's allusions to hagiography situate the *Heptaméron* in a long tradition of religious writing, while they also illustrate Marguerite's ability to creatively adapt the genre to serve her own purposes. The emphasis on Floride's virtue and faith and the circumstances surrounding her self-mutilation all serve to emphasize the parallels between her actions and the legend of Saint Eusebia.

In contrast, the connections between Amadour and his patronymic saint highlight the divergence between his violent threats to Floride's chastity and the behavior of a saint who selflessly dedicated himself to honoring the Virgin Mary. Marguerite incorporates elements of saints' vitae into tale 10, while she also questions hagiographic tradition, in that self-disfigurement does not successfully eliminate the threat of rape in her narrative. The next section explores how the twenty-second tale draws on hagiography in its depiction of Sister Marie's saintly response to her persecution by the evil prior of Saint Martin.

The Saintly Sufferings of Sister Marie Héroët

Geburon, one of the male storytellers most sympathetic to women, recounts the *Heptaméron*'s twenty-second tale. In the introduction, he refers to the Bible, citing Psalms that declare that "tout homme est menteur" (all men are liars) and "n'est celuy qui face bien aucun, non jusques à un" (there is not a single one who does good, not even one), but he also evokes God's goodness, noting that "s'il y a du bien, on le doit attribuer à celuy qui en est la source, et non à la créature" (2.328–329; if they do any good, it must be attributed to Him in whom it finds its source, and not to the thing He has created). Thus, he emphasizes human weakness and God's goodness before announcing that his story will illustrate that it is not impossible "que soubs extreme austerité ne se trouve extreme concupiscence" (2.329; for extreme lust to hide beneath extreme austerity). He then narrates the disturbing tale of a corrupt cleric who brutalizes, humiliates, and isolates a young nun when she resists his advances.

Marguerite's story serves to boldly denounce clerical abuse and corruption in the Renaissance church.[32] While the narrative underscores the progression of the moral depravity of a prior, it also consistently highlights the unswerving faith and holiness of Sister Marie Héroët. A close reading of her prolonged sufferings alongside selected hagiographic writings reveals that the virtuous nun's plight shares noteworthy parallels with saints' lives. More specifically, the repeated threats to her virginity, the specific nature of the physical and emotional humiliations that she endures, and her steadfast response to aggression throughout her lengthy tribulations encourage a comparative reading with the lives of Saint Catherine of Alexandria and Saint Margaret of Antioch. The portrayal of Sister Marie as a saint-like figure illustrates the influence of hagiographic narratives on Marguerite's tale, while the juxtaposition of a blameless nun with a lascivious cleric also serves to question the unlimited authority of the clergy in the Renaissance church and to discredit misogynistic arguments in the *querelle des femmes*. Marguerite's tale draws on hagiography to offer her readers an exemplary heroine and to strengthen her response to contentious debates about gender, religion, and ecclesiastical power in sixteenth-century France.

Although many of the *Heptaméron*'s tales briefly mention geographical locations involving the names of saints, Marguerite explicitly refers to both Saint Benedict and Saint Martin in the introduction to the story. In addition, the presence of various forms of the word "saint" in the introduction also supports a comparative reading with hagiography. The beginning of the tale underscores that the prior's "sainctеté" (2.330; reputation for being a pious man) was widely known. While his faith may have initially been sincere, his pride eventually corrupts him, and his holiness evolves into nothing more than a false appearance of sanctity. The contrast between the cleric's reputed holiness and that of Sister Marie, whom Marguerite initially presents as "une saincte religieuse," is compelling (2.330). Cotgrave writes that the word "saincte" can be defined as "a she saint" or "a most holie woman."[33] From a grammatical perspective, describing Sister Marie Heroët as "une saincte religieuse" merits analysis. The adjective "saincte" (saintly or holy) usually follows the noun that it modifies, thus the word's positioning suggests that it can be interpreted either as a noun or as an adjective that is placed before the noun for greater emphasis. Whatever interpretation one may prefer, Marguerite clearly emphasizes the saint-like qualities of this nun by intentionally creating a connection between the tale's heroine and saintly behavior. This emphasis on saints is intriguing, especially given that these are not the only references to saints in the tale.

Saint Benedict is mentioned twice, and Saint Martin is evoked more than seven times in the twelve pages of the novella. Even though there are no lengthy references to these saints' vitae, the fact that the priory of Saint Martin is repeatedly referenced in the tale merits attention, especially given that Marguerite demonstrated a strong personal attachment to Saint Martin. Around 1523 she requested an orthodox book of hours that featured various saints such as Jerome, Anne, and Joachim, but no saint receives as much attention as Martin in this manuscript.[34] In fact, this work includes a lengthy Mass to Saint Martin accompanied by multiple miniatures of Marguerite herself pictured with this saint. This book of hours demonstrates that not only did Marguerite have a certain affinity for Saint Martin, but she also possessed extensive knowledge of his life and works. Marguerite and her sixteenth-century readers would have been keenly aware of the stark contrast between the behavior of the lascivious prior of Saint Martin and the selfless actions of Saint Martin of Tours. This tale also engages in Renaissance debates involving gender and religion in that it highlights the moral divergence between the prior's corrupt actions and the holiness of Sister Marie.

Different facets of the young nun's multiple sufferings and steadfast faith serve to recall the lives of Saint Catherine and Saint Margaret. Devotion to these two saints experienced explosive growth in medieval and early modern France. These holy women were widely acclaimed in Renaissance France since they were among the Fourteen Holy Helpers. Along with Saint Barbara and Saint Dorothy, they were also among the *Quattuor Virgines Capitales,* or Four Capital Virgins. Another reason that Margaret and Catherine both received greater attention during this era was that they were the saints, along with Saint Michael, who had appeared together as divine counselors to Joan of Arc. As a result, these two saints were frequently depicted together in late medieval and early Renaissance art. Another factor that led to their growing popularity was that both of their stories were featured in Voragine's *Golden Legend.* His narratives highlight the strength and sacrifices of Saint Catherine and Saint Margaret, while they also underscore how these women suffered extensively to preserve their virginity. Strong emphasis on these very themes is also found in Christine de Pizan's *Le livre de la Cité des dames.* In Christine's text, Catherine and Margaret are the first two saints presented to readers; one also finds these saints depicted together in devotional works in Marguerite's close circles.

Renaissance devotional texts and objects typically reflect the specific interests of the works' owners. It is therefore noteworthy that Saint Catherine and Saint Margaret are both prominently featured in Queen Claude's prayer book. These two saints are depicted on pages facing each other in this manuscript (Figures 3.4 and 3.5). Louise de Savoie's book of hours, a manuscript that was passed down to Marguerite upon her mother's death, also presents the virgin martyrs Catherine, Barbara, and Margaret in direct succession (Figures 3.6 and 3.7).[35] Marguerite's given name and her enduring struggles with infertility and difficult pregnancies resulted in her having a special affinity for Saint Margaret, patron saint of childbearing. In addition, scholars note that Marguerite owned devotional objects depicting both Saint Margaret and Saint Catherine.[36] Saint Catherine's royal status often resulted in European queens adopting her as their own patron saint. Elsa Kammerer argues that it is likely that the Catholic humanist Jean de Vauzelles translated the life of Saint Catherine specifically for Marguerite de Navarre.[37] When analyzing the twenty-second tale along

Figure 3.4. *St. Catherine with a Sword and St. Catherine Surviving the Torture Wheels*, illuminated by the Master of Claude de France, 2¾ × 2 in. From *Prayer Book of Claude de France* (Tours, France, ca. 1517), MS M.1166, fol. 43v, The Morgan Library and Museum, New York. Gift of Mrs. Alexandre P. Rosenberg in memory of her husband, Alexandre Paul Rosenberg, 2008. Courtesy of The Morgan Library and Museum.

Figure 3.5. *St. Margaret Emerging from the Dragon* and *The Decapitation of St. Margaret*, illuminated by the Master of Claude de France, 2¾ × 2 in. From *Prayer Book of Claude de France* (Tours, France, ca. 1517), MS M.1166, fol. 44r, The Morgan Library and Museum, New York. Gift of Mrs. Alexandre P. Rosenberg in memory of her husband, Alexandre Paul Rosenberg, 2008. Courtesy of The Morgan Library and Museum.

Figure 3.6. "St. Catharine Debating Philosophers, Beside Wheel, Beheaded," 192 × 123 mm. From *Hours, use of Rome* (France, ca. 1500–1515), MS 411, fol. 144v, General Collection, Beinecke Rare Book and Manuscript Library, Yale University, New Haven, CT. Courtesy of Beinecke Rare Book and Manuscript Library.

Figure 3.7. "St. Margaret with Dragon, with Flock, Two Men on Horseback," 192 × 123 mm. From *Hours, use of Rome* (France, ca. 1500–1515), MS 411, fol. 146r, General Collection, Beinecke Rare Book and Manuscript Library, Yale University, New Haven, CT. Courtesy of Beinecke Rare Book and Manuscript Library.

with hagiography, one must recall that Catherine is the patron saint of nuns in the cloister and that Margaret is the patron saint of those who are falsely accused. These two different roles of Saint Catherine and Saint Margaret directly relate to the harrowing circumstances of Marguerite's heroine, a cloistered nun who is falsely accused by an evil prior.

Saint Margaret and Saint Catherine were among the most celebrated of the virgin martyrs in sixteenth-century France. Their unswerving commitment to Christ and the persecutions that they endured to maintain their chastity are reflected in the heroine's struggles in the *Heptaméron*'s twenty-second tale. The cleric initially tries to grab Sister Marie's breasts and throw her on a bed. When she adamantly refuses his advances, he admonishes her for even being aware that she has breasts. In response to his egregious statement, she defends herself with eloquence and reason. Much like the emperor and philosophers who debated with Saint Catherine, the prior recognizes Sister Marie's eloquence and intellect (2.332). When the cleric finds himself powerless to sway her with words, he resorts to brutally attacking her. Marguerite writes, "quand il veit toutes ses inventions et efforts estre tournez en rien, comme un homme furieux, et non seulement hors de conscience, mais de raison naturelle, luy meit la main soubs la robbe, et tout ce qu'il peut toucher des ongles esgratigna de telle fureur que la pauvre fille en criant bien fort, de tout son hault, tomba à terre toute esvanouye" (2.334; when he saw that all of his ruses and efforts had come to nothing, he put his hand under her dress, like a man in a fury, defying his conscience and natural reason. He scratched anything he could get his hands on with such fury that the poor girl cried out loudly, fainted, and fell to the ground). As a result of the ferocious attack, Sister Marie cries out, falls, and strikes her head when she faints from the pain caused by her injuries.

The progression from failed seduction, to threats, and ultimately to a violent physical assault in this tale reflects the similar sequence of events in legends of Saint Catherine. Christine de Pizan recounts, "Le tyran Maxence, qui convoitait fort la bienheureuse Catherine pour sa beauté, commença à lui prodiguer des flatteries pour tenter de la soumettre à son désir, mais quand il vit que rien n'y faisait, il en vint aux menaces, puis aux tortures" (The tyrant Maxentius, who was inflamed with desire for the beautiful, holy Catherine, began to pay court to her in an attempt to persuade her to do his bidding. However, when he saw that he was getting nowhere with her, his pleas turned to threats and then to torture).[38] The tale's references to Sister Marie's head injury and the severe violence of the attack recall the physical sufferings of Saint

Catherine and Saint Margaret, who both suffered from torn flesh and ultimately decapitation. In contrast to many other sexual assaults in the *Heptaméron*, Marguerite describes the prior's brutal attack and Sister Marie's injuries in a detailed and graphic manner. Similar to what is found in the violent attack of the mule-driver's wife, Marguerite's narrative places emphasis on the extreme brutality of the physical and sexual violence that women experienced in Renaissance France. Marguerite's depiction of the events immediately following the assault also merits further attention for its theological content.

Immediately after this brutal encounter, the prior publicly addresses the entire chapter. He even requests that the sisters sing a Salve Regina to honor the Virgin Mary. When he weeps on hearing the song, the other nuns assume that it is because he is such a holy man (2.336). Virginia Krause remarks, "Sister Marie is not deceived by the saintly aura surrounding her would-be seducer."[39] In fact, the young nun responds to his hypocritical actions with a silent prayer to the Virgin Mary: "Mais seur Marie, qui congoissoit sa malice, *prioit en son cueur la vierge Marie* de confondre celluy qui desprisoit tant la virginité" (emphasis added;[40] Sister Marie, who knew his malice, prayed in her heart to the Virgin Mary that she would be able to confound this man who had treated her virginity with such contempt).[41] Marguerite's portrayal of the nun's plea for the Virgin Mary to intercede is of particular interest given the intense debate between reformers and orthodox Catholics in Renaissance France over the intercession of Mary and the saints. Significantly, Marguerite not only depicts Sister Marie as praying to Mary, but the text also specifies that her prayers are answered at the end of the narrative. This detail serves to highlight the efficacy of this approach to prayer. This reference and the multiple images of the Virgin in Marguerite's own book of hours also suggest that despite certain reformist tendencies, Marguerite nevertheless held an enduring attachment to the traditional Catholic devotion to the Virgin Mary and a fervent belief in Mary's intercessory prayers.

The narrative emphasis on virginity appears once again when the prior falsely accuses the virtuous nun of sordid acts with another monk. He then attempts to convince her to allow him to "visit" her virginity by insisting that she cover her face and allow him to inspect her physically. Sister Marie adamantly refuses and reminds the prior that the sole threat to her virginity has come from him (2.340). Her refusal to acquiesce or indulge his demands results in the prior aggressively making threats of excommunication and public humiliation. Despite such forceful intimidation, he once again fails in swaying Sister Marie. In fact, as one commonly finds in saints' lives, she courageously responds to his egregious request with a steadfast profession of faith: "Celuy qui cognoist le cueur de ses serviteurs, me rendra autant d'honeur devant luy, que vous me ferez de honte devant les hommes. Parquoy puis que vostre malice en est jusques là, j'aime mieux qu'elle paracheve sa cruauté envers moy, que le desir de son mauvais vouloir : car je sçay que Dieu est juste juge" (2.340; He who knows the hearts of his servants will honor me as much before him as you could shame me before men. So, since your malice has gone this far, I would prefer that it act on its cruel intentions rather than succumb to its wicked desire, since I know that God is a righteous judge). Sister Marie's expression of her firm confidence in God throughout her harrowing plight recalls similar declarations of faith that Saint Catherine and Saint Margaret made amid their own sufferings and persecutions.

The cleric then threatens the innocent nun with excommunication and when she refuses to yield to his coercions, he proceeds to dishonor her in front of the entire chapter. The prior assembles the whole community of nuns together to watch as he humiliates Sister Marie by forcing her to come before him on her knees. He then proceeds to publicly accuse her of lascivious behavior, lowers her rank in the convent, and demeans her by forcing her to eat bread and water on the ground. It is a common motif in saints' lives to subsist on nothing but bread and water. According to legend, Saint Catherine was subjected to starvation, yet she was sustained by bread provided by doves sent from heaven.[42] Joan of Arc also survived on nothing but bread and water when she was imprisoned and on trial.[43] Although Joan was convicted of heresy and burned at the stake in 1431, her trial was nullified in July 1456 and she was rehabilitated.[44] While Joan's sanctity would have been widely recognized during Marguerite's lifetime, it was not until 1909 that she was beatified and 1920 when she was canonized.[45] Sister Marie's multiple persecutions recall saints' vitae, and so does her unshakeable faith in God throughout her sufferings. Marguerite writes, "Sœur Marie . . . endura ceste sentence, levant les yeux au ciel, et priant celuy, qui avoit esté sa resistance contre le peché, vouloir estre sa patience contre sa tribulation" (2.341; Sister Marie faced this judgment in silence, raising her eyes toward the heavens, and prayed to the One who had been her resistance against sin, asking him to be her patience in such tribulation). Marguerite's lexicon and motifs firmly place the story in the discourse of hagiography, as do Sister Marie's saintly actions of praying and raising her eyes toward heaven amid persecution.

Along with extreme physical suffering and humiliation, imprisonment and social isolation are recurrent themes in narratives of Saint Catherine's and

Saint Margaret's lives. The threat of imprisonment also looms large in the twenty-second tale. Early in the tale, the reader is told that the prior plotted to have relics stolen. This detail emphasizes the extent of his scheming and dishonesty, but it also merits attention in that it highlights the prior's complete disregard for relics, an important component of traditional devotion to the cult of saints. According to Catholic theology, these devotional objects exemplify Christ's presence in the body of the church's members. In his letter to Riparius, Saint Jerome noted, "colimus et adoramus: ne serviamus creaturae potius quam Creatori, qui est benedictus in saecula. Honoramus autem reliquias Martyrum, ut eum cujus sunt Martyres, adoremus" (we do not worship, we do not adore, for fear that we should bow down to the creature and not the creator, but we venerate the relics of the martyrs in order the better to adore Him whose martyrs they are).[46] Thus, for a sixteenth-century reader, Marguerite's description of the prior's utter disrespect for sacred relics would have served to underscore the extent of his false sanctity, his total disregard for the saints, and his lack of a true commitment to Christ. The narrative then explains that the prior proceeds to accuse and imprison an innocent man for the crime. When this wrongly accused man seeks to reveal the misdeeds of the cleric, he is unjustly imprisoned and treated so poorly that he is never seen again (2.338).

The narrative also underscores the threat to Sister Marie of perpetual imprisonment, noting that "Sœur Marie, estant advertie par une de ses compaignes qui entendoit tout son affaire, que si elle respondoit chose qui despleust au prieur, il la mettroit in pace, c'est à dire, en chartre perpetuelle" (2.341; Sister Marie had been warned by one of her sisters, who had heard everything about her case, that if she said anything that displeased the prior, he would put her *in pace*, that is to say, in prison forever). Marguerite specifies that the young nun is forced to endure a prolonged period of total isolation. In fact, she is prohibited from speaking or writing to her family for more than three years (2.341). Through these details Marguerite emphasizes the severity of Sister Marie's social isolation, while she also highlights the young nun's consistent privileging of her faith above any worldly comforts.

In this tale, the prior attempts to persuade Sister Marie to succumb to his desires by promising to make her abbess of one of the best convents in the kingdom. He states, "si vous me voulez aimer, je vous feray eslire abbesse d'une des meilleures abbayes de ce royaume" (2.335; if you choose to love me, I will have you elected abbess of one of the best abbeys in the kingdom). His repeated attempts to sway her, along with his strategy of trying to woo her with the promise to elevate her status in the kingdom, merit analysis. His words mirror those of Satan when he sought to tempt Christ in the desert, as depicted in the fourth chapter of the Gospel of Matthew: "The devil took him to a very high mountain and showed him all the kingdoms of the world and their splendor. 'All this will I give you,' he said, 'if you will bow down and worship me'" (4.8–9). They also share significant parallels with the tactics and words of the emperor when he tries to entice Saint Catherine in the *Golden Legend*. Voragine describes the emperor's attempts to woo Saint Catherine, saying, "O tresnoble vierge, aies pitié de ta majesté et tu seras appellee dame après la royne en mon palais; et ton ymage sera faite ou milleu du palais et adoree de tous comme deesse" (O damsel nobly born, take thought to your youth! In my palace you will be called second only to the queen. Your image will be erected in the center of the city, and you will be adored by all as a goddess!).[47] He tries to convince her a second time, saying, "se tu te repens, tu seras la premiere en mon palais" (if you have now come to your senses, you shall be first lady in my palace).[48] Along with the parallels in the temptations they experienced, Sister Marie's willingness to embrace sufferings also reflects the influence of the lives of Saint Catherine and Saint Margaret as depicted by Voragine.

The *Golden Legend* highlights how Saint Margaret replied to the prefect who tried to seduce her, saying, "Jhesucrist bailla soy mesme a mort pour nous et pour ce ne doubte je pas a mourir pour lui" (Christ gave himself up to death for me, and therefore I want to die for Christ!).[49] Saint Catherine replies to her torturer in a similar fashion, saying, "N'atens pas a faire quelxconques tourmens que tu vouldras ne yceulx veilles differés, car je desire offrir a Dieu mon sang et ma char comme il offrit pour moy" (Whatever torments you have in mind, don't waste time! My one desire is to offer my flesh and blood to Christ as he offered himself for me).[50] Saint Catherine insists on her sacrifice and position as bride of Christ once again, saying, "Il est mon Dieu, mon pasteur, et mon espoux seul" (He is my God, my lover, my shepherd, and my one and only spouse).[51] Marguerite depicts Sister Marie's response to the prior in a similar light when she writes, "elle aimoit mieux mourir en chartre perpetuelle, que d'avoir jamais autre amy que celuy qui estoit mort pour elle en la croix, avec lequel elle aimoit mieux souffrir tous les maux que le monde pourroit donner, que sans luy avoir tous les biens" (2.335; she would rather die in perpetual confinement than to have any friend other than He who died for her on the cross. She preferred to endure, with him, all the suffering that the world could inflict rather than to disobey him to receive all worldly pleasures). The tale's emphasis on Sister Marie's willingness to embrace death, isolation, and continual sufferings in order to honor her commitment to Jesus recalls hagiographic narratives, as does the insistence on her total devotion to Christ.

The depiction of Sister Marie as a bride of Christ also serves to evoke Saint Catherine's mystical marriage to Jesus. This facet of Saint Catherine's legend received sustained attention not only in literature, but also in the visual arts of the Renaissance. Renowned works such as Christine's *Le livre de la Cité des Dames* or the Master of the Legend of Saint Lucy's painting illustrate the artistic focus on Saint Catherine's mystical marriage during the fifteenth and sixteenth centuries. In addition, Sister Marie refers to "celuy qui estoit mort pour elle en la croix" (2.335; He who died for her on the cross); she thus explicitly evokes the cross, the ultimate symbol of Christ's sufferings as well as a widely recognized attribute of Saint Margaret. Moreover, in the tale's conclusion, the prior admits his misdeeds by describing Sister Marie as "une perle d'honneur et de virginité" (2.344; a pearl of honor and virginity). Like the cross, the pearl, or "marguerite," was also one of the well-known attributes of Saint Margaret that Voragine incorporated into her vitae in the *Golden Legend*.[52] The references to the pearl and the cross together with Marguerite's insistence on Sister Marie's persecutions and her steadfast faith recall the lives of Saint Catherine and Saint Margaret, while they also underscore the fact that Sister Marie successfully resisted the prior and maintained her chastity.

While the twenty-second tale establishes multiple parallels between Sister Marie and these virgin martyrs, there is one significant difference that merits further exploration. Nevanlinna and Taavitsainen remark, "The central issue in Saints' lives is the fight between good and evil, between Christians and pagans. . . . The plot is developed through the confrontation of the saint with worldly authorities in the form of an evil tyrant."[53] The saints are typically persecuted and accosted by pagan leaders, but Marguerite depicts a nun who suffers extensively within the walls of a religious sanctuary because of the egregious actions of a man of the cloth.[54] The queen of Navarre was clearly outraged at the prevalence of clerical abuse in sixteenth-century France and disheartened by the institutional structures of the church that made such crimes possible. In fact, after Sister Marie writes her story and shares it with her family, they seek Marguerite's help. The queen of Navarre represents herself as coming to the aid of the persecuted nun by confronting the cleric and taking the necessary measures to restore order to the convent. After Sister Marie's long-sufferings, her innocence and virtues are ultimately recognized. Moreover, she is eventually placed in a position where she has the power to reform religious institutions (2.345). In a certain sense, the tale's conclusion can be seen as a revisionist hagiography, for unlike Saint Margaret and Saint Catherine, who were ultimately martyred, Marguerite's narrative reverses the power structures that allowed the corrupt cleric to persecute a steadfast nun.

The discussion among the *devisants* also presents a persuasive challenge to the institutional structures of the church and patriarchal society through the use of Scripture. Geburon concludes with an encouraging message for the women in the group: "Voilà, mes dames, une histoire, qui est bien pour monstrer ce que dict l'Evangile, et sainct Paul aux Corinthiens : 'Que Dieu par les choses foibles, confond les fortes, et par les inutiles aux yeux des hommes, la gloire de ceux qui cuident estre quelque chose, et ne sont rien'" (2.345; There you have, my ladies, a story that shows very well what the Gospel says: that weak things confound the mighty; and through things that are useless in men's eyes, the pride of those who think they amount to something is reduced to nothing). He also refers to the exaltation of the persecuted nun and recalls Christ's admonition that "He who exalts himself will be humbled, and he who humbles himself will be exalted" (2.345–346).

Interestingly, Geburon is the only male storyteller to react to the story. After his remarks, it is the women who lead the discussion as Oisille, Nomerfide, and Ennasuite exchange their opinions on clerics. Oisille reminds readers that the evil prior was able to get away with such behavior because "on se fioit plus en luy qu'en Dieu" (2.346; people trusted him more than they trusted God). Nomerfide expresses that she is so horrified by clerics that she is unable to confess, since she finds them worse than all other men. In response, Oisille diplomatically notes that "il y en a de bons . . . et ne fault pas que pour les mauvais, ils soient tous jugez" (2.346; there are good ones . . . and they mustn't be condemned because of the actions of the bad ones). Ennasuite adds to the skepticism about the integrity of men of the cloth, noting that "moins on les voit, moins on les cognoist, et plus on les estime, pource que la frequentation les monstre tels qu'ils sont" (2.346; the less we know them, the more we respect them, because when you spend time with them, you see them for what they are). Oisille concludes the discussion and introduces the next tale by warning women about "l'hypocrisie de ceux, qui s'estiment plus religieux que les autres" (2.347; the hypocrisy of those who think themselves to be more pious than others). It is telling that the male storytellers remain silent after the tale while the women discuss their doubts about the integrity of clerics. While the male *devisants* frequently defend a man's right to take a woman by force, this discussion clearly shows that clerics are held to a different code of behavior.

Within the twenty-second tale, Marguerite depicts herself confronting the debauched cleric, but her actions also extend well beyond what is represented in the pages of this story. By adapting elements of saints' lives to a sixteenth-century context, Marguerite offers her readers powerful examples of women's holiness while she also boldly calls attention to the risks that men pose to faithful women. This chapter has demonstrated how the violent persecutions, saintly resistance, and heroic virtue of the *Heptaméron*'s heroines recall exemplary women from saints' lives, while they also respond to misogynistic commonplaces in Renaissance debates by highlighting the strength and faith of women in sixteenth-century France. The next chapter examines how the spirituality and admirable courage that Marguerite's heroines manifest during isolation, imprisonment, and abandonment reveal yet another influence of hagiography in the *Heptaméron*.

CHAPTER FOUR

Saintly Women Confined and Isolated

Je faictz oraison
Et ne craindz ny mort, ny prison,
Pour l'amour du Dieu que je croy.

[I pray
and fear neither death, nor prison,
For the love of God in whom I believe.]

—Marguerite de Navarre, *Les dernières œuvres de la royne Marguerite de Navarre*

In Renaissance France, women were at the mercy of the men in their families; it was the men who held the economic, legal, and social power. Consequently, at the whims of their male relatives, women could be confined and forced into isolation with no repercussions. Similarly, in hagiographic legends, male authority figures frequently use their unfettered power to imprison and sequester women. Female saints respond to their confinement and sufferings with prayer, patience, and unwavering faith in God. In the *Heptaméron,* Marguerite draws on hagiography by depicting her heroines in isolation as saint-like figures. Their persecutions, their strength throughout their trials, and their steadfast belief in God's faithfulness amid harrowing difficulties recall hagiographic legends. Through an analysis of depictions of saints in literature and visual arts, together with a close reading of tales 21, 32, 40, and 67, this chapter highlights how Marguerite both borrows from and revises saints' vitae in the portrayal of her isolated heroines. In so doing, she intervenes on behalf of women in various Renaissance controversies and questions the gender bias in certain hagiographical writings and the Catholic Church.

Women's Confinement, Piety, and Suffering in the *Heptaméron*'s Twenty-First and Fortieth Tales

Scholars have frequently examined the twenty-first and fortieth tales together.[1] This comparative approach is hardly surprising, since the novellas are explicitly linked in the *Heptaméron*'s frame. Aside from Parlamente's overt remarks establishing a connection between the narratives, the heroines in these tales are related. Rolandine is the niece of the unnamed heroine in the fortieth tale, and both women are tormented and imprisoned by the same nobleman. There are also numerous thematic parallels between the stories. Emily Thompson remarks, "The similarities between the two novellas are multiple; in each, a heroine's marital prospects are neglected by her family until she reaches an age at which she acquires some legal rights. She uses these to make her own choice of husband but marries him secretly. Their relationship is uncovered, and the woman is punished and kept in isolation."[2] Although these tales have received substantial critical attention, the connections between hagiography and these heroines have been mentioned only briefly.[3] Significantly, both women respond to their sufferings and confinement with prayer, patience, and faith in God. In fact, the trials of Marguerite's heroines recall the life and attributes of Saint Barbara. Through an analysis of various depictions of this saint in early modern literature and visual arts, together with a close reading of Marguerite's tales, this section highlights the many parallels between Saint Barbara and these heroines. It also sheds light on how textual and visual depictions of Saint Barbara reinforced Marguerite's response to religious and social debates and allowed her to bring greater attention to the injustices that women encountered in the patriarchal society of sixteenth-century France.

Although Saint Barbara is not explicitly mentioned in the *Heptaméron*, she was one of the most venerated saints of Renaissance France. She was one of the Fourteen Holy Helpers, as well as one of the *Quattuor Virgines Capitales*, or Four Capital Virgins. According to legend, she was held captive in a tower by her father, who persecuted her for her faith, subjected her to cruelties when she shunned marriage, and then tortured and eventually murdered her when she adamantly refused to recant her Christian faith. The sixteenth-century readers of the *Heptaméron* would have been cognizant of details of Saint Barbara's legend, especially the tower, her most widely recognized attribute. Christine de Pizan's *Le livre de la Cité des dames* introduces this saint saying, "son père l'avoit enclose en une tour" (her father locked her away in a tower).[4] Marguerite would have been familiarized with Saint Barbara's story through hagiographical narratives, as well as via representations of this saint within her family's possessions. Saint Barbara is one of the saints featured in Queen Claude's prayer book. Unlike many other saints in this work, there are multiple representations of her trials. The work features her tower, the martyr's palm, and her torture and beheading (Figures 4.1 and 4.2). She also holds a prominent place among the female saints in Louise de Savoie's book of hours, where her tower and baptism are both depicted (Figure 4.3). The suffrages typically represent the owner's devotional interests; thus, the fact that Saint Barbara is one of the few saints featured in a full-page illustration in Louise's book of hours is noteworthy. Marguerite undoubtedly encountered multiple representations of Saint Barbara throughout her life and different facets of this saint's iconography are integrated into the twenty-first and fortieth tales.

In Saint Barbara's legend and in Marguerite's tales, women are persecuted, punished, and isolated when they resist familial dictates regarding their marriages. When Saint Barbara refused her father's command to marry according to his wishes, he became so enraged that he imprisoned her in a tower. Like Saint Barbara, Rolandine and her aunt are also isolated in connection with marriage. However, while Saint Barbara refused marriage, these women choose their husbands and marry secretly. When they act on their own volition by selecting their spouses, they are persecuted by a close family member. In tale 21, Rolandine's wisdom and virtue elicit several auspicious marriage proposals, but her father's selfishness and the queen's dislike for her family result in her prospects being neglected. Consequently, the young woman lives a saintly life of solitude and prayer (2.299–300). Eventually, she takes consolation in a chaste friendship with an illegitimate nobleman, and they secretly marry. When the queen discovers their marriage, she persecutes Rolandine in a scene that recalls hagiography. Marguerite writes, "ceste correction devant plusieurs personnes ne procedoit pas d'amour qu'elle luy portast, mais pour luy faire une honte" (2.315; the queen was scolding her in front of people not out of love but to humiliate her). Throughout Rolandine's public humiliation, she calmly responds to the angry queen and emphasizes that her actions are in accordance with God's will. Scott Francis argues that Marguerite depicts Rolandine as a "beatific martyr."[5] During this heart-wrenching scene, Rolandine reminds the queen of her status as "la plus grande Princesse de Chrestienté" (2.318; the

celos per martyrii palmam per
uenire fecisti: concede nobis que
sumus vt eius exempla sectan-
tes: ad te venire mereamur. Per.
De Sancta Barbara. an.
Gaude Bar-
bara beata:
summe pol-
lens in doctri-
na: angeli mi-
sterio. Gaude
virgo deo gra-
ta: que bap-
tistam imitata: es in vite stadio
Gaude cum te visitauit chris-
tus vita & curauit: plagas ac-
tu proprio. Gaude quia meru-
isti: impetrare quod petisti: dã
te dei filio. Gaude nanqȝ eleua-
ta: es in celum & delata nobili
martyrio. Te laudantem fami-

Figure 4.1. *St. Barbara with Tower and Palm* and *St. Barbara Tortured*, illuminated by the Master of Claude de France, 2¾ × 2 in. From *Prayer Book of Claude de France* (Tours, France, ca. 1517), MS M.1166, fol. 44v. The Morgan Library and Museum, New York. Gift of Mrs. Alexandre P. Rosenberg in memory of her husband, Alexandre Paul Rosenberg, 2008. Courtesy of The Morgan Library and Museum.

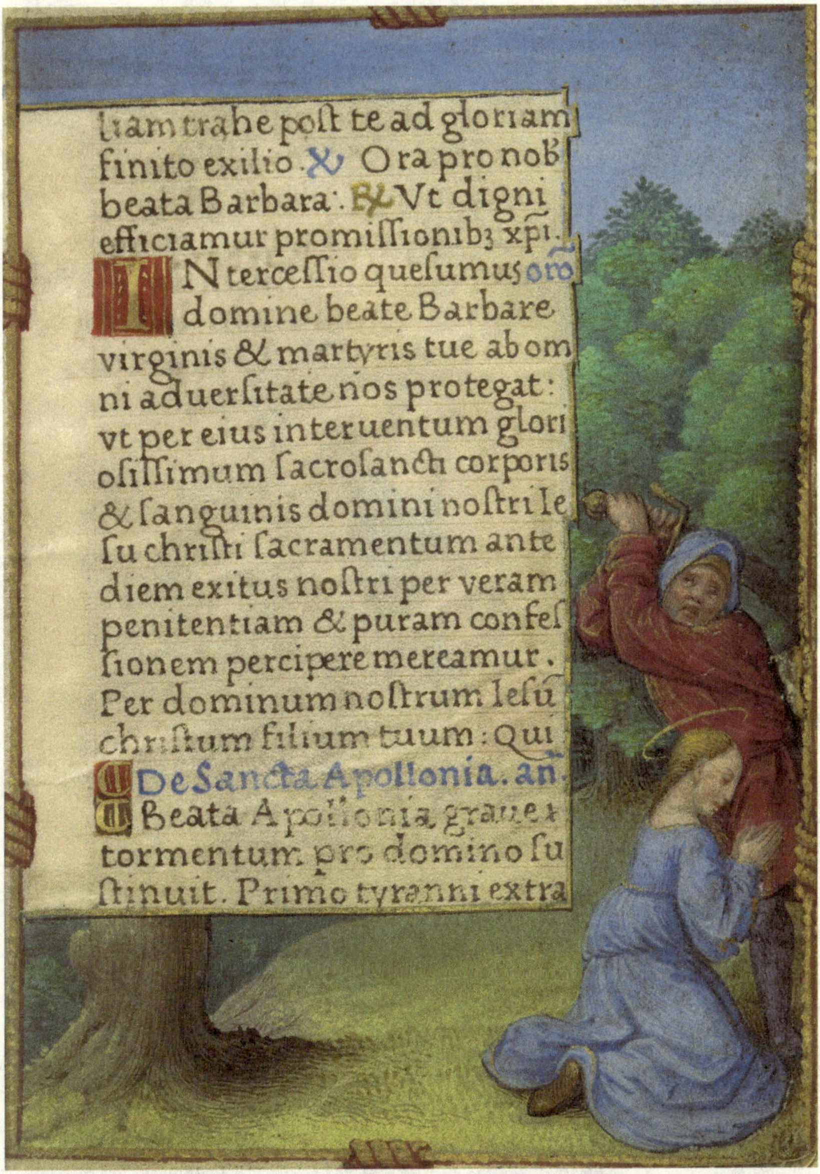

Figure 4.2. *Decapitation of St. Barbara,* illuminated by the Master of Claude de France, 2¾ × 2 in. From *Prayer Book of Claude de France* (Tours, France, ca. 1517), MS M.1166, fol. 45r, The Morgan Library and Museum, New York. Gift of Mrs. Alexandre P. Rosenberg in memory of her husband, Alexandre Paul Rosenberg, 2008. Courtesy of The Morgan Library and Museum.

Figure 4.3. "St. Barbara Baptized," 192 × 123 mm. From *Hours, use of Rome* (France, ca. 1500–1515), MS 411, fol. 145r, General Collection, Beinecke Rare Book and Manuscript Library, Yale University, New Haven, CT. Courtesy of Beinecke Rare Book and Manuscript Library.

greatest princess of all Christendom). The reference is notable in that it serves to underscore the monarch's lack of Christian charity, especially since her actions closely resemble those of pagan tormentors from hagiographic narratives.

Rolandine also refers to God repeatedly in defense of her own actions. For instance, she asserts that she has in no way offended God (2.317, 2.319). Moreover, she insists that God-given reason has governed her choices (2.317). She fearlessly remarks that she dares to speak in such a manner since God is with her: "Et voilà qui me fait parler sans crainte, estant asseurée que celuy qui veoit mon cueur est avec moy : et si un tel juge est avec moy, j'aurois tort de craindre ceux qui sont subjects à son jugement" (2.319; This is why I speak with no fear: I am certain that he who sees my heart stands by me; and if such a judge is on my side, I would be wrong to fear those who are subject to his judgment). In hagiographical writings, saints frequently insist on their oneness with the will of God.[6] It is Rolandine's persecution that allows her to publicly affirm her "perfect confidence in God" and to express her firm belief that her actions are in accordance with God's will. Moreover, akin to the portrayals of saints in hagiography, Rolandine's punishment elicits a compassionate response. In fact, her suffering serves to elevate rather than to debase her. Marguerite writes that when the king's deputies "la menerent devers son pere en si piteuse façon, que par où elle passoit chacun ploiroit . . . la punition fut si grande et sa constance telle, qu'elle feist estimer sa faulte estre vertu" (2.322; sent her to her father in such pitiful conditions that, as she passed, everyone was brought to tears . . . her punishment was so great and she faced it with such constancy that she made people think her misdeed was actually a virtue). Similarly, in tale 40, the aunt's holiness powerfully transforms a place of vengeful punishment into a locus of saintly devotion.

The same nobleman who isolates his daughter, Rolandine, imprisons his sister in the fortieth tale.[7] Parlamente introduces the novella by explaining why she recounts it: "Je vous promis . . . de vous dire l'occasion pourquoy le pere de Rolandine feit faire le chasteau, où il la tint si long temps prisonniere" (2.504; I promised . . . to tell you why Rolandine's father built the castle where she was imprisoned for a long time). Although Rolandine's aunt receives numerous marriage proposals from worthy suitors, her brother's greed and possessive nature impel him to reject them all. After he has neglected his sister's marital prospects, she secretly marries one of her brother's most trusted companions. When the infuriated brother confronts the couple, the heroine's husband does everything in his power to save his own life. Unable to escape by the door, he jumps out the window. In contrast to the husband who thought only of his own survival, the heroine immediately and selflessly offers to surrender her own life instead.

She throws herself on her knees before her brother and demands mercy for her husband as she offers herself up as a sacrifice, saying, "Monsieur, sauvez la vie de mon mary : car je l'ay espousé, et s'il y a offense, n'en punissez que moy" (2.507; My lord, spare my husband's life—I married him. If it was wrong, punish only me). In response to her pleas for her husband's life, her brother demands the man's immediate execution. The heroine again expresses her desire to sacrifice her own life, saying, "je vous supplie pour toute l'amitié, que vous m'avez jamais portée, me faire en ceste mesme heure compagne de sa mort, comme j'ay esté de toutes ses fortunes. Par ce moyen satisfaisant à vostre cruelle et injuste colere, vous mettrez en repos le corps et l'ame de celle, qui ne veult et ne peult vivre sans luy" (2.508; I beg you, in the name of all the friendship that you've ever felt for me, to send me to join him in death now, as I was joined to him in all of his fortunes. This way, in indulging your cruel and unjust anger, you will bring peace to the body and soul of the woman who cannot live without him). Her courage and willingness to sacrifice herself highlight her moral strength, especially when compared with her husband who quickly fled, thought only of preserving his own life, and left her alone to face her brother's wrath. Her words also emphasize the Christian perspective of death as peace for the body and soul and demonstrate her firm conviction that she will find rest in God. It is ultimately her faith and her love of God that enable her to find peace during the harsh punishment that her brother inflicts on her.

Along with the threat of death, the nature and severity of the punishment of the women in these tales is particularly striking. The imprisonment of these women in the castle borrows from Saint Barbara's legend. In visual depictions of Saint Barbara from medieval and Renaissance France, she is usually portrayed along with her characteristic attribute, the tower where she was held prisoner by her father. The depiction of the tower in visual and literary arts allowed for the immediate recognition of this saint. Catharine Randall has demonstrated the important role of objects in medieval hagiography and Marguerite's familiarity with this aspect of the genre.[8] Marguerite would have known that her contemporaries, who were steeped in the rich Catholic traditions of Renaissance France, would have inevitably made a connection between the women imprisoned in her tales and the story of Saint Barbara.

The tower that is the most prevalent attribute associated with Saint Barbara is always featured with three windows. This saint is associated with windows since according to legend she had three windows placed in her tower to honor the Trinity. Maurienne's early sixteenth-century *Histoire de Sainte Barbe* (Story of Saint Barbara) describes Saint Barbara's demand that masons add a third window to her tower, a request that is immediately followed by her declaration "O precieuse trinité, vray essence en unite" (O precious Trinity, true essence in unity).[9] This expression of Barbara's Christian faith enraged her father to the point that it was the primary reason that he handed her over to the authorities who brutally tortured her.

In tale 21 of the *Heptaméron*, there is also transgressive behavior associated with windows. When the queen forbids Rolandine and her suitor from speaking, they develop a strategy to communicate. They discreetly place themselves at adjoining windows in the castle, "car leurs deux fenestres estoient promptement au *triangle* du bout des deux corps de maison" (emphasis added; since the windows of the two rooms were just at the angle where the two wings of the house met).[10] Their clandestine meetings at the "triangle" between two windows allow them to defy the queen by engaging in lengthy conversations. The portrayal of windows in the fortieth tale also serves to recall Saint Barbara's legend, since the connection between transgression, rage, and windows is clearly present. When the brother discovers the couple together, the heroine's husband promptly jumps out the window into a garden. The brother then places himself at the window, from where he orders his servants to kill the gentleman. The text clarifies that the brother "se meit à la fenestre, et cria tout haut qu'on le tuast, ce qui fut faict promptement par son commandement, devant les yeux de luy, et de sa sœur" (2.507–508; went to the window and yelled out that the gentleman should be killed—orders that were executed before his and his sister's eyes). The window is also what allows the sister to witness her husband's brutal death. The fact that Marguerite incorporates windows, rage, and transgression into both tales is noteworthy as it creates yet another parallel with Saint Barbara's legend.

Much like the emphasis on imprisonment, persecution, and windows that readers find in portrayals of Saint Barbara's father in hagiography, Marguerite's narratives emphasize the gross injustice of the nobleman's cruel actions toward his daughter and his sister. He responds to his daughter's public humiliation with bitter silence and a prolonged imprisonment. "Le père sçachant ceste piteuse nouvelle, ne la voulut point veoir, mais l'envoya en un chasteau dedans une forest . . . et la teint là longuement en prison" (2.322; Having learned this pitiful news, her father chose not to see her but rather sent her to a castle in a forest. . . .

He held her imprisoned there for a long time). In the fortieth tale, the severe injustice of the gentleman's actions toward his sister are also highlighted. Marguerite writes that he "eust bien voulu jamais n'avoir commis un tel crime. Si est-ce que la crainte qu'il eut, que sa sœur en demandast justice ou vengeance, luy feit faire un chasteau au milieu d'une forest, auquel il la meit, et deffendit que aucun ne parlast à elle" (2.508–509; regretted having committed such a crime. However, for fear that his sister would ask that he be brought to justice or that she be avenged, he had a castle built for her in the middle of a forest. He put her there and forbade anyone to speak with her). Following his merciless acts, the text unambiguously characterizes his actions as a crime and evokes his regret. Although his actions are represented as a violation of the law, rather than trying to make things right, he allows his fear of legal repercussions and desire for revenge to govern his behavior. Thus, he decides to imprison his sister. In so doing, he attempts to silence and isolate her by removing her entirely from social life. The brother's belief that by holding his sister captive she could in no way work for justice underscores his selfish and cruel actions, but it also serves to highlight the limitations of his earthly perspective.

While the imprisonment of Rolandine and her aunt underscores the moral depravity of the nobleman, the heroines' responses to their captivity increase the reader's admiration for them as they are depicted as unequivocally saintly. Their reactions to their imprisonment illustrate their spiritual devotion and unshakeable faith in God. In tales 21 and 40, both women respond to their persecution and humiliation with affirmations of faith. Rolandine declares, "Mais j'ay un pere au ciel, lequel (je suis seure) me donnera autant de patience, que je me voy de grands maulx par vous preparez, et en luy seul j'ay ma parfaicte confiance" (2.320; But I have a father in heaven, who, I am certain, will give me as much patience as I need to face the great suffering that you have planned for me, and in him alone I put all of my confidence). Her aunt is also depicted as placing her hope solely in God, "nonobstant qu'elle fust foible et impuissante pour s'en venger, si esperoit elle en celuy, qui estoit vray juge, et qui ne laisse nul mal impuni, avec le seul amour duquel elle vouloit user le demeurant de sa vie en son hermitage" (2.509; even though she was weak and did not have the power to take revenge, she had hope in Him who is the true judge and who leaves no wrong unpunished, in whose love she wished to live her remaining days in her hermitage). This passage emphasizes that, like Saint Barbara, Rolandine's aunt spent her time imprisoned expressing her love for God and placing her faith and hope in divine justice.

The saint-like portrayal of the heroine is also underscored by Marguerite's use of the word "hermitage." While the expression can refer to an isolated dwelling, this word frequently has a religious connotation as it represents a place where one lives in religious seclusion. Randall remarks, "The *chasteau* is no longer a terrestrial prison; it has been transformed into a spiritualized dwelling, a *hermitaige*."[11] Moreover, the fact that the reference is included in a sentence that begins with emphasis on the heroine's hope in God alone encourages the spiritual interpretation of the word. Given the extreme isolation that her father forced upon her, Saint Barbara is often described as living a hermit's life. After the reference to the aunt's hermitage, Marguerite writes that she spent her life imprisoned but "vivant en telle patience et austerité, qu'après sa mort chacun y couroit comme à une saincte" (2.509; she lived there in such patience and austerity that after her death many visited the castle as if she had been a saint). Not only does this passage portray the heroine as living an exemplary life of holiness, but Marguerite unequivocally represents the aunt's prison as a site of pilgrimage after her death.

Saint Barbara is frequently honored as the patron saint of protection against sudden death. This role certainly increased her popularity during the Renaissance, when France was simultaneously confronting recurrence of the plague, religious strife, and ongoing wars over its borders. Saint Barbara's association with protection from sudden death stems from God's swift justice following her martyrdom. According to legend, after her father murdered her, he was immediately struck by lightning, consumed by flame, and died a miserable death. In both the twenty-first and fortieth tales, the reader finds examples of sudden death in which God's role is emphasized. In sharp contrast to Rolandine's faithfulness, the man that she had married abandons her and shamelessly seeks a financially profitable marriage elsewhere. God, however, takes pity on Rolandine and rewards her patience by ensuring that her husband's sudden death grants her freedom of conscience: "Parquoy la bonté divine, qui est parfaicte charité et vraye amour, eut pitié de sa douleur, et regarda sa patience, en sorte qu'après peu de jours le bastard mourut" (2.324; Divine goodness, which is perfect charity and true love, had pity on her suffering and took account of her patience in such a way that a few days later the bastard died). Grace Morgan Armstrong remarks, "The divine approval of her actions is confirmed in a striking way when her wayward husband dies unexpectedly."[12]

The narrative also depicts a similar turn of events with Rolandine's brother. After threatening her with death and isolating her, Rolandine's father eventually comes to regret his mistreatment of his daughter, saying, "Ma fille, vous estes plus juste que moy : car s'il y a eu faulte en vostre affaire, j'en suis la principale cause : mais puis que Dieu l'a ainsi ordonné, je veux satisfaire au passé" (2.324–25; My daughter, you are right and I was wrong, since if you were at fault in your actions, I was mainly to blame. But since this was God's will, I want to make amends for the past). Thus, he ultimately welcomes his daughter home and eventually arranges for a favorable marriage. Despite the father's forgiveness, Rolandine's brother obstinately holds a grudge. He constantly reminds her of her "disobedience," endeavors to deprive her of her inheritance, and leaves her with little means to live. Significantly, once again God intervenes to set things right: "En quoy Dieu pourveut : car le frere, qui vouloit tout tenir, laissa en un jour par une mort subite les biens qu'il tenoit de sa sœur et les siens ensemble. Ainsi elle fut heretiere d'une bonne et grosse maison, où elle vesquit honorablement et *sainctement* en l'amour de son mary. Et après avoir eslevé deux fils que Dieu leur donna, *rendit joyeusement son ame à celuy où de long temps elle avoit sa parfaicte confiance*" (2.325–326, emphasis added; But God provided for them, since the brother who wanted to keep everything for himself gave up in one single day, through his sudden death, both his sister's share and his share of the estate. Thus she inherited a rich and noble house, where she lived piously and honorably in the love of her husband. After having raised two sons that God had given them, she joyfully returned her soul to Him in whom she had always had perfect confidence). In contrast to her brother's sudden death, Rolandine lives with honor and holiness and eventually embraces death "joyfully," much like the saints in hagiographic legends.

While the cruel brother in the fortieth tale does not encounter the same dramatic death as Saint Barbara's father, Marguerite's novella highlights the rapid and disastrous decline of his entire household nonetheless. Marguerite notes, "la maison de son frere alla tellement en ruine, que de six fils, qu'il avoit, n'en demeura un seul, et moururent tous fort miserablement" (2.509; her brother's house declined to such an extent that only one of his six sons remained alive, and the others all died miserable deaths). Not only does the narrative emphasize that the cruel brother tragically loses his sons, but it specifies that they die miserably. In contrast, the heroine's life is widely recognized for its patience and austerity. Randall notes, "While she experiences a sort of sainthood, his refusal to follow scriptural mandates causes his ruin and that of his house."[13] These tales offer striking similarities with Saint Barbara's life. They also provide readers with a powerful message about God's ability to bring justice to mistreated women when they place their faith in Him.

The conversation following tale 21 exemplifies how Marguerite draws on saints' lives to offer readers depictions of women that persuasively dispel the misogynistic discourses of the *querelle des femmes*. Parlamente asserts that not only do Rolandine's constancy and faith disprove the typical negative stereotypes about women, but she also expresses skepticism that an equally powerful example of men's faithfulness exists when she declares, "je vous prie que les hommes, qui nous veulent peindre tant inconstantes . . . me monstrent un aussi bon mary comme ceste cy fut bonne femme, et d'une telle foy et perseverance" (2.326; I'd like to see the men who want to portray us as being so fickle come and show me an example of a husband who was as good as this good wife and who had as much faith and resolve). Moreover, she defends Rolandine by asserting that her actions bring honor to all women (2.326).

Despite what some *devisants* explicitly claim in the conversation following the fortieth tale, the favorable depiction of Rolandine's aunt and the negative portrayal of her brother also cast doubt on the idea that women should submit completely to their relatives' wishes regarding marriage. Geburon remarks that the gentleman's death was too cruel and refers to the legal justification for the woman's actions (2.511). Significantly, Nomerfide defends the aunt's actions with the very expression that Rolandine uses in tale 21 when she asserts, "Dieu n'y est point offensé" (2.511; it did not offend God). Even the typically misogynistic Simontault condemns the brother's cruelty (2.512). In contrast, Saffredent interjects with a commonplace argument of misogynistic tradition, declaring that "les philosophes tiennent, que le moindre homme du monde vault mieux, que la plus grande et vertueuse femme, qui soit" (2.513; the wise philosophers hold that the least among men is worth more than the greatest and most virtuous woman). However, the events of the tale and the fact that the majority of storytellers firmly condemn the brother's actions and describe the aunt with the saintly expression "bien heureuse" (blessed) cast doubt on the validity of his opinion and this misogynistic perspective (2.512).

Multiple parallels between Saint Barbara's iconography and the representation of Rolandine and her aunt encourage a reading of these tales with saints' lives. These intertextual connections lead one to ask why Marguerite would use hagiography as a source. Like the philosophers that Saffredent mentions, in sixteenth-century France many clerics and theological and literary texts argued for women's spiritual inferiority and moral weakness, and the need for them to be controlled through marriage. In contrast, saints' lives provided numerous examples of women's exemplary spirituality and unwavering faith. Moreover, traditional stories of female saints are often by their very nature antiauthoritarian. The lives of these holy women usually challenged both familial and religious authorities. Tales 21 and 40 have a similar didactic purpose in that they present Marguerite's readers with examples of God's faithfulness to two strong and saintly women who were unjustly imprisoned by their male relatives. Just as saints' vitae were meant to inspire faith, to show God's ability to work in human lives, and to provide models to emulate, the favorable portrayals of Rolandine and her aunt underscore women's great capacity for moral and spiritual strength. The next section examines how Marguerite incorporates elements of Saint Mary Magdalene's iconography into tale 32 to contest the traditional representation of this saint in works by clerics and male hagiographers.

"Le nom de Pecheresse": Saint Mary Magdalene and Tale 32

Saint Mary Magdalene played a significant role in the religious life of the royal family.[14] She is featured in both Louise de Savoie's book of hours and Claude de France's prayer book. Marguerite owned various religious objects depicting Mary Magdalene.[15] The royal family also sought this saint's intercession for Claude's and Marguerite's pregnancies.[16] Louise, Marguerite, and Claude displayed their fervent devotion to Mary Magdalene by making two pilgrimages to her shrine in the south of France; King Francis accompanied them on their second journey. In January 1516, the royal family venerated her relics at La Sainte-Baume.[17] This pilgrimage motivated Louise to ask François Demoulins de Rochefort to compose a new account of Mary Magdalene's life. In 1517, he produced *La vie de la belle et clere Magdalene* for Louise.[18] Demoulins's text was instrumental in fueling intense controversy about the identity of this saint, "la fameuse querelle de la Madeleine ou des trois Maries" (the famous quarrel of the Magdalene or the three Marys).[19] This debate revolved around questions surrounding the true identity of Mary Magdalene, namely whether she was one individual or three distinct people. Demoulins borrowed several arguments from Jacques Lefèvre d'Étaples's 1517 treatise *De Maria Magdalena*. In so doing, he disseminated Lefèvre's ideas on Mary Magdalene to a wider public who could not read Latin. Jonathan Reid argues that Lefèvre's work had serious ramifications beyond recounting the legend of one saint when he asserts that "Conservatives saw Lefèvre's tract as the thin end of a wedge that would open the door to disbelief. They warned that scholars would be tempted by Lefèvre's example to reassess the cult of saints and other practices accepted by the church, thereby undermining the laity's trust in the church and destroying their faith."[20]

In contrast to the official stance of the sixteenth-century Catholic Church and the common depictions in medieval hagiographies, Lefèvre et Demoulins argued that Mary of Bethany (Martha's sister), Mary Magdalene (who was healed of demonic possession and became a devoted follower of Jesus), and the unnamed sinner who anointed the feet of Jesus with her tears were three separate individuals.[21] Demoulins asserts that "il ya heu trois Mariez qui sont toutes trois appelleez Magdalenez" (there were three Marys that we call Magdalene).[22] In the text, he also explicitly asks for Saint Mary Magdalene's intercession for Louise, François, Claude, and Marguerite, thereby expressing a belief in the intercessory power of saints and drawing the royal family into the debate.[23] An examination of the *Heptaméron*'s references to Mary Magdalene with an analysis of the Bible, hagiographic legends, and texts associated with the Renaissance debate over this saint will demonstrate that Oisille's tale serves to contest both the depiction of Saint Mary Magdalene in medieval hagiographic writings and the position of the orthodox theologians in the Renaissance Catholic Church.

As discussed earlier, although many hagiographical references in Marguerite's text have received limited attention, tale 32 is a notable exception. François Rigolot has published two articles on connections between Mary Magdalene and this narrative. In "The *Heptameron* and the 'Magdalen Controversy': Dialogue and Humanist Hermeneutics," he addresses the prevalent theme of repentance in connection with debates over the saint's real identity, while in "Magdalen's Skull: Allegory and Iconography in *Heptameron* 32," he focuses on Mary Magdalene's iconography and Marguerite's personal experience with the saint's skull at the shrine at La Sainte-Baume in connection with the sixteenth-century fascination with this saint.[24] More recently, Gary Ferguson analyzed connections between the *Heptaméron*'s thirty-second tale and Saint Mary Magdalene in an article, "Veritable Histoire: *L'Heptaméron* et La Madeleine." While these scholars have examined the tale in association with the Magdalene controversy, it is useful to contextualize the story in connection with early hagiographies and women's writings, and alongside various references to saints and other tales of adultery in the *Heptaméron*.

In the haunting thirty-second tale, a German man cruelly punishes his wife's adultery through a "tourment continuel" (2.444; continual torment) that is even worse than death. She is forced to shave her head, drink from her lover's skull, and lead a life of silent confinement in a room with the skeleton of her lover. Ennasuite evokes Mary Magdalene in the conversation following the tale in response to the harsh statements of other *devisants* about the woman's adultery. Ennasuite states, "dictes moy si la Magdaleine n'a pas plus d'honneur maintenant entre les hommes, que sa sœur qui estoit vierge" (2.452; wouldn't you say that Mary Magdalene has more honor among men today than her sister who was a virgin?). Ennasuite emphasizes Mary Magdalene's great honor among men; she was among the most venerated saints in Renaissance France. However, she also highlights the traditional representation of Saint Mary Magdalene by evoking her alleged sexual sins. She had already made a similar comment at the conclusion of the nineteenth tale, saying, "l'on ne doit douter que celuy, duquel la fin de la loy est charité, ne leur dist à la fin de leur vie comme à *la Magdaleine*, que leurs pechez leur estoient pardonnez, veu qu'ils avoient beaucoup aimé" (1.283, emphasis added; we cannot doubt that at the end of their lives, He whose law begets charity said to them, as He said to Mary Magdalene, that their sins were forgiven, since they had loved greatly). According to Ennasuite, Mary Magdalene's sins had been forgiven, for she had loved much. Christ did indeed use these very words, but while speaking to the unnamed "sinful woman" in Luke's Gospel rather than to his faithful follower, Mary of Magdala. Rigolot remarks, "Ennasuite is not aware of the new distinction Lefèvre had drawn between Luke's popular contrite sinner and 'Mary called Magdalen' . . . [she] simply follows . . . the traditional teaching of the church."[25] To add to the confusion, Ennasuite also refers to Mary Magdalene's "sister," thereby including another common erroneous belief, namely the conflation of the saint with Mary of Bethany, Martha's sister. It is hardly surprising that scholars have referred to this phenomenon as the "muddle of Marys."[26]

While Ennasuite's declarations reflect the beliefs of the Renaissance Catholic Church, Marguerite was keenly aware of the controversy over the saint's identity. Thus, the final exchange between Ennasuite and Longarine merits examination. Longarine replies, "Je vous confesse . . . qu'elle est louée entre nous de la grande amour qu'elle a portée à Jesus Christ, et de sa grande penitence, mais si luy demeure il *le nom de pecheresse*" (2.452, emphasis added; I admit that we praise her for her great love of Jesus Christ and for her great penitence, but she is still called a sinner). Longarine refers to Mary Magdalene's love for Jesus; she also evokes her contrition, but she emphasizes her enduring designation as a sinner. For Longarine, despite Mary Magdalene's unwavering devotion to

Jesus, it is the label of sinner that most clearly defines her. Ennasuite replies by saying, "Je ne me soucie . . . *quel nom les hommes me donnent* : mais que Dieu me pardonne" (2.452, emphasis added; I don't care what men call me, as long as God forgives me). Ennasuite boldly asserts that she has no concern for the names that men may give her, rather it is God's opinion that matters most. This declaration is compelling, since the saint's designation as a sinful woman was in fact created by men in the Middle Ages.

Ennasuite's comment takes on additional importance when read alongside the Renaissance controversy over Mary Magdalene and the saint's life as represented in the Bible, the Catholic Church, and the *Golden Legend*. Diana Apostolos-Cappadona has demonstrated that the first representations of Saint Mary Magdalene honored her as the chosen first witness of the Resurrection, as well as extolled her powerful ministry and unwavering devotion to Jesus.[27] This is not surprising given how she is depicted in the Bible. Katherine Ludwig Jansen summarizes the New Testament portrayal of Saint Mary Magdalene, saying: "According to scripture, then, Mary Magdalene is the woman whom Christ heals of demonic possession, who becomes one of his loyal disciples, who ministers to him during his lifetime, who stands beneath the cross at his crucifixion, who is present at his burial, who brings ointments to the tomb after his death, who is the first person (in three of the four accounts) to witness the risen Christ, and is the person on whom he bestows the honor of announcing the good news to the other disciples . . . not only was she first to witness one of the central tenets of the Christian faith—the resurrection—she also received the paschal privilege of announcing it."[28] Interestingly, this had also been the official stance of the Catholic Church up until the sixth century, when Pope Gregory decided to meld three individuals: Mary Magdalene, Mary of Bethany, and the unnamed sinful woman in the Gospels.[29] After Pope Gregory conflated the three Marys, clerics and hagiographers dutifully transformed the faithful Mary of Magdala into a penitent sinner.

When recounting Saint Mary Magdalene's life in the *Golden Legend*, Voragine writes, "de tant soubzmectoit elle plus son corps a delices; et par ce perdit elle son propre nom et fut acoustumee d'estre appellee pecheresse" (she was no less known for the way she gave her body to pleasure—so much so that her proper name was forgotten and she was commonly called "the sinner")."[30] Moreover, he writes that she "se fut mise a toutes les delices du corps" (gave herself totally to the pleasures of the flesh).[31] Not only did hagiographers highlight her purported sexual sins, but at times they even combined Mary Magdalene's story with the legend of Saint Mary of Egypt, another alleged prostitute turned saint. From this point forward, hagiographers began to place greater emphasis on the invented narrative of Mary Magdalene's sexual misdeeds. Various accounts of Saint Mary Magdalene's life by male clerics exemplify Brigitte Cazelles's argument that "the achievements of the female saints are presented as almost inimitable conquests of 'woman's innate propensity to sin in the flesh.'"[32] In contrast to the clerics and hagiographers who focus on Mary Magdalene's sexual transgressions and sinfulness, women writers such as Christine de Pizan and evangelical reformers like Demoulins privilege the biblical representation of the saint's unswerving devotion to Jesus.

In *Le livre de la Cité des dames*, Christine specifically highlights Mary Magdalene's faithfulness to Jesus and the sharp contrast between her actions and those of the male Apostles who had forsaken him. She writes: "O grant foy de femmes et grant amour qui oncques le Filz de Dieu, qui de *tous ses apostres avoit esté abandonné et relenqui, ne le laissierent mort ne vif!* Et parut bien que Dieu ne reprouvoit mie tant amour de femme si que ce feust chose fraisle, comme aucuns font et que ilz veullent dire, quant ou cuer de la *benoite Magdeleine* et des autres dames mist etincelles de si fervant amour comme il y paru et que il tant aprouva" (emphasis added; What great devotion and unfailing love these women showed by never once abandoning the Son of God in life or in death, even when all the apostles had rejected and forsaken him! You can see just how much God values women's love, even though there are those who claim that it is such a paltry thing, for He sparked a flame in the hearts of both the Magdalene and these other ladies that caused them to reveal their burning devotion, a devotion which He so warmly appreciated).[33] In her text, Christine sought to rehabilitate the saint's reputation from the misogynistic representations that were widespread in literature, art, and religion.

Like Christine, Demoulins offers a positive portrayal of Mary Magdalene, saying, "Magdalene vous monstrez bien maitenant que en amour perfaict oncquez femme ne vous passa" (Magdalene, you now clearly show that in perfect love no other woman surpasses you).[34] He also highlights her role as Apostle of the Apostles and herald of the Resurrection: "C'est bien raison que Magdalene qui a este messagiere de Jesus Christ soit nomee Apostola" (It is right that Magdalene who was the messenger of Jesus Christ be called Apostle of the Apostles).[35] As an avid reader of saints' lives and the texts associated with the Magdalene controversy, Marguerite also sought to redress the focus on sinfulness in legends of Mary Magdalene. She may have found inspiration in the works of Christine de Pizan. Although Marguerite does not explicitly mention Christine, Paula Sommers has demonstrated that Marguerite had access to *Le livre de la Cité des dames* in the substantial collections of Christine's works in the royal libraries at Cognac and Blois.[36] Sommers also argues that "the *Heptaméron* makes it clear that she shares with her fifteenth-century precursor a sincere interest in the rights of women and a willingness to speak out in their defense."[37] Like Christine's text, in Marguerite's *Petit Œuvre dévot*, she emphasizes Mary Magdalene's faithfulness when she refers to "la devotion/De magdeleine" (the devotion of Magdalene).[38] Significantly, the thirty-second tale's use of hagiography is distinct as compared to other references to saints in the *Heptaméron*.

Aside from including well-known iconographic characteristics of saints in the positive depictions of the *Heptaméron*'s holy heroines, Marguerite's storytellers also display knowledge of the most common attributes of the saints by referring to Saint Peter's chains, Saint Anthony's temptations, and Saint Lawrence's instrument of torture. Tale 32 is intriguing in that it does not include some of the best-known attributes of Saint Mary Magdalene, namely her ointment jar, her long flowing hair, or her signature red clothing. Significantly, these very attributes are all portrayed in Claude's prayer book and Louise's book of hours (Figures 4.4 and 4.5). Rigolot argues that the alabaster jar is not included, as it "would have connoted sensuality and the worldly life."[39] However, if one rejects the narrative of Saint Mary Magdalene as a sinful woman, another viable explanation for the omission of the ointment jar could be that anointing is evoked in the New Testament in association with Mary of Magdala, who waits to anoint Jesus at his tomb, with Mary of Bethany in John's Gospel, and with the sinful woman in Luke's story. By omitting this attribute, Marguerite eliminates the possibility of confusion among these three distinct individuals. Moreover, the fact that Saint Mary Magdalene's flowing hair and signature red clothing are replaced with austere dress and a shorn head may have been another means of differentiating these women. Although the skull cup has been associated with Saint Mary Magdalene's relics, it can also be interpreted in connection with the tradition of the skull cup as depicted in medieval *chansons de geste*. In fact, Gabriele Sorice argues that it was common in Old French epic to make an enemy's skull into a cup after defeating them in battle.[40] Sorice also refers to the use of precious metals in the fashioning of these objects, just like the silver in the skull cup in Marguerite's narrative. Aside from the absence of

Figure 4.4. *St. Mary Magdalene with the Jar of Ointment* and *The Levitation of St. Mary Magdalene*, illuminated by the Master of Claude de France, 2¾ × 2 in. From *Prayer Book of Claude de France* (Tours, France, ca. 1517), MS M.1166, fol. 42v., The Morgan Library and Museum, New York. Gift of Mrs. Alexandre P. Rosenberg in memory of her husband, Alexandre Paul Rosenberg, 2008. Courtesy of The Morgan Library and Museum.

De scta maria magdalena a
Maria ergo unxit pedes ihu et
extersit capillis suis et domus
impleta est ex odore unguenti. V
Dimissa sunt ei peccata multa
R Quia dilexit multum. Oro
Largire nobis clementis
sime pater q sicut beata
maria magdalena dnm nrm
super omnia diligendo suor
obtinuit veniam peccami
num ita nobis apud tuam
misericordiam impetret bea
titudinem per xpistum.

Figure 4.5. "Assumption of Mary Magdalen, in Cave, at Mass, and with Ointment Jar," 192 × 123 mm. From *Hours, use of Rome* (France, ca. 1500–1515), MS 411, fol. 143r, General Collection, Beinecke Rare Book and Manuscript Library, Yale University, New Haven. CT. Courtesy of Beinecke Rare Book and Manuscript Library.

Mary Magdalene's attributes, the fact that there are no references to prayer or Jesus in the tale itself is particularly surprising, especially given that Oisille recounts the story.

While Oisille does eventually evoke God in the conversation, it is highly unlikely that she would draw on Saint Mary Magdalene's legend with no mention of prayer, God, or Jesus in the novella itself. Moreover, the woman in tale 32 is defined by her lack of faithfulness whereas in the Bible Mary of Magdala is the quintessential faithful follower of Jesus. A viable explanation could be that Marguerite depicts Oisille as the storyteller who knows Scripture better than the other *devisants*. The most fervent reader of the Bible among the storytellers would have known that in the New Testament Mary of Magdala is portrayed not as a sinful woman, but rather as the epitome of faithfulness. Thus, one must consider that in this tale Marguerite draws instead on the story of the unnamed adulteress. Like the sinful woman in Luke's writings, the wife in the thirty-second tale is unnamed. She is vilified for her sins by her husband, much like what one finds in Simon the Leper's disdainful response to the woman. Akin to the New Testament's "sinful woman," the wife in the tale must endure the judgment and accusations of men with no possibility of telling her side of the story. Thus, it is quite possible that the reference to Mary Magdalene and Ennasuite's insistence on God's perspective are meant to portray this woman not as a penitent sinner in the tradition of the invented narrative surrounding Mary Magdalene, but rather as Marguerite's attempt to join Lefèvre and Demoulins in their efforts to separate the biblical Mary Magdalene from the *pecheresse* (sinner). This interpretation is intriguing in that the predominant theme of the sinful woman's story is pardon.

Jesus did not harshly judge adulterous women; rather he showed forgiveness, saying to the woman in Luke's Gospel, "Your sins are forgiven" (7:48), or to the woman caught in adultery in John's Gospel, "Has no one condemned you? . . . Neither do I condemn you. Go, [and] from now on do not sin any more" (8:10–11). The behavior of men whose wives commit adultery in the tales of the third day could not diverge more radically from Christ's compassion. The president of Grenoble murders his wife by poisoning her salad and tale 32 highlights the cruel vengeance of the husband. The actions of these men not only deviate from Christ's example, but they also contrast sharply with the behavior of women in tales 37 and 38. These women have husbands who commit adultery, but they ultimately respond with patience and forgiveness. Significantly, Marguerite invites the reader to form connections between these tales and the thirty-second novella through the inclusion of shared material elements. In tale 32, the tapestry isolates the wife, and the skull cup is a cruel punishment. In story 38 the wife generously provides tapestries and a silver cup to her husband's lover so that his health does not suffer, and he can indulge in his extramarital affair in greater comfort; her lesson in generosity inspires him to lead a more virtuous life. The wife in tale 32 enters the dining room and washes before and after each meal in forced silence while in tale 37 the wife prays for her adulterous husband during his visits to his maid's bed and urges him to wash his hands after he returns in hopes of changing his sinful behavior. These forgiving women follow Jesus's example, in contrast with the brutal vengeance of the men who murder or torment their wives. Thus, although tale 32 certainly does not present a woman of admirable virtue like so many of Marguerite's other stories, when it is read alongside other tales on the third day a positive portrayal of women's mercy and forgiving nature does indeed emerge. Moreover, if one interprets the tale as an attempt to separate the unnamed adulteress from Mary Magdalene, it can also be seen as ultimately honoring Mary of Magdala, one of Christ's most devoted followers.

Not only did Marguerite attempt to redress the reputation of Saint Mary Magdalene, but she also clearly emphasized women's tendency to follow Christ's model of forgiveness in other tales of the third day. Finally, although Lefèvre, Demoulins, and Marguerite endeavored to set the record straight in the sixteenth century, it was not until 1969 that the Catholic Church officially returned to its earlier position on Mary Magdalene. Apostolos-Cappadona notes, "In 1969 the Roman Catholic Church formally revised the canonical definition of Mary Magdalene. . . . She was returned to the early Christian description of faithful follower and first witness, and not the unnamed adulteress or sister of Lazarus and Martha."[41] However, the enduring influence of Pope Gregory's decision and the medieval hagiographies remains pervasive. For instance, Zegura recently argued that in tale 32, Marguerite portrays "a fallen but repentant matron who is eventually forgiven, in an echo of the New Testament's Mary Magdalene."[42] As a woman who had been slapped in the face for discussing theology, as a writer who had had a skirmish with the theologians at the Sorbonne, and as the sister of a king who showed diminishing support for any unorthodox ideas, Marguerite would not have been in a position to directly contradict the official stance of the Catholic Church regarding Saint Mary Magdalene, but her readers would have known that clerics and male hagiographers had transformed the positive, powerful New Testament Mary of Magdala into a reformed prostitute and penitent. Like Demoulins's text, Marguerite's tale also revises this traditional portrayal in that it seeks to separate the unnamed sinful woman in Luke's Gospel from the "Apostle of the Apostles." Just as tale 32 engages in sixteenth-century debates by representing a notable revision to Saint Mary Magdalene's legend and contesting the official stance of the Renaissance church and the gender bias in hagiography, the next section argues that Marguerite raises her voice in literary and theological controversies by offering important revisions to Saint Mary of Egypt's story through the depiction of the heroine of tale 67.

Saint Mary of Egypt and the Steadfast Heroine of Tale 67

The *Heptaméron*'s sixty-seventh tale relates the circumstances surrounding a couple's marooning on an isolated island during Captain Roberval's 1542 colonizing mission to the New World. During the crossing from France to Canada, the husband betrayed the captain and was to be put to death; however, because of his wife's faithful service, his life was spared. When the group approached Canada, Captain Roberval punished the man's treachery by abandoning the couple on an unforgiving island inhabited by wild beasts. Left to survive on their own, they confronted the harshest conditions. They built a makeshift shelter and were forced to hunt and forage for food. Their potential for survival was unlikely. In fact, the man perished not long after the marooning. The young woman was left alone to fend for herself in the most inhospitable of environments. Against almost impossible odds, she survived the grueling ordeal. After an extensive period in utter isolation, the young woman was rescued, and she returned to France. This remarkable story of betrayal, struggle, and survival undoubtedly fascinated the French, who were hungry for insights into the mysteries of the New World.

While there is no incontestable proof surrounding these events in the historical documents associated with Roberval's journey, Marguerite would have had privileged access to details about the expedition because of her position at court and her close relationship with King Francis. In fact, early in the tale she writes, "Roberval faisant un voyage sur la mer . . . en l'isle de Canadas, auquel lieu avoit deliberé, si l'air du pays eust esté commode, de demeurer, et y faire villes et chateaux" (2.721; Roberval was named as the leader of an expedition across the seas to the island of Canada, where he planned to stay and build cities and forts if the climate was suitable). Marguerite's language in this passage mirrors King Francis's official document commissioning the Canadian expedition, a detail that demonstrates her intimate knowledge of the affair.[43] In addition, it was after this voyage that Roberval's chief navigator, Jean Alphonse de Saintonge, started to refer to the "Ysles de la demoiselle" in his works.[44] Subsequently, this nomenclature began to appear on maps such as Cornelius Wytfliet's 1597 map of Nova Francia et Canada.[45] While Cartier's other journeys are typically well documented in his *Relations*, at the end of this specific expedition with Roberval one finds the following declaration: "la suite de cette relation se trouve perdue" (the rest of this relation is lost), a fact that gives credence to Elizabeth Boyer's hypothesis of a "conspiracy of silence" surrounding the affair.[46] However, an exhaustive overview of the historicity of the marooning is not within the scope of the present study; thus this section focuses on the literary accounts published during the Renaissance in order to demonstrate how the representation of the saintly heroine of Marguerite's tale both borrows from and revises hagiography.[47]

This compelling story of the marooning of a young woman was the inspiration for several literary accounts in sixteenth-century France. Marguerite de Navarre's 1558 tale was the first to be published, François de Belleforest's version appeared in his 1570 *Le Cinquiesme Tome des Histoires tragiques* (The fifth volume of tragic stories), and André Thevet included the story in his 1575 *Cosmographie Universelle* (*The Universal Cosmography*). Thevet later penned two additional versions, one in his 1586–1587 *Grand Insulaire* (*The Great Island Book*) and the other in his 1588 *Description de plusieurs isles* (Description of several islands).[48] While each story has merits, the *Heptaméron*'s tale deserves greater attention for various reasons. It was the first version of the events and the first literary text set in Canada. It was also the only work published while the people involved were still living. Moreover, Marguerite's unique standing at court undoubtedly provided her with privileged information about Roberval's journey. Michel Bideaux argues that the *Heptaméron*'s version is the most historically accurate.[49] Scholars like Frank Lestringant and Arthur Stabler have argued that Marguerite's account of the events is simplistic and lacking in complexity as compared to Thevet's and Belleforest's works.[50] In contrast, Margaret Ferguson argues that the *Heptaméron*'s version can be seen as a carefully crafted critique of men's approach to the colonial empire through its representation of "an idealized and feminized version of Christianity."[51] Carrie Klaus develops an insightful analysis of the tale in association with labor, interpreting it as Marguerite's advocacy for expanded roles for women in sixteenth-century France.[52]

This section provides another interpretation by arguing that an intertextual reading with hagiography reveals another facet of the richness and complexity of the sixty-seventh tale. Marguerite's narrative skillfully borrows from Saint Mary of Egypt's iconography to engage in sixteenth-century debates about women and religion, while it also offers her readers a revisionist saint's vitae by questioning the gender bias and misogynistic commonplaces in depictions of this saint from earlier hagiographies.

Simontault introduces the tale by stating, "Ce *m*'est chose si nouvelle, mesdames, d'ouïr de vous quelque acte vertueux : que s'il s'en offre quelqu'un, il me semble ne devoir estre celé, mais plutost *escrit en lettres d'or*, à fin de servir aux femmes d'exemple, et aux hommes d'admiration : voyant en sexe fragile, ce que fragilité refuse" (2.719–720, my emphasis; It is so unusual for me to hear about some virtuous deed done by you, my ladies, that it should not be kept secret but rather written in gold letters to serve as an example to women and as something for men to admire. Seeing in the weak sex what weakness itself rejects). Simontault's mention of the fragile sex and his skepticism of women's capacity for virtue serve to recall misogynistic commonplaces of the *querelle des femmes*.[53] However, Marguerite de Navarre is behind the scenes orchestrating the frame story. Thus, Simontault's suggestion that virtuous acts by women should not be hidden, but rather "written" merits attention. This assertion serves to affirm Marguerite's own project of writing the *Heptaméron*, especially since her work frequently foregrounds the actions of saintly women. Simontault's statement also recalls Jacobus de Voragine's compendium of saints' lives. When he evokes "letters of gold," an early modern reader would have formed an immediate association between this tale and the *Golden Legend*. Thus, this reference encourages a reading of tale 67 with hagiography and incites the reader to view the heroine in connection with saints' vitae. The fact that Marguerite's narrative not only borrows from but also serves to cast doubt on earlier depictions of Saint Mary of Egypt is also compelling.

Throughout the *Golden Legend*, the male saints who spent years in isolation in the desert are typically referred to as "hermits."[54] In contrast, despite her extensive period of solitude and prayer in the wilderness, Voragine initially presents Saint Mary of Egypt with emphasis on her sinfulness. He writes, "Marie egipcienne qui fut appellee pecheresse mena tresdestroicte vie XL VII ans au desert" (Mary the Egyptian, who is called the Sinner, led a most austere life in the desert for forty-seven years).[55] He insists on her sinfulness, referring to her once again as a "vile pecheresse."[56] Voragine also has the saint use excessively self-deprecating language to describe herself through direct discourse. In his text she proclaims, "se je te disoie mon estat, tu t'en fuyeroies de moy tout espouventé ainsi comme d'ung serpent. Et tes oreilles seroient conchiees de mes paroles et l'air seroit honny de mes ordures" (if I tell you who and what I am, you will flee as if frightened by a serpent, your ears will be contaminated by my words, the air will be polluted with filth).[57] Significantly, throughout Voragine's work, he labels only female saints as sinners. Male saints who led dissolute lives before their conversions are free from this moral judgment. Simon Gaunt argues that hagiographers' tendency to focus on sinfulness in Mary of Egypt's story negatively impacts female readers, saying, "in the *Marie l'Egyptienne* narratives, women readers are implicitly enjoined to contemplate their own bodies as the incarnation of sin and as a threat not only to their own spiritual wellbeing, but to that of all the men they encounter."[58] As an avid reader of saints' lives, Marguerite was certainly cognizant of hagiographers' tendency to focus on female sinfulness. This may have compelled her to draw on Saint Mary of Egypt's vitae in order to transform the narrative and offer her contemporaries a revisionist hagiography.

Like Mary Magdalene, Saint Mary of Egypt is extolled for her holiness and life of privation, and yet medieval hagiographies emphasize that she became a prostitute at a young age and that she initially led a life of sinful pleasures. Significantly less emphasis has been placed on the narrative that she was a nun who simply longed for a solitary existence in the desert. The earliest accounts of her life were written as didactic texts for monks and they simply depict her as a hermit who withdrew to the wilderness.[59] Ronald Pepin and Hugh Feiss remark that it was Sophronius, patriarch of Jerusalem in the seventh century, who "expanded Mary's story and made her an Egyptian harlot."[60] Like Sophronius, rather than focusing on Saint Mary of Egypt's solitary life of prayer in the wilderness, Voragine also emphasizes her fleshly temptations: "en ce desert moult molestee des temptacions de la char dix et sept ans, mais, par la grace de Dieu, je les ay vaincus maintenant" (for seventeen years I was troubled by temptations of the flesh, but now by the grace of God I have conquered them all).[61] Akin to what readers find in different portrayals of Saint Mary of Egypt, Thevet's and Belleforest's Renaissance accounts reflect, albeit in varying degrees, the misogynistic discourse of the sinful woman.

Hagiographies of Saint Mary of Egypt recount that she offered her body to sailors to pay for her journey by ship from Egypt to Jerusalem; the portrayals of the heroine in Thevet's and Belleforest's accounts also focus on her sinful behavior as she crossed the Atlantic en route to Canada. In André Thevet's *Cosmographie universelle*, the couple, especially the young woman, was guilty of fornication on the journey to Canada: "Estans sur mer, ce Gentilhome ne faillit d'acoster si privément ladite Damoiselle, que nonobstant les perils & dangers qui s'offrent ordinairement à ceux qui courent à la mercy des vents, jouerent si bien leur roullet ensemble, qu'ils passerent plus avant que promesses et vaines paroles" (Being on the ocean, the gentleman did not fail to approach the maiden, and notwithstanding the perils and dangers that present themselves to those who pass swiftly to the mercy of the winds, played their roulette so well together, that they passed well beyond promises and vain speech).[62] He also writes that Roberval longed to solely punish the young woman, rather than the man.[63] François de Belleforest offers a more sympathetic portrayal of Marguerite de Roberval than Thevet by highlighting the young woman's "chaste desir, & amour plein de vertu" (chaste desire and fully virtuous love) and emphasizing Captain Roberval's cruelty.[64] However, his narrative nonetheless includes Roberval's accusations that she had prostituted herself on board the ship: "Qui eust jamais pensé, ma sœur, qu'une Damoiselle de si bon lieu que vous, eust voulu faire tort aux siens, que de se prostituer, comme une publique, dans un navire à la veue de chacun?" (Who would have ever thought, my sister, that a lady of good standing like yourself, would wrong her family, by prostituting herself, like a whore, on a ship in full sight of everyone?).[65] In contrast, in the *Heptaméron* they are punished uniquely because of the husband's treachery. It is the male in the couple who is portrayed as entirely responsible for the betrayal. Marguerite writes:

> un homme, qui fut si malheureux, qu'il trahit son maistre, et le meit en danger d'estre prins des gens du pays. Mais Dieu voulut, que son entreprinse fut si tost cogneuë, qu'elle ne peut nuire au capitaine Roberval, lequel feit prendre ce meschant trahistre, le voulant punir comme il avoit merité. Ce qui eust esté faict sans sa femme, laquelle, ayant suyvi son mary par les perils de la mer, ne le voulut abandonner à la mort : mais avec force larmes feit tant envers le capitaine, et toute la compagnie, que tant pour la pitié dicelle, que pour les services qu'elle leur avoit faicts, luy accorda sa requeste. (2.721)

> [there was a man so wretched that he betrayed his master and put him in danger of being captured by the inhabitants of the land. But God's will was such that the man's plan was quickly discovered and so did not pose any danger to Captain Roberval, who had the wicked traitor ar-

> rested in order to punish him as he deserved. And that is what would have happened if it had not been for the man's wife, who had accompanied her husband on the dangerous voyage. She would not abandon him and allow him to die. Shedding many tears, she implored the captain and all the members of the crew so persistently that out of pity for her and because of the services she had rendered to them, they agreed to grant her request.]

Unlike the depiction of the woman in Thevet's and Belleforest's accounts, the *Heptaméron*'s heroine is entirely blameless. She intervenes on her husband's behalf and his life is spared uniquely because of her faithfulness, service, and eloquence. Marguerite's emphasis on her loyalty and virtues contrasts with other versions of the story, while it also questions misogynistic commonplaces of the time.[66] One must entertain the possibility that Marguerite would have heard similar arguments from Roberval to justify his actions, or perhaps she encountered other gender biases as the story circulated in France after the voyage. Margaret Ferguson offers an intriguing interpretation, positing that Marguerite's version was "a deliberate revision of an oral narrative known to many members of her courtly circle."[67] Marguerite also shows foresight in that she insightfully anticipated how male writers would later interpret the events through the lens of prevalent misogynistic discourses. The *Heptaméron*'s representation of the heroine's strength and moral probity responds to detractors of women in the *querelle des femmes* while the allusions to hagiography in the tale question the earlier literary representations of Mary of Egypt that highlight her sinfulness and supposedly weak female nature.

Along with narrative emphasis on Mary of Egypt's triumph over her feminine debilities, medieval hagiographers frequently depict her as a holy woman renouncing the world and doing penance alone in the wilderness. Textual and visual representations of Saint Mary of Egypt often represent her in isolation in the desert, praying and subsisting only on bread. For instance, a statue at the entrance of the church of Saint-Germain-l'Auxerrois (where Francis I hosted a procession in 1535) depicts Saint Mary of Egypt holding three loaves of bread (Figure 4.6).[68] In the *Golden Legend*, Voragine writes, "Et quant je eu adouré tresdevotement la saincte croix, ung homme me donna trois deniers desquelz je achetay trois pains. . . . Et les trois pains que je apportay avec moy s'en durcirent par le long temps et m'ont souffist par quarante et sept ans que j'en ay mangé" (When I had worshiped the cross with the utmost devotion, someone gave me

Figure 4.6. Photograph, "Saint Mary of Egypt, Église de Saint-Germain-l'Auxerrois," by Marie-Lan Nguyen, 2008. Image courtesy of Marie-Lan Nguyen / Wikimedia Commons, Creative Commons Attribution 3.0 Unported (CC-BY-3.0).

three coins with which I bought three loaves of bread. . . . The loaves I had brought with me turned hard as stone, but they have sufficed me for food all these years).[69] Interestingly, references to the desert, bread, and God's provision in legends of Saint Mary of Egypt are also reflected in Marguerite's novella about a young woman stranded in Canada.

In tale 67, Marguerite de Navarre characterizes the Canadian island where the heroine was marooned as a "desert," a portrayal that serves to recall Saint Mary of Egypt's iconography. In the *Heptaméron,* Marguerite clarifies that soon after the marooning, the couple runs out of bread; this is one factor that leads to the husband's death. The narrative also emphasizes that while the couple nourishes themselves with bread, the heroine alone sustains herself with the Bible. Marguerite writes, "comme celle qui avoit toute sa consolation, en luy, porta pour sa sauve-garde, *nourriture,* et consolation le Nouveau Testament, qu'elle lisoit incessamment" (2.722, my emphasis; as God was her sole consolation, she had taken with her the New Testament, which she read constantly to serve as protection, nourishment, and consolation). Like Saint Mary of Egypt, the young woman is depicted as responding to her plight in the wilderness by nourishing herself with bread and sustaining herself with prayer and the Word of God.[70] Moreover, when the heroine is eventually rescued, the men who come to save her are reminded that "Dieu est autant puissant de nourrir en un desert ses serviteurs" (2.723; God has the power to nourish his servants in the wilderness). This reference to God's servants being provided for in the desert recalls the life of Saint Mary the Egyptian, while it also highlights this woman's service to God. These lexical and thematic choices reveal Marguerite's intent to depict the heroine as a saint-like figure, as does the reference to lions in the tale.

In this novella, Marguerite makes multiple references to wild beasts on the Canadian island, but she offers only one specific description of the animals that dwell there by evoking the "lions" (2.722). Critics have typically viewed the lions in the *Heptaméron*'s tale as a colorful misperception of the New World, likening them to Belleforest's mention of Florida or Thevet's palm tree in their accounts of this young woman's tribulations.[71] However, the reference makes sense if one does a comparative reading of the tale alongside hagiographic narratives of Mary of Egypt. Like her association with bread in the desert, the lion has also become an attribute incorporated into narratives and visual portrayals of Mary of Egypt (Figure 4.7). The *Golden Legend* relates how after Mary of Egypt's death, a lion came to serve her. When Father Zosimas discovered the saint's body in the desert, he longed to bury her but lacked the physical strength to

Figure 4.7. "Saint Mary of Egypt in Penitence," 178 × 120 mm. From *Horae ad usum Romanum* (Toulouse, France, ca. 1490), MS 2842, fol. 164r, Bibliothèque municipale de Toulouse. Courtesy of the Bibliothèque municipale de Toulouse.

give her a proper burial. At that point, a lion appeared to help dig her grave: "Lors commença le lyon a fouyr et fist une convenable fosse. Et quant il l'eut parfaicte et elle y fut mise, le lion s'en ala comme ung de bonnaire agniel et le bon homme vint a son monastere glorifiant Dieu" (The lion began to dig and prepared a suitable grave, and when that was finished went away like a gentle lamb, while the old man made his way back to his monastery, glorifying God).[72]

Significantly, in Marguerite's tale, she also depicts beasts in association with a grave: "Si est-ce que les bestes en eurent incontinent le sentiment, qui vindrent manger la charongne : mais la pauvre femme, de sa petite maisonnette defendoit à coups de harquebuze, que la chair de son mary n'eust tel sepulchre" (2.722; However, wild beasts were immediately drawn to the scent of the corpse and came to eat it, but the poor woman in her little house shot the harquebus to keep her husband's flesh from having such a sepulcher). There is certainly a difference in the sense that the young woman works diligently to protect her husband's corpse from being unearthed and consumed by the lions on the island. However, the text emphasizes that it is solely her efforts that prevent his body from being consumed by these beasts. Thus, like Mary of Egypt, it is the woman's faithfulness that eliminate the threat of lions. Her devotion to reading the Word of God also serves as protection.

Given the virulent debates over the translation of the Bible and the laity having free access to it, the representation of the young woman's reading of the New Testament in the tale merits further exploration. In a certain sense, it was Marguerite de Roberval's isolation in Canada that gave her total freedom to contemplate Scripture and devote herself to prayer. Along with the mention of her reading of the New Testament, Marguerite insists on the heroine's spiritual activities, noting that she "passoit son temps en lectures, contemplations, prieres et oraisons" (2.723; spent her time reading, contemplating, and praying). The explicit reference to the heroine's reading of the New Testament is particularly important since no mention is made of this in other sixteenth-century accounts of her story. Marguerite's depiction of the young woman reading the Bible highlights her heroine's active faith while it also demonstrates the queen of Navarre's engagement in contemporary debates about the laity's access to Scripture. More specifically, it underscores Marguerite's strong support for women to have unfettered access to sacred texts.

In the *Heptaméron*, Marguerite makes the revolutionary choice to have Oisille, a female layperson rather than a male cleric, lead the daily biblical lessons. In the Prologue, she also insists on gender parity regarding reading

Scripture by noting that all of the storytellers had read the Bible. While orthodox Catholic clerics fervently opposed the laity's direct access to the Word of God and sought to prohibit the French translation of the Bible, the *Heptaméron*'s depiction of women having equal opportunity to study and teach Scripture contests such views. In contrast with other Renaissance versions of Marguerite de Roberval's story, the *Heptaméron*'s tale is the only account that specifies that the heroine earns a living by teaching young girls after her return to France. "Et quand ils eurent faict entendre aux habitans la fidelité et perseverance de ceste femme, elle fut receuë à grand honneur de toutes les dames, qui volontiers luy baillerent leurs filles pour aprendre à lire, et à escrire" (2.723–724; When they told the inhabitants of the city about this woman's loyalty and perseverance, she was received very honorably by all the ladies, who had her teach their daughters to read and write). Reading this passage with a biblical intertext is valuable.

Jesus spent forty days in the desert in preparation for his ministry. It was only after his temptation in the desert that his ministry and teaching flourished. It is important to remember that the word "ministry" comes from the Latin word for "service." On her Canadian voyage, Marguerite's heroine repeatedly demonstrates that she is indeed a faithful servant. First, she saves her husband's life because she has faithfully served the captain, then she effectively serves her husband as physician and confessor. Finally, in the narrative's conclusion she is depicted as serving young girls as a teacher because she has proven her faithfulness and steadfastness during a harrowing trial. Margaret Ferguson remarks, "Presumably, these daughters learn more than just basic literacy from this humble woman who has already demonstrated her authority as a minister to her husband and as a critical reader of Scripture."[73] While the tale notes that the heroine teaches her students to read and write, the conclusion emphasizes that it is her experiences with God's mercies that have prepared her to effectively teach others about His love. Just as Jesus returned from the desert to start his ministry, Marguerite's heroine returns from Canada to teach young women in France about spiritual matters. The fact that the narrative concludes with emphasis on the heroine's position as a teacher illustrates the powerful potential of women's contributions to ministry and education.

Simontault initiates the conversation after the tale by praising God's greater work in women due to their inherent weaknesses. Oisille promptly repudiates his claim by asserting, "à dire vray, toute vertu vient de luy : mais il fault passer condamnation, que aussi peu favorise l'homme à l'ouvrage de Dieu, que la femme : car l'un et l'autre par son courir, ny par son vouloir, ne faict rien que planter *et arroser*, et Dieu seul donne l'accroissement" (2.724; to tell the truth, all virtue comes from him. But we must acknowledge that men contribute just as little as women to God's works. Through their heart and their will, men and women do nothing more than sow a seed; God makes it grow). Her beginning her rebuttal by saying "to tell the truth" casts doubt on the veracity of Simontault's declaration. She also insists on the perfect equality of men and women before God. Saffredent responds to Oisille by arguing that if she had "bien leu," or carefully read, the Scriptures of Saint Paul, she would know that he does not mention the works of women. His suggestion that Oisille is not well acquainted with Saint Paul's writings lacks credibility, since the storytellers trust her religious authority enough for a daily biblical lesson (often on Saint Paul's texts) even though they are situated in an institution of all male religious authorities.

Parlamente responds by stating, "Vous voudriez suyvre . . . l'opinion des mauvais hommes, qui prennent un passage de l'escriture pour eux, et laissent celuy qui leur est contraire. Si vous avez leu sainct Paul jusques au bout, vous trouverez qu'il se recommande aux dames, qui ont beaucoup labouré avecques luy en l'Evangile" (2.724; You're following the example of those vile men who cling to one passage in Scripture that supports their view and leave aside another that goes against it. If you had read Saint Paul to the end, you would see that he speaks of women who worked hard alongside him to defend the Gospel). Parlamente questions men's interpretations of Scripture as she recalls those who take a Bible verse out of context to support their claims while they ignore the verses contradictory to their opinions.[74] In contrast to Simontault, Saffredent, and the questionable interpretations of the men who misconstrue the word of God, the *Heptaméron*'s *devisantes* are portrayed as capable interpreters of God's word. Marguerite de Navarre takes full advantage of the polyphonic nature of the frame story to depict her female storytellers as sagacious interpreters of Scripture. By highlighting women's capacity for biblical exegesis, she emphasizes the necessity of offering them opportunities to contemplate and interpret Scripture on their own. Not only does the depiction of a saintly heroine in tale 67 dispel the misogynistic discourses that were so common in the debates of Renaissance France, but Marguerite also presents her own work as glorifying God.

Before the young woman is rescued, Marguerite writes that God, "qui n'abandonne jamais les siens au besoing, et qui au desespoir des autres, monstre sa puissance, ne permeit que la vertu, qu'il avoit mise en ceste femme, fust ignorée des hommes : mais voulut qu'elle fust cogneuë à sa gloire" (2.723; who never abandons his own—and who displays his power to the despair of all others—would not allow the virtue he had placed in this woman to remain hidden from men but rather willed it to be known, to His greater glory). The author's choice to portray God as intervening to ensure that this young woman and her story become known is a powerful narrative device. It emphasizes the heroine's exemplarity, while it also underscores the value of the *Heptaméron*'s account, since Marguerite de Navarre was the first writer to publish this narrative. Much like medieval hagiographers, Marguerite presents herself as doing God's work by writing this exemplary story of a saintly woman's experiences. Her tale allows for this woman's virtue to be widely known and in so doing it ultimately serves to bring glory to God. Through this compelling narrative, Marguerite underscores the admirable faith and strength of her heroine, while she also demonstrates her own ability to lead her readers to reflect more profoundly on depictions of women in Renaissance debates and to question the gender bias in portrayals of Saint Mary of Egypt in hagiographic tradition.

The next chapter explores another influential element of hagiography in the *Heptaméron,* namely how Marguerite draws on the life of Saint Francis to challenge misogynistic commonplaces in the *querelle des femmes* and to question gender inequalities in hagiography and the Renaissance Catholic Church. An exploration of Marguerite's allusions to Saint Claire underscores the relationship between equals that existed between Saint Francis and this holy woman, while her references to the holiness of Saint Francis highlight how the behavior of Franciscans in Renaissance France diverged drastically from that of their esteemed founder.

CHAPTER FIVE

Holiness and False Sanctity

Saint Francis, the Franciscans, and Ungodly Clerics and Women

Holy Charity confounds all diabolical and fleshly temptations and all fleshly fears.

—Saint Francis of Assisi

Saint Francis is among the most celebrated saints in Catholic tradition. Given Marguerite's close relationship with her brother and the royal family's possession of various artistic works portraying King Francis's patronymic saint, the queen of Navarre was undoubtedly cognizant of Saint Francis of Assisi's iconography. Furthermore, she was actively involved in advocating for reforms in the Franciscan order.[1] Marguerite also exhibited a strong interest in Saint Clare. She offered financial support to the Poor Clares and she frequently withdrew to spend time in their convents.[2] She would have been familiar with both the legends of Saint Clare and the details of Clare's relationship with Francis. This chapter explores tale 19 in conjunction with lives of Saint Francis, Saint Clare, and Saint Mary Magdalene. It also examines the portrayal of lascivious and violent Franciscans in the *Heptaméron* together with Saint Francis's legend and iconography to demonstrate that Marguerite utilizes hagiography to highlight clerical corruption and to redress inequalities about men and women in traditional saints' lives and in Renaissance debates. Finally, this chapter analyzes how hagiographical references in two tales featuring corrupt clerics and adulterous women illustrate her creative and nuanced response to sixteenth-century controversies.

Tale 19: Saint Francis, Saint Clare, and a Sixteenth-Century French Novella

The *Heptaméron*'s nineteenth tale recounts how familial and social pressures prevent a couple from marrying. Realizing that there is no possibility for their marriage to take place, the young man becomes a Franciscan and the tale's heroine, Pauline, joins the Poor Clares. The tale includes references to the religious orders of Saint Francis and Saint Clare, and Marguerite de Navarre also mentions Saint Mary Magdalene in the tale's conclusion. Scholars have briefly remarked on the similarities between tale 19 and these saints' lives.[3] However, a detailed analysis of the multiple parallels between the *Heptaméron*'s tale and the lives of these three saints deserves more consideration. This chapter argues that thematic similarities between hagiographic legends and Marguerite's tale such as the couple's rebellion against familial pressures to marry, the desire to forsake riches for a life of asceticism and poverty, and the transformation of earthly love into complete devotion to God, point to saints' lives as one of the primary sources for this novella. An analysis of the intertextual echoes between tale 19 and hagiographic legends sheds new light on the narrative traditions incorporated into this tale. The queen of Navarre's adaptation of these saints' lives to a sixteenth-century context also offers unique insights into her response as a reader of traditional hagiography and clarifies her position on controversies involving gender and theology in Renaissance France.

Saint Francis was born in 1181 into a family of wealthy merchants and he was expected to follow in his father's footsteps. His decision to defy his family's wishes and embrace a life of poverty for Christ provoked familial ire and discord. In fact, he was ridiculed, beaten, and held captive by his own father. Ultimately, Francis rejected the material wealth and luxuries that his family offered him; he chose to give away his possessions and live in radical poverty for Christ. One reason that Francis embraced what he called "Holy Lady Poverty" was his disenchantment with the abuses of wealth in the institutional Church. Thus, in strict accordance with the teachings of Jesus, the first rule of his order was that the friars live without any possessions of their own. Francis's commitment to poverty was so extreme that he was commonly referred to by his contemporaries as "poverello," or little poor man. Given these facts, it is hardly surprising that the account of Saint Francis's life in the *Golden Legend* repeatedly evokes the theme of poverty. Voragine writes, "Moult de nobles et non nobles et clercs et lais, ont despité ce siecle et se sont prins a le ensuyr et le saint Pere leur enseigna a emplir la perfection de l'euvangile, prendre povreté et aller par voye de simplesse" (Many people, of noble and of humble birth, both clerical and lay, put away the world's vanities and followed his path. Like a father, this holy man taught them to strive for evangelical perfection, to embrace poverty, and to walk the way of holy simplicity).[4] Like Saint Francis, Saint Clare also chose to spurn her family and their riches.

Saint Clare was born in 1194 into a prominent noble family in Assisi and she was destined to marry a wealthy gentleman. After Clare heard Francis preach, they secretly met several times over the course of a year and their spiritual friendship blossomed. Ultimately, she resisted her family's wishes when she rejected an arranged marriage to secretly join Francis. Clare then sought to lead a life inspired by his teachings and founded an order for women in the Franciscan tradition. Her order, the Poor Clares, is primarily characterized by its ascetic lifestyle and radical pledge to poverty.[5] In fact, Saint Clare frequently battled with church authorities for the right to maintain her unflinching commitment to total poverty. Considering the emphasis on the rejection of familial pressures and the voluntary embrace of poverty in legends of Saint Francis and Saint Clare, Marguerite's multiple references to these very themes in tale 19 merit scrutiny.

This novella repeatedly emphasizes that the young couple rejects more financially profitable marriages for each other despite extreme societal and familial pressure. The gentleman is first described as such a "pauvre et tant gentil compaignon, qu'il devoit chercher . . . quelque femme riche" (1.267; poor and such an honorable man, . . . that . . . he should have tried to marry some rich woman). Nevertheless, he resists a more economically favorable marriage because of his belief that "tout le tresor du monde estoit en Pauline" (1.267; in Pauline he had found all the treasures in the world). The gentleman is described with the adjective "pauvre" multiple times in the narrative; he is most frequently referred to as a "pouvre serviteur" (poor servant) throughout the tale. Similarly, the marquise wants Pauline to marry someone richer, so the marquise reminds her that if she were to marry the gentleman, they would be "les plus pauvres et miserables de toute l'Italie" (1.267; the poorest, most miserable couple in all of Italy). The description of the couple in association with extreme poverty in Italy recalls the saints from Assisi who were widely renowned throughout their country for their commitment to abject poverty.

The couple's desire to marry and reject more financially beneficial marriages is met with great resistance. They are reminded of "la pauvreté . . . où il leur faudroit tous deux vivre" (1.269; they would have to live in poverty). The text also underscores that their families voice their unfavorable opinions of the match (1.269). While it is important to recognize that the couple does not initially make these personal and financial sacrifices for God, it is nevertheless significant that they rebel against their families by willfully privileging their relationship over material wealth. When the young man ultimately decides to join the Franciscan order, he clarifies that "leur fin est de nous marier bien et richement chacun : car ils ignorent que la vraye richesse gist au contentement" (1.270; their goal is to marry each of us to someone very rich, since they do not know that true riches lie in happiness). Moreover, much like Saint Francis, who gave everything to the poor, the gentleman also distributes his worldly possessions when he goes to the monastery. Marguerite clarifies that he "eut departy à ses serviteurs le peu de bien qu'il avoit" (1.273; divided among his servants the few belongings that he had). The emphasis on this theme arises once again when the gentleman writes Pauline a song that proclaims, "Laissons les biens / Qui sont liens / Plus durs à rompre que fer" (1.277; Let's give up pleasures / Which imprison / Better than a cell). The emphasis on privileging spirituality over materiality in the tale's song echoes Saint Francis's Canticle of Exhortation to Saint Clare and her sisters, in which he addresses them as "little poor ones called by the Lord," thereby encouraging their life of sacrifice.[6] The couple's resistance to familial and social pressure and their deliberate embrace of poverty vividly recall the lives of Francis and Clare.[7] Along with their choice to lead a life of poverty, the couple's gradual transformation from having an earthly focus to a purely spiritual perspective also reveals the influence of hagiography.

There are numerous commonalities between the life of Saint Francis and the spiritual evolution of the young gentleman in the tale. For instance, in his youth, Saint Francis joined the military and was taken captive and spent a year in prison.[8] It was not long after Francis's time in captivity that he decided to reject the world and its pleasures. In Marguerite's tale, the young man also joins the military, fights in war, and spends almost a year imprisoned. Like Francis, his imprisonment also leads to his decision to join the religious orders. It is during his captivity that he decides that if his sacrifices and service are not enough to convince the marquise to allow him to marry Pauline, then "il s'en iroit rendre cordelier, et ne serviroit jamais maistre que Dieu" (1.268; he would become a cordelier and would serve no master other than God). His companion is in disbelief at his declaration, "ne voyant en luy un seul signe de la religion, fors la devotion qu'il avoit en Pauline" (1.268; since the only religious sentiment he had seen in him was his devotion to Pauline). The gentleman's decision is also met with astonishment from the superior at the monastery (1.273–274). The marquis and the marquise also find his choice to join the religious orders so strange that they could hardly believe it (1.274). The fact that his entourage interprets his actions in a less than favorable light also reflects commonplaces of saints' vitae.

It is typical in hagiography for saints to defy the expectations of those around them by undergoing a profound transformation. For instance, the *Golden Legend*'s narrative about Saint Francis begins with the mention that he led a frivolous life until he turned twenty.[9] According to Thomas of Celano, "the young man was raised indulgently and carelessly . . . and was taught shameful and detestable things full of excess and lewdness. . . . He boiled in the sins of youthful heat and was steeped in 'every kind of debauchery.'"[10] Moreover, the notion of transformation is also a recurring topos in hagiography as the genre frequently portrays radical conversions. These transformations ultimately serve to manifest the power of God to drastically change hearts and lives. The representation of the gentleman and his evolution in the tale reflect Saint Francis's own conversion.

In contrast to depictions of Saint Francis's youth, hagiographic legends frequently relate that Saint Clare was reputed for her religious devotion from a tender age.[11] Despite her renowned piety, Clare's decision to join Francis was nevertheless viewed as radical. Saint Clare was so moved by the teachings of Francis that she eventually decided to forsake the world and join him in his utter devotion to live in imitation of Christ. When her family realized that she had fled, they sent armed guards to force her to change her mind. Clare refused to be swayed by the brutal tactics of her family; she clung to the altar and adamantly declared that she would have no husband other than Jesus Christ.

In Marguerite's tale, when Pauline prepares to join the convent of Saint Clare, she attends Mass where her suitor has joined the Franciscans. On seeing each other, they are both overcome with emotion. She coughs to better hide the flush of her cheeks while he falls to the ground to conceal his desire. She then meets with him in a chapel of the Franciscan monastery on her way to join the Poor Clares. This passage is significant for its rich spiritual content as well as its multiple resonances with the meeting of Saint Francis and Saint Clare. The scene in the chapel begins with Pauline's explanation of her reasons for waiting to join the religious orders, namely that social strictures prevented her from doing so earlier. She then reveals her plans to the gentleman, saying, "suis deliberée de prendre l'estat, la robbe, et la vie, telle que je voy la vostre" (1.281; I am determined to adopt the same condition, dress, and way of life as I see you have taken). Her speech emphasizes her desire for the spiritual unity that is only available to them in the context of the religious life. Pauline also declares, "Car par tel chemin que vous irez en paradis, je vous veux suivre : estant asseurée que celuy qui est le vray, parfaict, et digne d'estre nommé amour, nous a tirez à son service par une amitié honneste et raisonnable, laquelle il convertira par son Sainct Esprit du tout en luy. Vous priant que vous et moy oublions ce corps qui perit et tient du vieil Adam, pour recevoir et revestir celuy de nostre espoux Jesus Christ" (1.281; Whatever path you tread to paradise, I want to follow you, as I am sure that He who is true, perfect, and worthy of being called Love has drawn us to his service through an honorable and reasonable love which he will convert completely, through his Holy Spirit, to a love for Him. Let's both forget the body that is mortal and comes from the old Adam to receive and put on that of our spouse Jesus Christ). Marguerite represents the couple's actions as ordained by God by underscoring that it is He who has drawn them to a life of devotion and service.

Furthermore, her heroine professes her faith that the Holy Spirit will convert their earthly love into love for God, concluding with emphasis on "nostre espoux Jesus Christ" (1.281; our spouse Jesus Christ). Later, when the marquise learns of Pauline's decision to become a nun and pleads with her to reconsider, Pauline once again insists that she is a bride of Christ. Marguerite writes, "si elle avoit eu puissance de luy oster un mary de chair (l'homme du monde qu'elle avoit le plus aimé) elle s'en devoit contenter, sans chercher de la vouloir separer de celuy qui estoit immortel et invisible" (1.282; as the marquise had succeeded in taking an earthly husband from her—the man she had loved the most in the world—she should be satisfied with that, without trying to separate her from the husband who was immortal and invisible). Pauline's words recall the language of Saint Clare, who frequently used variations of the expression "sponsa Christi," or "bride of Christ," in writings such as her letters to Agnes of Prague.[12] Other religious elements that are integrated into the chapel scene also share notable commonalities with the celebrated saints from Assisi.

Marguerite writes that the gentleman responds to Pauline's decision to join the Saint Clares by "pleurant d'amour et de joye luy baisa les mains, mais elle abbaissa son visage jusques à la main, et se donnerent par vraye charité le sainct baiser de dilection" (1.282; with tears of love and joy he kissed her hand, but she lowered her face toward his, and in the spirit of true Christian charity, they gave each other a holy kiss). Not surprisingly, this section of the text has received attention in the scholarship. Vernqvist states, "The Holy Kiss of Love is a religious gesture performed between Christians. But at the time of the novella's writing and its plot setting, the sixteenth century, it was no longer practiced outside of mass."[13] Given the heroine's first name, Pauline, on one hand, this kiss can be viewed in association with repeated emphasis on this theme in Saint Paul's writings, since he frequently closes his works with an exhortation to believers to share a kiss of love. On the other hand, it is essential to recognize that it is following Pauline's expression of her desire to join religious orders that the gentleman first kisses her hands and then they share the Holy Kiss of Love. Although this aspect of the text has not received attention, Marguerite's description of these two different kisses is important, particularly when interpreted in connection with long-standing Catholic traditions associated with joining religious orders.

The kissing of hands as an expression of reverence for those entering the religious life remains a common Catholic tradition even at the present time. Furthermore, it is an enduring ritual in the Catholic Church that at the conclusion of one's religious vows, one receives a kiss of peace. What is most striking is that it is typically the laity who approach the altar to kiss the hands of a newly ordained priest or the priest who gives the kiss at the ordination of another priest. Marguerite's representation of Pauline being received into the religious life in this manner serves to underscore the equal value of women's ministry. Moreover, much like Pauline, Saint Clare also received a rather unorthodox entry into religious life.[14] Marguerite's representation of the chapel scene shares notable similarities with the lives of Saint Francis and Saint Clare, as does her depiction of the couple's remarkable spiritual unity.

In contrast to the couple's "deux cueurs" (two hearts) evoked early in the tale, this passage portrays them as "vivans en un estat d'un amour, d'un cueur et d'un esprit, tirez et conduicts de la bonté de Dieu" (1.282; living in a state of one love, one heart, and one spirit emerging from and guided by the goodness of God). Scholars have offered different interpretations of the representation of their spiritual union. Philip Ford notes that "a Christianized form of Platonism underpins Marguerite's presentation of love in this story."[15] Vernqvist argues for a reading in association with the "metaphor of the androgyne."[16] While these approaches are valuable, an intertextual approach with hagiographic narratives provides unique insights. To interpret the couple's representation of having "one love, one heart, and one spirit" in association with the lives of Clare and Francis, it is essential to recall that Saint Clare was so devoted to the ideals and teachings of Saint Francis that she was widely referred to by their contemporaries as an "alter Franciscus," or another Francis. Interestingly while Saint Clare was often called "another Francis," Saint Francis was frequently referred to as "another Magdalen."[17] Thus, Marguerite's declaration at the end of the tale is particularly intriguing: "Et depuis vesquirent Pauline et son serviteur si *sainctement* et devotement en leur observance, que l'on ne doit douter que celuy, duquel la fin de la loy est *charité*, ne leur dist à la fin de leur vie comme à *la Magdaleine*, que leurs pechez leur estoient pardonnez, veu qu'ils avoient beaucoup aimé" (1.282–283, emphasis added; From that time on, Pauline and her loyal servant lived so piously and devoutly according to the rules of the Observant order that we cannot doubt that at the end of their lives, He whose law begets charity said to them, as He said to Mary Magdalene, that their sins were forgiven, since they had loved greatly). This phrase emphasizes the saintly behavior and Christian love of both Pauline and her *serviteur*. The spiritual equality represented in the nineteenth novella may be interpreted as Marguerite's response to what she had observed in written and visual representations of the lives of Saint Francis and Saint Clare.

Saint Francis is one of the most revered saints in Catholic tradition. In contrast, Saint Clare's story has received significantly less attention.[18] Moreover, historically, Clare has often been perceived as a follower of Saint Francis who played a mere "auxiliary role".[19] Fortunately, scholars are increasingly recognizing Clare's substantial influence on Francis. For instance, Carney notes: "The relationship between Clare and Francis was the relationship of equals. Clare had already achieved a reputation for holiness prior to her first meetings with Francis. Francis respected her ability to govern her community and deferred to her judgment in certain matters. Clare, on her part, likewise saw Francis as an essential presence in her vocational story, but both retained and exercised independent judgment and responsibility."[20] However, Clare's important spiritual influence was not as widely recognized in sixteenth-century France. Certain visual representations of these saints in works that circulated within Marguerite's close circle are particularly revealing in this regard. Louise de Savoie's book of hours and Claude's prayer book both feature images and prayers to Saint Francis, but there is no mention whatsoever of Saint Clare. Similarly, Saint Francis's life is recounted in the *Golden Legend*, but Saint Clare is absent from Voragine's text. When analyzing tale 19, it is intriguing that Marguerite names her heroine while she leaves the gentleman in the tale unnamed. Consequently, readers must entertain the possibility that the *Heptaméron*'s representation of Pauline underscores the importance of recognizing the invaluable contributions and substantial influence of holy women and their spiritual leadership, especially given the importance of Marguerite's frequent personal interactions with the order of Saint Clare.

Scholars have observed that this religious order played a substantial role in Marguerite's own spiritual life.[21] In light of Marguerite's close ties with the Poor Clares and the fact that she regularly withdrew to spend time in their convents, there is no doubt that she would have known that Saint Clare was the first woman to write a religious rule for women and that she was a remarkable political figure in her own right. Marguerite's devotion to the Poor Clares and her retreats to their cloisters would have given her a profound appreciation for Saint Clare's legacy as well as a desire to bring greater attention to this holy woman's important role. This interpretation is also supported by Marguerite's reference to Mary Magdalene at the conclusion of the tale. Saint Mary Magdalene is a figure who epitomizes women's faithfulness to Christ. Marguerite's references in the *Petit Œuvre dévot* and the *Heptaméron* follow the model of her literary predecessor, Christine de Pizan, who praised Mary Magdalene's devotion.[22] Thus, while Marguerite's direct association of the couple with Saint Mary Magdalene highlights their total devotion to Christ, it also serves to remind readers of the steadfast nature of women's faith.

The storytellers' lengthy conversation following the tale is intriguing in that, unlike many of the conversations, it is not characterized by a clear division between the men and the women. In addition, it is rich with religious references. Simontault refers to Saint John and the storytellers also directly evoke God six times in the discussion. Unsurprisingly, Hircan categorizes the chaste lovers as fools (1.283). Oisille questions him by insisting on their honorable love, which they converted to a love of God (1.283). Hircan laughs while declaring, "Si melencolie et desespoir sont louables, je diray que Pauline et son serviteur sont bien dignes d'estre louëz" (1.283; If melancholy and despair are praiseworthy, I would say that Pauline and her loyal servant are very deserving of praise). Interestingly, Geburon sides with Oisille, saying that "Dieu . . . a plusieurs moyens pour nous tirer à luy, dont les commencemens semblent estre mauvais, mais la fin en est tresbonne" (1.283; God has ways to draw us to him that at first seem bad, but are good in the end). In an oft-quoted passage that has received much attention in scholarship, Parlamente then offers an extensive reflection on the concept of "perfect love."[23] While lamenting that he cannot do it properly in

Latin, Simontault paraphrases a verse about love from the Gospel of John. It is fitting that he evokes Saint John, the patron saint of love and loyalty, following a tale that exemplifies these very themes. Ennasuite responds to Simontault by demonstrating her own facility with Latin. The conversation concludes with Dagoucin and Saffredent expressing opinions that are at odds with each other and readers are left to form their own opinions.

The elements of the lives of Saint Francis and Saint Clare that are incorporated into tale 19 would have been easily recognized by Marguerite's Renaissance readers. Although traditional hagiographies privileged Saint Francis and either neglected Saint Clare, or at least portrayed her as a lesser saint, this tale can be interpreted as a revisionist hagiography in that Marguerite borrows from these saints' lives to craft a narrative that recalls both of their important contributions to the church and their religious communities. By recalling Clare's vibrant ministry and Mary Magdalene's important influence on Francis, Marguerite's tale also responds to contemporary debates about women and religion by emphasizing women's capacity for holiness and spiritual leadership. Just as the nineteenth tale effectively highlights Pauline's saintly qualities in connection with the lives of Clare, Francis, and Mary Magdalene, the next section explores how Marguerite draws on hagiographic tradition to emphasize that the Franciscans in Renaissance France have little in common with the holiness of the venerable founder of their order.

Saint Francis and the False Sanctity of the Franciscans in the *Heptaméron*

It is hardly surprising that Marguerite de Navarre's anticlericalism has been the focus of significant critical attention, as several tales in the *Heptaméron* highlight the clergy's misdeeds. While there are some positive depictions of clerics, Marguerite consistently evokes the clergy's crimes, with pointed emphasis on the Franciscan order.[24] Many scholars have analyzed the representation of abuses by the Franciscans in the text.[25] Given Marguerite's extensive attention to the topic, it is not within the scope of the present study to explore all of the tales depicting corrupt Franciscans. Thus, this section will focus more specifically on the *Heptaméron*'s references to Saint Francis's life and iconography. Although direct references and subtle allusions to the revered saint from Assisi are interspersed throughout the tales evoking clerical abuse, this aspect of the stories has received little attention in the scholarship. While modern readers may not immediately recognize the connections to Saint Francis's life and attributes, he was one of the most celebrated saints in sixteenth-century France, and Marguerite's references would have been readily apparent to her Renaissance readers. This section analyzes Marguerite's representations of Franciscans in connection with visual images from early modern devotional texts as well as hagiographic works such as the *Golden Legend* or *I Fioretti di San Francesco* (*The Little Flowers of Saint Francis*). It also demonstrates how Marguerite creatively drew on Saint Francis's life and iconography to highlight the rampant corruption of the Franciscan order in Renaissance France.

Marguerite explicitly refers to the association between Saint Francis and the Franciscans in tale 5. In this story, two friars decide to rape a ferrywoman or throw her into the river if she refuses. When she appears to be willing to yield to their desires, they make an oath to her swearing by the name of "leur bon sainct François" (1.63; their good saint Francis). Marguerite's reference to Saint Francis recalls his moral goodness, while this characterization also contrasts sharply with the two Franciscans in the tale who outwardly claim to be the saint's followers, but instead prove themselves capable of unfettered abuse and malice. The direct reference to Saint Francis in the tale is also accompanied by an indirect allusion to one of the most iconic moments of his life. When the ferrywoman succeeds in outsmarting and then escaping from the monks, Marguerite writes, "laissans ces deux beaux-peres aux desers, ausquels elle cria tant qu'elle peut : 'Attendez messieurs, que l'Ange de Dieu vous vienne consoler'" (1.65; leaving the two good fathers in the wilderness, then she called out to them as loudly as she could, "Wait for the angel of God to bring you comfort"). Numerous texts and visual representations from the Renaissance highlight how Saint Francis withdrew to the wilderness to pray when a winged seraph appeared in the sky. This celebrated event in Francis's vita was well known in Marguerite's entourage. It is visually depicted in both Louise de Savoie's book of hours and Queen Claude's prayer book (Figures 5.1 and 5.2). Moreover, Marguerite refers to this iconic moment of Saint Francis's life in detail in her *Petit Œuvre dévot*.[26] Scholars have briefly remarked on the connection between Saint Francis and this reference in tale 5.[27]

Marguerite incorporates this element of Saint Francis's story into the tale of the malicious Franciscans to underscore their exceedingly immoral behavior. In contrast to their esteemed founder, the fact that these monks arrive in the wilderness, or "desers," has nothing to do with prayer. It is also telling that the verb "prier" (to pray or to implore) appears frequently in the tale (1.63, 1.65). The term "prier" for these Franciscans has no connection whatsoever to spiritual

Figure 5.1. "St. Francis Receiving the Stigmata," 192 × 123 mm. From *Hours, use of Rome* (France, ca. 1500–1515), MS 411, fol. 142v, General Collection, Beinecke Rare Book and Manuscript Library, Yale University, New Haven, CT. Courtesy of Beinecke Rare Book and Manuscript Library.

Figure 5.2. *Stigmatization of St. Francis*, illuminated by the Master of Claude de France, 2¾ × 2 in. From *Prayer Book of Claude de France* (Tours, France, ca. 1517), MS M.1166, fol. 37v, The Morgan Library and Museum, New York. Gift of Mrs. Alexandre P. Rosenberg in memory of her husband, Alexandre Paul Rosenberg, 2008. Courtesy of The Morgan Library and Museum.

devotion; rather it involves the monks beseeching the ferrywoman to give in to their carnal desires. Similarly, Marguerite portrays the friars ending up on bended knee. However, unlike Saint Francis, who is frequently depicted as a supplicant on his knees in the humility of prayer, the Franciscans take this position to beg for mercy from the ferrywoman once they realize that they have been outsmarted and will be punished for their misdeeds. The tale's references to Saint Francis all serve to emphasize the marked contrast between the holy man from Assisi and the false sanctity of these clerics.

One finds a similar depiction of the moral divergence between Saint Francis and his purported followers in tale 31. Although the Franciscan in this story comes from what is regarded as an esteemed monastery (2.437), Marguerite's novella highlights the rampant deceit and vicious nature of these monks. In fact, tale 31 is one of the most violent stories in the entire collection. A cleric is so infatuated with a noblewoman that when he discovers that her husband is away from his home, he brutally stabs three servants to get her alone. After ruthlessly murdering the servants, he intimidates the woman by showing her their lifeless bodies, threatening her with death, and ordering her to do his bidding or suffer the same fate. Wanting to prolong his pleasures with her, he refrains from raping her right away. He decides to disguise her as a Franciscan and kidnap her so that he can keep her at his monastery and rape her repeatedly. Marguerite describes the scene in vivid detail:

> À l'heure le meschant, qui n'en vouloit point jouïr d'elle pour une heure seule, ne la voulut prendre par force, mais luy dist : «Ma damoiselle, n'ayez peur, vous estes entre les mains de l'homme du monde qui plus vous aime.» Disant cela, il *despouilla son grand habit, dessoubs lequel en avoit un plus petit, qu'il presenta à la damoiselle, en luy disant, que si elle ne le prenoit, il la mettroit au rang des trespassez, qu'elle voyoit devant ses yeux.* La damoiselle *plus morte que vive*, delibera de feindre luy vouloir obeïr, tant pour sauver sa vie, que pour gaigner le temps *qu'elle esperoit* que son mary reviendroit. Et par le commandement dudict Cordelier, commença à se descoëffer, le plus longuement qu'elle peut : Et quand elle fut en cheveux, le cordelier ne regarda à la beauté qu'ils avoient, mais *les couppa hastivement* : et ce faict, la feit despouïller toute en chemise, et *luy vestit le petit habit* qu'il portoit. (2.439, emphasis added)

> [But the wicked man had no intention of taking his pleasure with her for just one hour and did not take her by force. Rather, he said, "Madame,

don't be afraid. You are in the hands of the man who loves you more than any other in the whole world." In saying this, he took off his habit, under which he was wearing a smaller one. He gave the smaller one to the young lady, telling her that if she didn't put it on, he would add her to the ranks of the deceased she saw before her. More dead than alive, the young lady decided to pretend that she would obey him, as much to save her life as to stall for time, hoping that her husband would return. Following the Cordelier's orders, she started to take off her coif as slowly as she could. When her hair was uncovered, the Cordelier did not look at how beautiful it was but rather quickly cut it all off. Having done this, he had her get undressed until she was wearing nothing but her chemise, and he had her put on the small habit he was wearing.]

The terrified noblewoman is threatened with a brutal death if she does not submit to the Franciscan's demands. Despite her terror, she actively does what she can to protect herself, taking her time to let her hair down in hopes that her husband will arrive. The friar proceeds to brusquely chop off her hair, and then he forces her to wear one of his habits. While the scene is remarkable for its violence, the passage is particularly intriguing for its parallels with a famous scene in Saint Francis's life.

The circumstances of Francis welcoming Saint Clare into religious life are as follows: "The day after Palm Sunday, 1212, St Clare visited St Francis at his chapel of the Portiuncula. Before the Blessed Virgin's altar Clare took off her fine cloak and St Francis cut off her hair, giving her a penitential habit of coarse cloth tied with a robe. As there was no convent nearby, St Francis took Clare to the Benedictine convent of St Paul."[28] It was at Clare's request and for purely spiritual reasons that Saint Francis cut Saint Clare's hair, gave her a Franciscan habit to wear, and then took her to a convent. In contrast, the Franciscan in Marguerite's tale forcibly cuts the noblewoman's hair, coerces her into wearing his habit to disguise his evil activities, and attempts to take her to a monastery against her will so that he can sexually assault her repeatedly. By drawing on hagiographic legend and incorporating these details into her tale, Marguerite underscores the extreme contrast between the honorable Italian saint and these Franciscans.

This very theme is also emphasized in tale 48, a story that has received little attention in the scholarship. This novella recounts how two Franciscans take a meal in a room at an inn since they were not welcome at a wedding feast because of their social status. Feeling slighted at having been excluded from the festivities, one of the Franciscans endeavors to take advantage of the marriage bed. He waits for the bride to leave the party and then quickly sheds his habit and stealthily sneaks into her bedroom where he sexually assaults her while the other monk willingly serves as a watchman. Later, when the couple figures out what the Franciscans have done, the entire wedding party goes after them. Marguerite writes, "ils les attraperent dans les vignes, et là furent traictez comme il leur appartenoit. Car après les avoir bien battuz, leur coupperent les bras et les jambes, et les laisserent dedans les vignes en la garde du dieu Bacchus et de Venus, dont ils estoient meilleurs disciples, que de *saint François*" (2.586, emphasis added; they caught them in the vineyard. And the cordeliers were treated as they deserved to be: after they had been beaten, their arms and legs were cut off, and they were left in the vineyard in the hands of Bacchus and Venus, since they were better disciples of these gods than of Saint Francis). Ultimately, the search party finds the guilty friars hiding in a vineyard, where they are beaten and then dismembered. Along with the violent nature of the punishment of these clerics, it is the reference to Saint Francis at the end of the story that merits attention.

Marguerite unequivocally expresses the idea that these Franciscans in no way adhere to the moral and spiritual teachings of Saint Francis. In fact, she explicitly remarks that they follow Bacchus and Venus, the pagan god of wine and goddess of love, much more than the saint from Assisi. Marguerite draws on her knowledge of hagiography and takes advantage of her readers' familiarity with Saint Francis's life to powerfully demonstrate the moral divergence between the saint and the lascivious Franciscans. This ethical divide is apparent in the *Heptaméron*'s representation of their actions, as well as in Marguerite's allusions to important elements of Saint Francis's iconography throughout these tales.

Another well-known iconographical element of Saint Francis's life is his role as patron saint of animals. While Saint Francis is renowned for his gentleness and love for all creatures, Marguerite's text offers a sharply different view of Franciscan friars. According to legend, Saint Francis preached to birds, animals obeyed his commands, and he would walk with utmost care so as not to tread on any of God's creatures. In the *Golden Legend*, Voragine writes, "le benoit François, plain de tresgrande simplesse columbine admonnestoit a toutes creatures a amer leur createur" (Blessed Francis was filled with the simplicity of the dove. He exhorted all creatures to love their Creator).[29] It cannot be mere coincidence that the behavior of the Franciscans in the *Heptaméron* leads to them consistently being likened to animals, and to one animal specifically. A close examination of these metaphors in Marguerite's text is particularly revealing. In tale 5, the Franciscan friars are depicted as "loups enragez" (1.65; ravenous wolves). The exceedingly violent Franciscan in tale 31 is also depicted as a wolf (2.442). The wolf metaphor has frequently been used in literature to symbolize predators; thus Marguerite's choice to repeatedly refer to these lascivious Franciscans with this term undoubtedly emphasizes their predatory nature and sexual aggressions.

Given the queen of Navarre's extensive knowledge of Scripture, Marguerite's repeated references to the Franciscans as wolves can also be interpreted in association with Matthew 7:15, where Jesus says, "Beware of false prophets, who come to you in sheep's clothing, but underneath are ravenous wolves." The fact that Marguerite specifically refers to malevolent Franciscans as wolves can also be interpreted in connection with a legendary episode in Saint Francis's life, namely the taming of the wolf of Gubbio. The fourteenth-century *Fioretti di San Francesco* recounts one of the saint's most celebrated miracles. Marguerite may have possibly read a version of the manuscript in Italian.[30] Her close ties to Franciscan reform and convents of the Poor Clares would have also familiarized her with detailed aspects of Francis's legend. When a wolf was terrorizing and attacking residents of the town of Gubbio, Saint Francis confronted the wolf armed with nothing but the sign of the cross. As the wolf aggressively approached him, he commanded "frate lupo," or "Brother Wolf," to do no harm.[31] The wolf then lay down at Francis's feet and henceforth the wolf and residents of Gubbio peacefully coexisted. While hagiographic legends recount that Saint Francis succeeded in preventing "Brother Wolf" from continuing with his violent attacks in Gubbio, Marguerite unequivocally depicts the Franciscan brothers as wolfish predators who travel throughout France terrorizing innocent women with physical and sexual violence until they are duly punished for their crimes.

Along with narrating the transgressions of the Franciscans, Marguerite's novellas frequently portray the grisly punishments meted out to these clerics. The punishments are brutal, but particularly so when compared to the *Heptaméron*'s depictions of members of the laity who sneak into women's beds and commit similar crimes with no repercussions whatsoever.[32] The malevolent clerics are punished by being bound, dismembered, or burned alive, a level of brutality that recalls the fate of saints in the *Golden Legend*. The fact that several of these clerics end up bound, or *lié*, serves a dual purpose. On one hand, it highlights the need for their physical restraint to prevent further abuses from taking place. On the other hand, as Gary Ferguson has demonstrated, the term also shares a noteworthy linguistic connection to the word *cordelier*.[33] While Saint Francis's habit was adorned with a knotted cord, or *corde liée*, with three knots symbolizing the vows of chastity, obedience, and poverty, Marguerite's Franciscans end up having their hands and feet bound as a punishment for their sexual aggressions. Although some saints in the *Golden Legend* have their hands and feet bound for their resolute faith, these corrupt clerics are punished for using their privileged position in the church to commit rape and murder. Thus, not only does Marguerite draw on Saint Francis's iconography to highlight the extreme contrasts between the Franciscans and their humble and holy founder, she also draws on hagiographic narrative tradition to highlight the fact that saints suffered for their holiness while the Franciscans in sixteenth-century France encounter brutal punishment for using their appearances of sanctity to perpetrate violent abuses.

While Saint Francis declared, "Sanctify yourself and you will sanctify society," the *Heptaméron* consistently emphasizes that the Franciscan friars of sixteenth-century France had abandoned the saint's ideals of chastity and holiness to the point that they caused more harm than good in society.[34] Marguerite explicitly warns readers not to believe that "tous ceux qui portoient cest habit, debvoient estre semblables au bon sainct" (2.348; all those who wore the habit of his order must be as holy as this good saint). The fact that Marguerite consistently weaves references to Saint Francis's legend and iconography into her collection of tales reveals another facet of hagiography's influence on the *Heptaméron*, while these depictions also serve to question the gender divisions in the hierarchy of the Renaissance Catholic Church. Marguerite juxtaposes these disturbing patterns of Franciscan abuses with depictions of women as saint-like figures. In contrast to the corrupt clerics, Marguerite's heroines demonstrate unyielding sanctity and spiritual strength even while they are martyred and persecuted. This disparity in the representation of holiness in women and men serves to question the hierarchy of the Renaissance church, while it also responds to the unfavorable stereotypes of women's capacity for holiness in the misogynistic texts of the *querelle des femmes*. These same tales also illuminate Marguerite's views on the controversy over the cult of saints with her emphasis on the "good" Saint Francis. Marguerite's stories about Franciscans recall the goodness and holy ideals of Francis while they also illustrate that the clerics who bear his name often have little in common with their esteemed founder. Along with drawing on hagiography to emphasize the unholiness of the Franciscans, Marguerite also participates in sixteenth-century debates by incorporating saints' vitae and pilgrimage traditions into the stories of immoral clerics who engage in affairs with ungodly women in tales 60 and 61.

Saintly Words, Holy Sacraments, and Ungodly Behavior: Tales 60 and 61

Virtuous and holy women appear throughout the *Heptaméron*. From the mule-driver's wife to the courageous heroine in tale 67, women's moral strength and holiness are consistently emphasized in Marguerite's text. Countless novellas also relate how clerics and their false appearances of sanctity enable them to rape, assault, and endanger women. In contrast, tales 60 and 61 depict extramarital affairs that women willingly engage in with men of the church. In these stories, confession, the Eucharist, and extreme unction play central roles in the female characters' deceptive behavior. Ironically, a vocabulary traditionally associated with holiness is used in connection with these adulterous women and immoral clerics. This section examines the portrayal of sacraments and the lexicon associated with sanctity in these tales together with saints' lives. It also demonstrates how Marguerite's creative use of her knowledge of the sacraments as well her familiarity with the saints and pilgrimage traditions associated with religious institutions in Blois and Autun relate to her work's unique engagement in debates about gender and religion in Renaissance France.

While the sixtieth and sixty-first tales have received less scholarly attention than Marguerite's other stories, they have not been entirely neglected. André Tournon has explored the pair of stories in an article on doubles and hybrids, arguing that the comic use of pious expressions incites readers' laughter, but also their self-examination.[35] Carrie Klaus has published a persuasive reading of the tales in connection with Marguerite's representation of Louise de Savoie's regency and women's political authority in France.[36] Jan Miernowski has thoughtfully analyzed the representation of the sacraments in tale 61.[37] Although these tales have been explored in scholarly literature, their intertextual connections merit further analysis. In a first (and rare) occurrence in the *Heptaméron*, Geburon, the storyteller who recounts tale 60, does not choose who tells tale 61. In a break with the established conventions in the text, it is Oisille who selects Saffredent to recount the next story even while expressing that he will undoubtedly not share something that will be "in favor of women" (2.682). This atypical transfer of voice encourages the reader to examine these tales in dialogue with one another as do the many notable similarities in the narratives.

The sequential stories have many parallels. Not only do the two main female characters pretend to be dying, but they both request the presence of a group of devout women to witness their agony. In theatrical scenes, the women feign serious illness and death, or being on the brink of death, to flee their marriages. After their escapes, these women willingly engage in affairs with clerics for the exact same duration (a period of fourteen or fifteen years). Although church officials intervene at various points, they do not successfully put an end to the affairs. It is ultimately the women in France's royal family who restore order and preserve the marriages. Along with these similarities, the sacraments play a central role in both stories.

In fact, the tales involve five of the seven sacraments of the Catholic Church, and the only two sacraments that are not included, baptism and confirmation, generally involve children and youths. Obviously, by having extramarital affairs, the wayward wives and corrupt clerics display complete irreverence toward the sacraments of matrimony and the holy orders. Marguerite's representation of the other sacraments also merits analysis. When these women feign such grave illness that they appear to be at death's door, they receive three sacraments: penance, the Eucharist, and extreme unction. From a Catholic perspective, the sacrament of reconciliation, or confession, involves the forgiveness for sins, but it also provides the strength to resist temptations, a sort of spiritual inoculation against sin. Similarly, extreme unction not only comforts and strengthens the sick in their sufferings, but it is also associated with the forgiveness of sins. In addition, it is seen as a preparation for the passing over to eternal life and thus is sometimes referred to as *sacramentum exeuntium*, or the sacrament of those departing. While the Eucharist is by its nature always holy, when combined with the sacraments of penance and extreme unction it has added importance. In this instance, it is referred to as holy viaticum, or provision for the journey, as this final partaking in the body and blood of Christ is seen as the ideal spiritual nourishment for the journey heavenward.

Ironically, the sacraments are taken in the tales not in preparation for the passage from the earthly life to heaven, but for a journey from a marital bed to that of a corrupt cleric. Through these references, Marguerite cleverly draws on both her knowledge and her readers' familiarity with Catholic traditions to emphasize the utter disregard for the sacraments on the part of these women, but also of the clerics. The cantor in tale 60 fully participates in the ruse and abuse of the sacraments, even preparing the grave and then disinterring his lover himself under the cover of darkness. In tale 61, it is the woman alone who is behind the nefarious abuse of the sacraments. Although the canon is not complicit in her ruse, he demonstrates no reluctance whatsoever in welcoming her into his arms immediately after her sacrilegious farce. In both tales, the very sacraments meant to enable the faithful to resist temptation and grant the grace of forgiveness are used instead to create the opportunity to sin more freely. While the adulterous affairs with clerics are shocking, it is this sacrilegious abuse of sacraments that is portrayed as particularly egregious.[38]

These instances of abuse of sacraments are not alone in the text. In fact, Marguerite repeatedly uses the term "manteau" (cloak) in association with the behavior of these clerics, emphasizing how they conceal their true nature and evil intentions under a false appearance of holiness. In tale 61, the husband who is aghast at his wife's behavior remarks, "Qui eust pensé que sous le manteau des saincts sacrements de l'Eglise, on eust peu couvrir un si vilain et abominable cas!" (2.687; Who would have thought that someone would use the holy sacraments to conceal such a vile and abominable plan!). The same term is used to refer to the incestuous priest in tale 33 whose "sainct manteau" (2.458; holy cloak) hides his monstrous behavior. One finds a similar expression in tale 41 with the confessor, who attempts to engage in lascivious activities under the cloak of confession (2.522). In the discussion of tale 61, even Hircan notes that a sacrament "lequel n'estant receu en foy, et charité, est en damnation eternelle" (2.691; which when it is not received with faith and charity leads to eternal damnation). By having a storyteller known for scandalous remarks express shock at the immoral behavior, Marguerite strongly emphasizes the gravity of the offense.

Along with underscoring the abuse of the sacraments, Marguerite represents another transformation of holy traditions into ungodly behaviors by weaving allusions to saints and pilgrimage into these stories. One tale takes place in Blois while the other is set in Autun. The two locations are noteworthy given the royal family's well-documented visits to these religious sites. Not only did they stay in both locations, but King Francis was instrumental in extensive building projects done at the cathedral at Blois. In 1523, Marguerite composed a letter from Blois about a matter involving the bishop of Autun, thus showing she was keenly aware of the ecclesiastical activities in these areas.[39] Marguerite often situates her stories geographically with a brief reference early in the tales, but in these short narratives she mentions Blois four times and Autun on seven occasions. This atypical and repeated insistence on geography may relate to Marguerite's detailed knowledge of the saints associated with the religious institutions there, namely Solenne, Lazarus, and Peter.

An examination of the pilgrimage traditions and saints' relics associated with these holy sites offers new insights into Marguerite's narratives. While the cathedral at Blois was renamed the Cathedral of Saint Louis in the seventeenth century, during the Merovingian era it was originally called Saint Peter's, a compelling reference given that this saint is explicitly referred to in the conclusion of tale 61. When the relics of the esteemed bishop, Saint Solenne, were transferred from Chartres to Blois during the tenth century, the church was renamed Saint Solenne and subsequently attracted a multitude of pilgrims.[40] By situating the tale in this renowned pilgrimage site, Marguerite highlights the divergence between devout pilgrims making a journey of faith to Saint Solenne's relics at Blois and the errant wife traveling there only to engage in an affair with a cleric. Moreover, Saint Solenne's faithful service in his role as bishop resulted in his canonization, a striking contrast with the cantor in the tale who uses his religious position to exploit the sacraments and the proximity of his clerical home to the church cemetery to hide his immoral activities.

Marguerite and her contemporaries would have known that, like Blois, Autun was an important center of pilgrimage. Not only was the cathedral there a common stop on the famous Way of Saint James, but it was a celebrated pilgrimage site in its own right. The journey the woman makes to her canon-lover is particularly compelling in connection with the saint honored there. Notably, the cathedral in Autun is the Cathedral of Saint Lazarus. The site's affiliation with a saint who had been miraculously raised from the dead makes Marguerite's lexicon and the events in the tale particularly ironic. The wayward wife pretends to be on the brink of death, then sneaks out of her home to join the cleric. As she travels on foot to Autun, Marguerite explicitly portrays her as a "pilgrim" making her way to a "saint" in 2.686 and 2.687. The extreme irony of a woman who attempts to fake her own death and then follows the pilgrimage path to a resurrected saint's shrine to continue her adulterous affair with a cleric is striking.

Along with the ironic portrayal of the woman as a pilgrim and the canon as a saint, Marguerite insists on the woman's "bare feet" and "chemise" during her journey, two references that relate to the early modern tradition of walking barefoot in a tunic during pilgrimage (2.686).[41] Marguerite's insistence on the woman's attire in the cold weather is especially ironic, for she notes that she does not suffer from the frigid temperatures since she has been warmed by the fires of hell. When the canon discovers her on his doorstep, he verifies that she has flesh and bones and is neither a spirit nor a phantom (2.687–688). Just as this is clearly not a miraculous resurrection like that of Saint Lazarus, the clerics in these tales have little in common with another saint that Marguerite explicitly evokes.

Saffredent finishes tale 61 with a reference to a saint and the sacraments and a warning to women about evil ministers: "Voilà, mes dames, comme les chaisnes de Sainct Pierre sont converties par les mauvais ministres, en celles de Sathan, et si fortes à romper, que les sacrements, qui chassent les diables du corps, sont à ceux cy les moyens de les faire plus longuement demeureur en leurs consciences" (2.690; That, my ladies, is how the chains of Saint Peter are converted by bad ministers into the chains of Satan. They are so hard to break that the sacraments that expel devils from the body are for these people the very thing that make devils remain longer in their conscience). Nicole Cazauran notes, "Ici ces 'chaînes' figurent les vœux prononcés par les prêtres, dont celui du célibat et de chasteté, qui en font serviteurs de Dieu. Les mauvais prêtres deviennent serviteurs et prisonniers de Satan" (Here these "chains" represent the vows taken by priests, including that of celibacy and chastity, that make them servants of God. The bad priests become servants and prisoners of Satan).[42] By evoking Saint Peter's chains, Marguerite emphasizes how the clerics disregard their vows and abuse the sacraments, while she also recalls a saint who was imprisoned as a punishment for preaching about Jesus. In contrast, the behavior of a cleric in these tales leads to a woman being imprisoned. Moreover, the reference has a connection to Autun, where Saint Peter is one of two saints prominently featured in the tympanum of the Last Judgment, but it also connects the two tales, since the cathedral at Blois was originally named after this very saint. By drawing on these connections between the hagiographic and pilgrimage traditions in Blois and Autun, Marguerite highlights the extent to which these women and clerics lack morality, but she also weaves an engaging and ironic tale.

While the queen of Navarre frequently finds inspiration in saints' lives to compose tales that highlight women's virtue and faith, these two stories exemplify the Prologue's endeavor to tell the truth in that Marguerite offers an honest portrayal of the variations and complexities of human behavior. The tales also display her more balanced representation of the sexes as compared to other writers in the *querelle des femmes*, who typically offer highly polarized opinions of men and women. Along with Marguerite's many tales of lascivious Franciscans and unholy men of the cloth, these stories add to her portrayal of widespread clerical corruption by underscoring immorality in various levels of the ecclesiastical hierarchy, with a canon and a cantor, and in diverse geographical regions, with settings in Autun and Blois. However, her portrayals of the clergy in the stories are not systematically negative as each tale also overtly refers to clerics who are honorable men such as the confessor and the archdeacon (2.675, 2.684). The portrayal of women in the two tales is also not entirely negative or positive.

Although Geburon and Saffredent recount stories that prominently feature female characters who lack integrity, Marguerite nonetheless spins the tales in a way that ultimately highlights women's positive actions in society. The female members of the French royal family are represented in favorable terms. They effectively use their authority to bring about order by ensuring that the affairs cease and the marriages are restored.[43] Along with the positive portrayal of women's political power, Marguerite also emphasizes their spiritual authority. In fact, there is a dramatic role reversal as the women in the royal family "prescherent . . . ce chantre" (2.678; lectured the cantor) so well that that he ceased his affair. Significantly, the verb "prescher" is also used favorably in reference to the faithful women who do not hesitate to console and pray for the wayward wives when they feign illness. Marguerite explicitly highlights their sound teaching on God's mercies in contrast to the message of so many "prescheurs indiscrets." The pious women "se meirent à la consoler, en luy disant, que Dieu n'estoit pas si terrible, que *beaucoup de prescheurs indiscrets* le peignoient : et que jamais il ne luy refuseroit sa misericorde" (2.675, emphasis added; consoled her, telling her that God was not as cruel as many preachers made him out to be and that he would never refuse her his mercy). Marguerite's word choice is noteworthy for its criticism, especially since Cotgrave offers "witlesse" and "unadvised" as definitions of "indiscret."[44] Moreover, while these tales are consecutive, they are also recounted on different days. Thus, in between the novellas, the prologue to the seventh day also serves to remind readers of women's spiritual authority as it emphasizes how Oisille's effective teachings inspire such deep devotion that the *devisants* momentarily forget about their storytelling venture (2.681). Along with the repeated emphasis on women's religious authority, the tales conclude with an intriguing representation of women sharing stories.

While many writers in the *querelle des femmes* offer negative portrayals of women talking among themselves, tale 61 challenges this unfavorable stereotype.[45] In contrast to a text like François Rabelais's *Tiers Livre*, which mocks the "interminable bavardage des femmes" (endless chatter of women), Marguerite depicts women communicating with one another as a force for good.[46] She writes that several good women were murmuring among themselves about the scandalous behavior of the canon and his lover, but they were powerless to do anything. And yet, these women's words are clearly not without consequence, as it is precisely because of their murmurings that a humble servant girl is cognizant of the situation. While doing laundry the young girl recounts the story to a chambermaid. The chambermaid then shares the story with Marguerite, who promptly informs the other two female members of the royal family. Then Louise, Claude, and Marguerite request a firsthand account of the events from the woman in question. This elaborate chain of women talking and sharing the story is ultimately what leads to the wife's repentance as well as to the reconciliation and restoration of the marriage; it may also serve to highlight the value of Marguerite's own storytelling project. For even though Oisille will lament the corruption of the age in the prologue to day seven, through these evocative tales Marguerite offers encouragement to her readers by illustrating how women sharing stories can in fact be an effective and powerful means to bring about positive social change. The final chapter considers how Marguerite integrates hagiographical references throughout her collection of tales while she also makes intriguing revisions to traditional hagiography.

Conclusion

The Final Tale, Revising Hagiography, and Offering Hope

> Je pourrais te parler d'innombrables dames de diverses conditions, vierges, veuves ou femmes mariées, en qui Dieu a montré sa puissance par leur force et leur constance extraordinaires.
>
> [I could tell you endless stories about women of all different social ranks, whether virgins, wives, or widows, whose wonderful strength and constancy revealed how God was working through them.]
>
> —Christine de Pizan, *Le livre de la Cité des dames*

While the Prologue of the *Heptaméron* recalls Mary's nativity and establishes the storytellers at a site of Marian devotion, the work's final tale also includes explicit references to Christ's mother, the most celebrated of the saints. Given that the Virgin Mary is present at the beginning and the end of Marguerite's text, this section begins with an examination of the portrayal of the Virgin and the assault of a virgin in the seventy-second tale. Although Marguerite espoused certain reformist ideas, she also repeatedly demonstrated a fervent attachment to Christ's mother. Jean-Marie Le Gall has argued that Marguerite's repeated pilgrimages to sites of Marian adoration illustrate her deep affection for the Virgin Mary.[1] Damien Plantey has demonstrated that Marguerite's library and collection of sacred objects exemplify her devotion to Christ's mother.[2] Gary Ferguson has shown that Mary is a consistent presence throughout Marguerite's poetry.[3] A close reading of tale 72 with Marian iconography and recent research on rape will further our understanding of the young nun's behavior in the tale and elucidate Marguerite's personal beliefs regarding the mother of Jesus and the cult of saints more generally.

The seventy-second tale offers unique insights into Marguerite's views on Mary with its repeated references to the Virgin as well as the circumstances surrounding Marguerite's own appearance in the narrative. In this novella, a young nun is helping an older monk with the burial of a poor man. While performing this corporal work of mercy together, the monk speaks of spiritual matters so piously that he brings her to tears. This gives the cleric such pleasure that while continuing to talk about God, he puts his arms around the young woman. Given his spiritual words and austere reputation, she does not dare resist and he has his way with her. Immediately after the event, the young nun proceeds to say her usual Marian devotions. On pronouncing the words "Virgin Mary," she suddenly remembers that she is no longer a virgin (2.776). At this point, she falls prostrate before an image of Mary sobbing uncontrollably. The monk hears her cries and worries that he will lose his sensual pleasures, thus he speaks sharply and demands that she confess only to him. Their relationship continues until she falls pregnant, a fact that distresses her so much that she finally reports the events to her superior. The corrupt prioress and prior chide her by saying that she is old enough to defend herself and insisting that the monk is a good man. However, to prevent her from revealing their own immoral lifestyle, they ultimately encourage her to make a pilgrimage to Rome in hopes of recovering her virginity from the pope. When she stops in Lyon during her trip, she fortuitously encounters Marguerite de Navarre in a church. The queen listens to the nun's story and comforts her, then she intervenes to have the monk removed from his position and sends the young woman back to her convent.

Critical work on the young nun in the seventy-second tale has often focused on her foolishness and has hesitated to depict this as an assault. For instance, Marie-Claire Thomine-Bichard and Véronique Montagne argue that she loses her virginity "par sottise et naïveté" (out of foolishness and naivety).[4] François Cornilliat writes that she loses her virginity "sans véritable cause" (without real cause).[5] Although Dagoucin is the male storyteller who is typically most sympathetic to women's plights, he notes that the sexual encounter happened "sans force ny amour" (2.776; not by way of force nor on account of love). However, Marguerite's representation of the events merits further exploration for its psychological acuity, especially when read alongside recent research on sexual assault.

Marguerite describes the nun as one of the youngest and specifies that the young woman fears the monk more than anyone else (2.775). Reading this in the post-#MeToo era, one must reflect more extensively on Marguerite's lexical choices and her representation of the threatening dynamics of this hierarchical relationship. The tale specifies that when the monk puts his arms around the young nun as he speaks about God, she does not dare resist. The nun's silence and lack of resistance should not be interpreted as her being complicit. Mary McKinley argues that "she is intimidated by the priest's reputation as *devost* and *austere* and overcome more than seduced."[6] Moreover, in Jen Percy's 2023 *New York Times* article "What People Misunderstand about Rape," she notes that freezing, or "tonic immobility," is in fact a common reaction to sexual assault and an involuntary response to trauma.[7] In tale 72, the startling disconnect between the monk's austere reputation and pious speech amid a religious duty and his lecherous actions could easily explain the young girl's shock and paralysis.

The traumatic experience of rape could also explain why the nun only recalls that she has lost her virginity when she prays before the Virgin. A delayed realization of the trauma of sexual assault is common. Rape survivors often dissociate during sexual assault as the circumstances are often too much or too painful for them to process. This interpretation of the young nun having a delayed response to the trauma is supported by Marguerite's depiction of the timeline of her emotions. The fact that she cries and sobs only later, and not during the attack, is also backed by research on rape. Percy notes, "Freezing tends to come early in an attack, and extreme responses tend to come later."[8] Moreover, other studies emphasize that rape victims who fail to actively resist are frequently haunted by overwhelming feelings of guilt. Sunda TeBockhorst argues that victims who misunderstand their "tonic immobility" often blame themselves.[9] These are the exact circumstances depicted in Marguerite's tale. The nun's self-recrimination is yet another common characteristic of victims of sexual assault. The fact that the evil monk is a master manipulator only exacerbates the situation. He continues to control the young girl by speaking to her sharply and silencing her by insisting that she not reveal what happened and only confess to him. While some might argue that her continued relationship and eventual pregnancy are evidence of her consent, rape experts note that it is not unusual for victims to continue relationships with their attackers. Elizabeth Jeglic explains that victims often do so as a result of the "lack of control" they experienced during the rape.[10] Marguerite's tale offers surprisingly modern insights into the psychology of sexual assault, while it also provides a unique window into the author's views on the Virgin Mary.

Immediately after the assault, the nun makes her way to a chapel dedicated to the Virgin Mary. Her actions are not unexpected; early in the tale Dagoucin emphasizes that, along with dedicating themselves to service, the nuns recite the Hours of the Virgin each day. Mary's role as patroness of nuns in the cloister would also have drawn the young nun to her. However, when she begins her usual devotional prayers and pronounces the words "Vierge Marie" (2.776), she is suddenly struck by the reality of the events and she falls prostrate before the Virgin and weeps uncontrollably. Mary McKinley observes that "she speaks for the first time in the story, addressing her words to another woman: 'Vierge Marie!'"[11] Given her youth and gender, Mary's maternal role would have been a great source of comfort to the nun. Perhaps more importantly for the traumatized young woman, Mary was widely celebrated in early modern devotional prayers as the Comforter of the Afflicted, Mother of Sorrows, Lady of Pity, Refuge of Sinners, and Mother of Mercy. These different roles would explain why the nun's first response on realizing the gravity of the events is to pray and grieve before the Virgin. François Cornilliat argues that the nun's loss of virginity "seulement par crainte" (only because of fear) prevents her from praying to Mary.[12] This interpretation not only underestimates the power of fear, but it is also questionable given that prostration is a form of devotion and prayer.[13]

Marguerite's portrayal of the nun's plea to the Virgin Mary is of particular interest given the debates in Renaissance France over the intercession of the Virgin and the saints. Significantly, Marguerite first depicts this nun as crying out to Mary, and then praying to God when she exclaims, "Helas! mon Dieu, ayez pitié de ceste pauvre pecheresse" (2.778; Alas, my Lord, take pity on this poor sinner!). From a Catholic perspective, when asking for intercession from the saints or the Virgin, one ultimately draws closer to the Lord; Marguerite's narrative aptly reflects this spiritual progression.

Although François Cornilliat has argued that the Virgin Mary disappears from the narrative after the scene with the young nun in the chapel, the portrayal of Marguerite's prayers and intervention in the seventy-second tale reflects important connections to Marian tradition.[14] Marguerite represents herself at the church of Saint John of Lyon praying a novena, a traditional Catholic devotion that involves a cycle of prayers over the course of nine consecutive days that is most often associated with the intercession of the Virgin or the saints: "ma dame la Duchesse d'Alençon, qui depuis fut Royne de Navarre, alloit secrettement faire quelque *neufveine,* avecques trois ou quatre de ses femmes" (2:778, emphasis added; the duchess, who has since become the queen of Navarre, would go secretly to make novenas in the rood loft of the church with three or four of her ladies in waiting). Patricia and Rouben Cholakian interpret this reference in negative terms, saying, "The fact that her prayers take the form of what she dismissively refers to as 'a few novenas' suggests that when she wrote the novella Marguerite no longer approved of such devotional practices, which the evangelistic reformists considered a form of medieval superstition."[15] In contrast to this interpretation, however, the fact that Marguerite does not simply represent herself in prayer, but more specifically as doing a novena, should be viewed in more positive terms.

This reference to Marguerite's practice of a novena unequivocally communicates her belief in these Catholic devotional prayers. Given her extensive biblical knowledge, Marguerite would have been cognizant of the fact that this spiritual practice is firmly based on Scripture, namely the first chapter of Acts, when the Apostles, the Virgin Mary, and other women spent nine days in the upper room devoting themselves "with one accord in prayer," from the Ascension of Christ until Pentecost. Moreover, the tale specifically highlights that Marguerite says this novena "devant le crucifix" (2.778; before the crucifix). In so doing, Marguerite places herself before the quintessential Catholic symbol of Christ's love and sacrifice. Moreover, this detail also silences the potential critics who might claim that this devotional practice detracted from Jesus by highlighting the Christocentric nature of her prayers.

As is clear by the reference to the crucifix and the detail that Marguerite hears the nun come up the stairs, this scene takes place in the rood loft of the church. This precise location is noteworthy given that Marguerite's Renaissance readers would have been sufficiently familiar with both church architecture and hagiography to know that the rood loft typically featured a large crucifix (the Holy Rood) flanked by statues of Saint John and the Virgin Mary. Significantly, Saint John is referred to both in the name of the church and in the Prologue to the eighth day. In addition, he is the saint most strongly associated with Mary because of his own virginity and since Jesus entrusted his mother and John to each other as he was suffering on the cross. The details on Marguerite's specific location in the church together with the references to Saint John and the Virgin in the tale reveal that Marguerite was praying her novena before the Rood group.

The fact that the Hours of the Virgin are a central component of Marguerite's own book of hours and that the young nun in tale 72 faithfully said the Hours of the Virgin could also explain Marguerite's motivation for representing her fortuitous meeting with the nun in the rood loft at this precise time of day. The reference to Marguerite holding a lamp is also intriguing in that this object is an attribute of the Virgin Mary. Moreover, the need for a lamp suggests that both women were there for the prayer to the Virgin customarily said at vespers. The fact that the young nun explicitly states that she will share her secrets solely with Marguerite de Navarre, and that Marguerite happens to be praying in the very church where the nun stops to pray, is not merely coincidental. Just as the monk on a Marian pilgrimage helps bring about the safe arrival of the *devisants* at Notre-Dame de Serrance, it is Marguerite's presence in a Catholic church and her participation in a novena before the Rood group that lead her to a nun in desperate need of an answered prayer.

The prologue to the eighth day clarifies that stories will recount either foolishness or truth. While the scholarship has often focused on the nun's foolishness in tale 72, the narrative can also be viewed as telling the truth about sexual assault and clerical corruption. Not only was Marguerite clearly ahead of her time in her depiction of different facets of the sexual abuse of women, but she was also innovative in the representation of the multiplicity of truths about early modern Catholicism. The *Heptaméron*'s final tale highlights the dark truths of institutional corruption and clerical abuse, while it also emphasizes that women's faith either in the form of praying a novena or through consistent devotion to the Hours of the Virgin can be a powerful force for change.

Revising Hagiography and Offering Hope

From references to Saint Savin and Our Lady in the Prologue to the representation of Marguerite praying a novena before the Rood group in the final tale, this volume has explored the influence of hagiography on the *Heptaméron*'s frame narrative and novellas. God protects the *devisants* during their dangerous pilgrimage-like trek from Cauterets through the Pyrenees to a monastery. Like pilgrims arriving at holy sites, the storytellers praise God for his protection on their miraculous safe arrival at Notre-Dame de Serrance. Despite the presence of clerics, Marguerite makes the transgressive choice to have Oisille, a female layperson, offer daily lessons on Scripture. Marguerite even represents the widow's teachings as more effective than any other sermons that the *devisants* had heard. However, the storytellers also devoutly participate in traditional masses at the abbey. Moreover, they ask for grace from the Holy Spirit as they prepare their stories. These narratives consistently represent saintly women. The mule-driver's wife, Floride, Pauline, Sister Marie Héroët, Rolandine and her aunt, and the indefatigable heroine of tale 67 offer the storytellers, and Marguerite's readers, powerful examples of women's sanctity and courage amid harrowing trials. The reader can understand why Parlamente likens the stories to a devotional gift akin to the rosaries and icons acquired on pilgrimages. Much like the sacred encounters during a pilgrim's travels, the *devisants* and the *Heptaméron*'s readers contemplate diverse models of women's exemplary holiness as they undertake their journey through Marguerite's text.

Like the female saints in hagiography, the heroic virtue of the *Heptaméron*'s heroines and the storytellers' interpretations and conversations about the tales incite readers to reflect on women's capacity for holiness and spiritual strength. These representations encourage a questioning of the traditional portrayals of sanctity, gender, and spiritual authority in literary and hagiographical texts and Renaissance debates, especially since Marguerite's saintly women frequently stand in marked contrast to the actions of the men.[16] Along with this disparity in the representation of holiness and spiritual authority, Marguerite's text consistently highlights gender-based violence. Emily Butterworth asserts, "Women are not safe in the world of the *Heptaméron*, where the general atmosphere is one of menace and terror, in which women are put in danger by the very people who should protect them."[17] Multiple tales recount instances of men who rape, threaten, persecute, and confine women.[18] While Marguerite's stories and discussions underscore men's violent acts toward women in general, she repeatedly draws attention to the fact that corrupt clergy pose a particularly grave threat, given that they exploit their privileged position and appearance of holiness to prey on women. The *Heptaméron*'s narratives question the power structures of the sixteenth-century Catholic Church by emphasizing how the institutional hierarchy limited women's participation in religious leadership and routinely placed faithful women in harm's way. Thus, Marguerite's stories highlight both the necessity for substantial reforms in the ecclesiastical hierarchy and the need to question the traditional portrayals of sanctity and gender in literary and theological writings.

The queen of Navarre's text also incites readers to reflect on marriage and representations of women in relation to this sacrament. An analysis of the connections between saints' vitae and women's marital status in the *Heptaméron* demonstrates that Marguerite consistently used hagiographic narratives as a source, while she also revised certain commonplaces of traditional hagiography. Marriage, laws governing matrimony, and women's freedom to choose their own spouses were all topics of intense debate in Renaissance France. The misogynistic writers in the *querelle des femmes* argued that marriage was necessary as it established a man's authority over a woman and allowed him to control her purportedly wayward nature and serve as the spiritual head of the family. Significantly, the *Heptaméron*'s tales offer a revisionist hagiography regarding marriage. A comparison of depictions of saintly women and their marital status in hagiographic tradition and in Marguerite's text is intriguing. While female saints were typically unmarried and virgins, the *Heptaméron*'s saintly women offer a different perspective on the relationship between marriage and sanctity. The mule-driver's wife, Floride, Rolandine, her aunt, and the heroine of tale 67 were all married; in no way did marriage prevent them from exemplifying holiness. Pauline and Sister Marie Héroët were both unmarried; they chose to take vows, consecrate themselves to the Lord, and spend their lives in convents. Marguerite's portrayal of saintly women who were married, unmarried, cloistered nuns, or widows offers an important revision to hagiographical tradition. In contrast to traditional saints' vitae and texts in the *querelle des femmes,* the *Heptaméron*'s stories illustrate women's capacity for holiness, heroic virtue, and unwavering faith regardless of their marital status.

Marguerite draws on saints' lives while simultaneously making noteworthy revisions to the genre. While hagiography emphasizes the evil actions of pagan tormentors and godless persecutors, the *Heptaméron* repeatedly portrays corrupt clerics and the harmful actions of men in the predominantly Catholic society of sixteenth-century France. Paula Sommers refers to Marguerite's "belief that virtue is rare, that it may be even more elusive for men than for women because the world which accords so many privileges to Hircain, Saffredan and Symontaut can easily distort their spiritual perspective and frustrate their moral growth."[19] Although writers on both sides of the *querelle des femmes* generally displayed a tendency toward extreme arguments, Marguerite nonetheless avoids excessively categorical generalizations. For instance, the representations of clerics in the *Heptaméron* are not systematically negative. The generous abbot of Saint-Savin, the faithful monk on pilgrimage in the Prologue, or the fifth tale's father superior, who was a "good man," avoid a situation where all clerics are depicted in purely negative terms (1.67). Moreover, even after a story of a violent Franciscan, Oisille remarks, "il y en a de bons . . . et ne fault pas que pour les mauvais, ils soient tous jugez" (2.346; there are good ones . . . and they mustn't be condemned because of the actions of the bad ones). Marguerite skillfully avoids the extreme rhetorical stances that characterized most texts in the *querelle des femmes*. However, with few exceptions, it is primarily women who display saint-like behavior in the *Heptaméron*'s tales. Marguerite not only distances herself from misogynistic writers in the *querelle* with her repeated emphasis on the sanctity of women, but she also diverges from hagiographic tradition in her depiction of sexual assault.

Another principal characteristic of medieval hagiography is that women are often threatened, but are ultimately protected from sexual violence. Even though female saints were tortured or martyred, traditional hagiographers shy away from depictions of rape and sexual assault. Clearly, this is not the case in the pages of the *Heptaméron*. Although Marguerite draws on hagiography, she departs from her source materials in that she offers readers brutally realistic depictions of women's traumatic experiences with sexual assault. The mule-driver's wife prays and lifts her hands and eyes to heaven after she has been viciously raped and repeatedly stabbed. After Amadour attempts to sexually assault Floride, she resorts to self-mutilation and strikes her face forcefully with a stone to prevent a second attack. Her painful sacrifice does not dissuade Amadour. Despite her lengthy and heroic resistance to a corrupt prior's advances, Sister Marie Heroët cannot escape from her aggressor's violent attack on everything "under her robe" (2.334). The seventy-second tale underscores the devastating psychological impact of sexual assault on a young nun. Marguerite's tales deviate from the customary norms of hagiographic narrative in their descriptions of the brutal physical and emotional realities of sexual assault from a woman's perspective.

Although the *Heptaméron* offers a more realistic portrayal of sexual assault and consistently depicts the gross injustices that women encountered in the highly patriarchal society of Renaissance France, Marguerite's stories do not leave readers with a hopeless vision of the world. Women experience countless trials and tribulations throughout the *Heptaméron*, but Marguerite avoids an utterly dismal portrayal of the world through her consistent depiction of women's fervent faith in God. Her heroines often illustrate a "parfaite confiance," or perfect trust, in God's faithfulness. Throughout the collection, when the tales relate the unjust treatment of women by their husbands, male relatives, or men of the cloth, God is frequently represented as actively intervening on women's behalf. Marguerite depicts God as an advocate, just judge, and protector of women. In fact, different variations of the subordinating construction "But God" at the opening of dependent clauses recur throughout the *Heptaméron* in instances where women confront serious injustices. When the vicious Franciscan commits murder and kidnaps a woman in tale 31, God intervenes to rescue her before the evil monk can rape and sequester her. Marguerite writes, "*Mais Dieu*, qui a pitié de l'innocent en tribulation, regarda les larmes de ceste pauvre damoiselle" (2.439–440, emphasis added; But God, who takes pity on the tribulations of the innocent, saw the tears of this poor young lady). Thus, divine intervention prompts her husband to return home earlier than expected so that he, and especially his insightful servant, can save her.

God is also instrumental in orchestrating the rescue of the heroine who had been marooned on a Canadian island in tale 67: "*Mais celuy*, qui n'abandonne jamais les siens au besoing, et qui au desespoir des autres, monstre sa puissance, ne permeit que la vertu, qu'il avoit mise en ceste femme, fust ignorée des hommes : mais voulut qu'elle fust cogneuë à sa gloire" (2.723, emphasis added; But He who never abandons his own—and who displays his power to the despair of all others—would not allow the virtue he had placed in this woman to remain hidden from men but rather willed it to be known, to His greater glory). In tale 72, God intervenes to help a young nun by ensuring that Marguerite is in a church saying a novena at the very moment when the young woman cries out for her help specifically (2.778). God also intervenes on Rolandine's behalf in tale 21: "*la bonté divine*, qui est parfaicte charité et vraye amour, eut pitié de sa douleur, et regarda sa patience" (2.324, emphasis added; divine goodness, which is perfect charity and true love, had pity on her suffering and took account of her patience). In tale 22, the evil prior extensively persecutes Sister Marie Héroët, but her faith does not waver. Eventually God intervenes and her honor is restored. Despite multiple portrayals of grave injustice and violence, the *Heptaméron* depicts how God actively works to protect women. Although Marguerite frequently emphasizes the Lord's faithfulness to women, she does not offer readers an unrealistically optimistic portrayal of the world. The violent rape and death of the mule-driver's wife, the demise of the mother, child, and father in tale 23, and the brutal murders of servants and terrifying kidnapping of the woman in tale 31 undoubtedly demonstrate that horrific events do take place; however, the text's frequent representation of God's protection of women nevertheless offers readers a source of hope in a society plagued by gender-based violence.

The *Heptaméron* also provides an encouraging message to readers through the depiction of the empowering force of women sharing stories. In tale 22, Sister Marie writes down her traumatic experiences, and her mother then enlists Marguerite de Navarre's help to set things right in the convent. The sixty-first tale demonstrates how a chain of women sharing and expressing their frustrations with each other, and ultimately with the women of the royal family, effectively brings an end to a couple's sinful existence. In tale 67, when Marguerite writes that her story will ultimately bring glory to God, she highlights the power and potential of women's writing. Thus, along with offering hope by representing God's frequent intervention on behalf of women, Marguerite also encourages her readers by emphasizing the power of women's stories to bring about positive social change.

Since the Renaissance, women have made significant strides in their fight for equality and justice. However, while some of the issues of the debate have changed since the sixteenth century, today's readers of the *Heptaméron* cannot fail to notice the continued relevance of the very challenges that women confront in Marguerite's text. Consistently high rates of femicide, rape, and domestic abuse across the globe illustrate the sobering reality of violence toward women that remains shockingly pervasive in society. In a recent high-profile and exceedingly disturbing case in France involving a husband who repeatedly drugged his wife and invited other men to rape her while she was unconscious, Gisèle Pelicot chose to waive her anonymity during the trial; her courage has made her a feminist icon and compelled women to mobilize and call for substantial legal and social change.[20] Along with the omnipresent scourge of gender-based violence, ongoing reports about widespread sexual abuse by Catholic priests and ministers in other denominations demonstrate that Marguerite's concerns about corruption and the dangerous consequences of patriarchal power structures in religious institutions have not yet been adequately addressed.[21] Moreover, the ever-increasing divisions in the contemporary political climate surrounding issues of gender and women's rights often reveal extreme linguistic tendencies that recall the polarized rhetorical stances and blanket generalizations of the *querelle des femmes*. However, recent movements like #MeToo, #BalanceTonPorc, or #NousToutes illustrate that women at the present time recognize the power of female solidarity and understand that sharing their experiences can be an impetus for important social change.

Marguerite's depiction of women's sufferings and virtues reveals her unwavering commitment to revealing the complex truths of their experiences, while the text's portrayals of women's courage and the emphasis on giving voice to their stories offer readers a formidable reminder of their individual and collective strength. The *Heptaméron*'s tales recall women's past achievements in the religious realm while they also highlight the admirable faith and strength of women in Renaissance France. Marguerite's saintly heroines exemplify how the queen of Navarre effectively advocated for women through her engagement in sixteenth-century societal and religious debates, while their triumphs and struggles also demonstrate the timeless value of her powerful and thought-provoking text. Clearly, we still have much to learn from stories of centuries past, especially from a book as engaging, insightful, and perpetually relevant as the *Heptaméron*.

Notes

Introduction

Epigraph: Marguerite de Navarre, *Marguerites de la Marguerite des princesses, tresillustre royne de Navarre* (Lyon: Jean de Tournes, 1547), 498, my translation.

1. Virginia Reinburg, *French Books of Hours: Making an Archive of Prayer, c. 1400–1600* (Cambridge: Cambridge University Press, 2012), 173.

2. Sarah Ann Long, *Music, Liturgy, and Confraternity Devotions in Paris and Tournai, 1300–1550* (Rochester, NY: University of Rochester Press, 2021), 2.

3. Virginia Reinburg notes, "A new proliferation of religious images appeared in the second half of the fifteenth and early sixteenth century. The creation of sculptures, stained glass, paintings, tapestries, illustrated books and prints for both public places and private settings displayed the economic prosperity enjoyed by the nobility and bourgeoisie after the Hundred Years War ended (1453)" (*French Books of Hours*, 113).

4. Long, *Music, Liturgy, and Confraternity*, 28.

5. Virginia Reinburg remarks, "Although the book of hours is often called the medieval European best-seller, this was true of France as nowhere else, and truer of the fifteenth and early sixteenth centuries than the middle ages" (*French Books of Hours*, 1–2).

6. The Fourteen Holy Helpers were invoked either separately or as a group for help with various diseases. They are Saints Acacius (headache), Barbara (fever and sudden death), Blaise (throat issues), Catherine of Alexandria (sudden death), Christopher (the plague and travels), Cyriacus (temptations on the deathbed and eye issues), Denis (headache and demonic possession), Erasmus of Formia (abdominal ills), Eustace (family troubles), George (herpetic diseases), Giles (the plague and mental illness), Margaret of Antioch (childbirth), Panteleon (patron of physicians and midwives), and Vitus (epilepsy and chorea). For a brief introduction to the Fourteen Holy Helpers, see David Farmer, *The Oxford Dictionary of Saints* (Oxford: Oxford University Press, 1997), 190–191; J. Dünninger, "Fourteen Holy Helpers," in *New Catholic Encyclopedia*, 2nd ed. (Detroit, MI: Gale, 2003), 5:836–837; Long, *Music, Liturgy, and Confraternity*, 1–2.

7. See Stanley Weed, "Venerating the Virgin Martyrs: The Cult of the 'Virgines Capitales' in Art, Literature, and Popular Piety," *Sixteenth Century Journal* 41, no. 4 (2010): 1065–1091.

8. Eamon Duffy, introduction to *The Golden Legend: Reading on the Saints* by Jacobus de Voragine, trans. William Granger Ryan (Princeton, NJ: Princeton University Press, 2012), xii.

9. Scott Francis, "Cross-Dressed Monks in Saints' Lives and Their Parodies: A Source for *Heptaméron* 31," in *Subject/Object and Beyond: Women in Early Modern France*, ed. Nancy M. Frelick and Edith Benkov (New York: Iter, 2023), 157.

10. Jean de Vignay, *Le miroir historial*, ed. Mattia Cavagna (Paris: Société des Anciens Textes Français, 2017).

11. Simon Gaunt asserts, "In patristic writing, women were associated with the flesh, men with the spirit. Women had to transcend the body in a way men did not" in *Gender and Genre in Medieval French Literature* (Cambridge: Cambridge University Press, 1995), 185. For more on gender and hagiography, see Emma Campbell, *Medieval Saints' Lives: The Gift, Kinship and Community in Old French Hagiography* (Cambridge: D. S. Brewer, 2008); Renate Blumenfeld-Kosinski and Timea Szell, eds., *Images of Sainthood in Medieval Europe* (Ithaca, NY: Cornell University Press, 1991); Jocelyn Wogan-Browne and Glyn S. Burgess, trans. and eds., *Virgin Lives and Holy Deaths: Two Exemplary Biographies for Anglo-Norman Women* (London: J. M. Dent, 1996).

12. Brigitte Cazelles, *The Lady as Saint: A Collection of French Hagiographic Romances of the Thirteenth Century* (Philadelphia: University of Pennsylvania Press, 1991), 13.

13. Virginia Reinburg remarks, "Some five hundred texts survive from the period 1450–1550, the golden age of mystery plays. Plays were widely performed and attended in French cities and towns" (*French Books of Hours*, 148). She also notes, "The language of mystery plays, so familiar to those who frequented cities and towns in this era, helped to form the ways devotees spoke to God and the saints" (149).

14. In addition to the *Comédies bibliques*, Bruce Hayes convincingly argues that "religious questions dominate most, if not all, of Marguerite's dramas, including the farces"; "De rire ne me puys tenir: Marguerite de Navarre's Satirical Farces," in *La Satire dans tous ses états: Le "meslange satyricque" à la Renaissance française*, ed. Bernd Renner (Geneva: Droz, 2009), 183–202.

15. Jean Calvin, *Institution de la religion chrestienne, en laquelle est comprinse une somme de pieté, et quasi tout ce qui est necessaire a congnoistre en la doctrine de salut* (Geneva: Michel du Bois, 1541), 532; John Calvin, *Institutes of the Christian Religion: 1541 French Edition*, trans. Elsie Ann McKee (Grand Rapids, MI: William B. Eerdmans, 2009), 468.

16. Jean Calvin, *Traité des reliques suivi de l'excuse à messieurs les Nicodémites*, ed. Albert Autin (Paris: Bossard, 1921), 87–88; John Calvin, *Treatise on Relics* (Amherst, NY: Prometheus, 2008), 54.

17. Martin Luther, *Selected Political Writings* (Philadelphia: Fortress, 1974), 145.

18. Charles Fantazzi, "The Handbook of the Christian Soldier / Enchiridion Militis Christiani," in *Spiritualia: Enchiridon / De Contemptu Mundi / De Vidua Christiana*, vol. 66, ed. John W. O'Malley (Toronto: University of Toronto Press, 1988), 71.

19. Fantazzi, "Handbook," 72.

20. See Jonathan A. Reid, *King's Sister—Queen of Dissent: Marguerite of Navarre (1492–1549) and her Evangelical Network*, 2 vols. (Leiden: Brill, 2009). Reid addresses various evangelical reformers and their beliefs on the cult of saints; see 1:21, 1:54, 1:66, 1:117, 1:135–137,

1:199, 1:244, 1:258–259, 261, 1:264, 1:290–295, 1:297, 1:305, 1:310, 2:413–414, 2:423, 2:483, 2:521, 2:530–532, and 2:568.

21. Jacques Lefèvre d'Étaples and François Demoulins de Rochefort, *Petit livret faict à l'honneur de madame Saincte Anne et de la royne, sa fille, vierge pure, mere de Jesus-Christ*, 1501–1525, MS 4009, fol. 69v–70r, Bibliothèque nationale de France (BnF), https://gallica.bnf.fr/ark:/12148/btv1b55005729x/f142.item.

22. Carol Thysell, *The Pleasure of Discernment: Marguerite de Navarre as Theologian* (Oxford: Oxford University Press, 2000); Jacob Vance, *Secrets: Humanism, Mysticism, and Evangelism in Erasmus of Rotterdam, Bishop Guillaume Briçonnet, and Marguerite de Navarre* (Leiden: Brill, 2014); Emily Butterworth, *Marguerite de Navarre: A Critical Companion* (Martlesham, UK: Boydell and Brewer, 2022).

23. Theresa Brock, *The Visionary Queen: Justice, Reform, and the Labyrinth in Marguerite de Navarre* (Newark: University of Delaware Press, 2024).

24. Elizabeth Chesney Zegura, *Marguerite de Navarre's Shifting Gaze: Perspectives on Gender, Class, and Politics in the Heptaméron* (New York: Routledge, 2017).

25. Marie-Claire Thomine-Bichard and Véronique Montagne, *Marguerite de Navarre, L'Heptaméron* (Neuilly-sur-Seine: Atlande, 2020).

26. Gary Ferguson, *Mirroring Belief: Marguerite de Navarre's Devotional Poetry* (Edinburgh: Edinburgh University Press, 1992).

27. Katherine Kong, "Writing Love in the Thirteenth Nouvelle: Marguerite de Navarre's Epistolary Fictions," *Romance Quarterly* 58, no. 2 (2011): 144–157.

28. See Elizabeth Archibald, *Incest and the Medieval Imagination* (Oxford: Oxford University Press, 2001), chap. 3.

29. Scott Francis, "'Cheminer apres les plus parfaictzs': Les pèlerinages et le culte des saints dans les *Comédies Profanes* et l'*Heptaméron*," *Le Verger* 20 (January 2021): 1–22; Francis, "Cross-Dressed Monks," 167–188.

30. Leanna Bridge Rezvani, "Pilgrimage and the Prologue of Marguerite de Navarre's *Heptaméron*," *Romance Notes* 61, no. 3 (2022): 451–461; Rezvani, "Saint Sebastian and the Mule-Driver's Wife: Marguerite de Navarre's Renaissance Martyr," in "Women in the World and Works of Marguerite de Navarre," ed. Judy Kem, special issue, *L'Esprit Créateur* 57, no. 3 (2017): 46–57.

31. Gary Ferguson, "'Veritable Histoire': L'*Heptaméron* et la Madeleine," *Le Verger* 20 (January 2021): 1–21; François Rigolot, "The *Heptameron* and the 'Magdalen Controversy': Dialogue and Humanist Hermeneutics," in *Critical Tales: New Studies of the* Heptameron *and Early Modern Culture*, ed. John D. Lyons and Mary B. McKinley (Philadelphia: University of Pennsylvania Press, 1993), 218–231; Rigolot, "Magdalen's Skull: Allegory and Iconography in *Heptameron* 32," *Renaissance Quarterly* 47, no. 1 (1994): 57–73.

32. For a study of Marguerite's work and the *querelle des femmes*, see Émile Telle, *L'œuvre de Marguerite d'Angoulême, reine de Navarre et la Querelle des Femmes* (Toulouse: Lion et Fils, 1937).

Chapter 1 Beyond Boccaccio

Epigraph: Marguerite de Navarre, *Dialogue en forme de vision nocturne entre très noble et excellente princesse Madame Marguerite de France, . . . et l'âme saincte de défuncte Madame*

Charlote de France, . . . Le Miroir de l'âme pécherresse. . . . Discord estant en l'homme par la contrariété de l'esperit et de la chair, et sa paix par vie spirituelle. Une oraison à Nostre Seigneur Jésus Christ (Alençon: S. Du Bois, 1533), https://gallica.bnf.fr/ark:/12148/bpt6k706153.

1. See Barbara Stephenson, *The Power and Patronage of Marguerite de Navarre* (Aldershot: Ashgate, 2004), especially chap. 5.

2. Eugenio Albèri, *Relazioni degli ambasciatori veneti,* 1st series, vol. 4, Florence, 1860, in-8, p. 48, https://babel.hathitrust.org/cgi/pt?id=hvd.32044019262674&seq=9. This English translation is my own.

3. Pierre Jourda, *Marguerite d'Angoulême, duchesse d'Alençon, reine de Navarre (1492–1549): Étude biographique et littéraire* (Paris: Honoré Champion, 1930), 1069. For a variety of insights into Marguerite's religion, see Jourda's concluding chapter in its entirety.

4. Abel Lefranc, *Les idées religieuses de Marguerite de Navarre d'après son œuvre poétique* (Paris: Fischbacher, 1898; repr. Geneva: Slatkine, 1969), 33; my translation.

5. Lucien Febvre, *Amour sacré, amour profane: Autour de l'Heptaméron* (Paris: Gallimard, 1944), 206.

6. Jean-Marie Le Gall, "Marguerite de Navarre: The Reasons for Remaining Catholic," in *A Companion to Marguerite de Navarre,* ed. Gary Ferguson and Mary B. McKinley (Leiden: Brill, 2013), 59–87.

7. Reid, *King's Sister.*

8. Theresa Brock remarks that Marguerite "may not have approved of all aspects of the Catholic Church in her lifetime, but neither did she break with the Church nor renounce all of its traditions"; *Visionary Queen,* 60.

9. Nicolas Russell, *Transformations of Memory and Forgetting in Sixteenth-Century France: Marguerite de Navarre, Pierre de Ronsard, Michel de Montaigne* (Newark: University of Delaware Press, 2011), 11.

10. Elizabeth Chesney Zegura notes, "Her book's inclusion on the official index of proscribed publications, along with her representation in a contemporary farce as a religious fanatic, attests to negative perceptions about the queen's religious politics among orthodox Parisian Catholics"; *Marguerite de Navarre's Shifting Gaze,* 47. Gary Ferguson and Mary B. McKinley state, "Marguerite also came under attack from reformers who had broken with the Church of Rome and established the Reformed Church of Geneva. They criticized her for what they saw as her lukewarm support for their cause and her accommodations toward the pope"; "Introduction," *A Companion to Marguerite de Navarre* (Leiden: Brill, 2013), 11. Patricia Francis Cholakian and Rouben Charles Cholakian have demonstrated in *Marguerite de Navarre: Mother of the Renaissance* (New York: Columbia University Press, 2006), 147, that while both orthodox Catholics and progressive reformers were openly critical of Marguerite, they also fervently longed for her support.

11. Jeanne d'Albret to the Vicomte de Gourdon, August 22, 1555, Français 17,044, Portefeuilles Vallant, fol. 446, BnF. For an English translation of the letter, see Nancy Lyman Roelker, *Queen of Navarre: Jeanne d'Albret* (Cambridge, MA: Belknap Press of Harvard University Press, 1968), 127.

12. D'Albret to de Gourdon, August 22, 1555; Roelker, *Queen of Navarre,* 127.

13. D'Albret to de Gourdon, August 22, 1555; Roelker, *Queen of Navarre,* 127.

14. D'Albret to de Gourdon, August 22, 1555; Roelker, *Queen of Navarre,* 127.

15. Thysell, *Pleasure of Discernment*, 99.

16. See John D. Bernard, "Realism and Closure in the *Heptaméron:* Marguerite de Navarre and Boccaccio," *Modern Language Review* 84, no. 2 (1989): 305–318; Nicole Cazauran, "*L'Heptaméron* face au *Décaméron*," in *La Nouvelle: Boccace, Marguerite de Navarre, Cervantès*, ed. Jean Bessière and Philippe Daros (Paris: Honoré Champion, 1996), 69–108; Yves Delègue, "Autour des deux prologues: *L'Heptaméron* est-il un anti-Boccace?," *Travaux de linguistique et de littérature* 4, no. 2 (1966): 23–37; P. B. Diffley, "From Translation to Imitation and Beyond: A Reassessment of Boccaccio's Role in Marguerite de Navarre's *Heptaméron*," *Modern Language Review* 90, no. 2 (1995): 345–362; Lance K. Donaldson-Evans, "The Narrative of Desire: Boccaccio and the French *Decamerons* of the 15th and 16th Centuries," *Neophilologus* 77, no. 4 (1993): 541–552; Silvia Ruffo Fiore, "Boccaccio in Marguerite de Navarre's *Heptaméron*: The Muted Confronts the Dominant," *Rivista di Studi Italiani* 14, no. 2 (1996): 54–63; Krystyna Kasprzyk, "Marguerite de Navarre, lecteur du *Décaméron*," *Studi francesi* 34 (1990): 1–11; Arnaldo Moroldo, "Réception du *Decameron* à la Renaissance française," in *Études sur "l'Heptaméron" de Marguerite de Navarre*, ed. Christine Martineau-Génieys (Nice: Publications de la Faculté des Lettres, Arts, et Sciences Humaines de Nice, 1996), 97–108; Aldo Scaglione, "From the *Decameron* to the *Heptaméron*," in *Approaches to Teaching Boccaccio's* Decameron, ed. James H. McGregor (New York: Modern Language Association, 2000), 127–133; Mihoko Suzuki, "Gender, Power, and the Female Reader: Boccaccio's *Decameron* and Marguerite de Navarre's *Heptameron*," *Comparative Literature Studies* 30, no. 3 (1993): 231–252; Nora Viet, "*Caméron, Décaméron, Heptaméron*: La genèse de l'*Heptaméron* au miroir des traductions françaises de Boccace," *Seizième Siècle* 8 (2012): 287–302; and Elizabeth C. Wright, "Marguerite Reads Giovanni: Gender and Narration in the *Heptaméron* and the *Decameron*," *Renaissance and Reformation / Renaissance et Réforme* 15, no. 1 (1991): 21–36.

17. Irina Dzero, "From Exile to Escape: Frame Narratives of the *Decameron* and the *Heptameron*," in *Topodynamics of Arrival: Essays on Self and Pilgrimage*, ed. Gert Hofman and Snjezana Zoric (Amsterdam: Rodopi, 2012), 177.

18. See Christine Martineau-Génieys, "La *lectio divina* dans l'*Heptaméron*," in *Études sur l'Heptaméron de Marguerite de Navarre*, ed. Christine Martineau-Génieys (Nice: Publications de la Faculté des Lettres, Arts, et Sciences Humaines de Nice, 1996), 21–42.

19. See Marguerite de Navarre, *Œuvres complètes*, vol. 8, *L'Heptaméron*, ed. Nicole Cazauran and Sylvie Lefèvre, 3 vols. (Paris: Honoré Champion, 2013); Marguerite de Navarre, *The Heptameron*, ed. and trans. Mary B. McKinley; and Nicolas Russell, *The Other Voice in Early Modern Europe* (Toronto: Iter, Centre for Reformation and Renaissance Studies, forthcoming). For the quote from 1.6, I added "in the morning" as it does not appear in the forthcoming translation.

20. Jourda, *Marguerite d'Angoulême*, 905; Betty J. Davis, *The Storytellers in Marguerite de Navarre's* "Heptaméron" (Lexington, KY: French Forum, 1978), 190.

21. *Hours, Use of Rome*, 1500–1515 (Louise's Book of Hours), MS 411, General Collection, Beinecke Rare Book and Manuscript Library, Yale University Library, https://collections.library.yale.edu/catalog/2029198; *Prayer Book of Claude de France*, Tours, France, ca. 1517, MS M.1166, Morgan Library and Museum, New York, https://www.themorgan.org/collection/Prayer-Book-of-Claude-de-France; *Horae ad usum Parisiensem, dites*

Heures de Charles d'Angoulême, MS Latin 1173, BnF, https://gallica.bnf.fr/ark:/12148/btv1b52502694t/f113.item; *Hours of Francis I*, 1539–1540, 2011.353, Metropolitan Museum of Art, New York, https://www.metmuseum.org/art/collection/search/238581.

22. *Heures de Marguerite de Valois, sœur de François Ier*, NAL 83, BnF, https://gallica.bnf.fr/ark:/12148/btv1b105127516/f15.item.

23. Jourda, *Marguerite d'Angoulême*, 24; Reid, *King's Sister*, 1.109.

24. Jonathan Reid, "Marguerite de Navarre and Evangelical Reform," in Ferguson and McKinley, *Companion to Marguerite de Navarre*, 33.

25. Reid, *King's Sister*, 1.104, 1.133.

26. The event is depicted in an image of King Francis kneeling before the saint in the Master of François de Rohan, *Hours of Francis I*, 1539–1540, parchment, 8³⁄₁₆ × 5¾ × 1½ in., 2011.353, Metropolitan Museum of Art, New York.

27. Cholakian and Cholakian, *Marguerite de Navarre*, 53.

28. Marguerite de Navarre, *Œuvres complètes*, vol. 8, *Chrétiens et mondains: Poèmes épars*, ed. Nicole Cazauran and Richard Cooper (Paris: Honoré Champion, 2007), 54.

29. *Heures de Marguerite de Valois, sœur de François Ier*, NAL 83, BnF.

30. Jourda, *Marguerite d'Angoulême*, 61.

31. Francis, "Cross-Dressed Monks," 170.

32. Marguerite de Navarre, *Chansons spirituelles*, ed. Georges Dottin (Geneva: Droz, 1971), 33; Marguerite de Navarre, *Œuvres complètes*, vol. 1, *"Pater Noster" et "Petit Œuvre dévot"*, ed. Nicole Cazauran and Sabine Lardon (Paris: Honoré Champion, 2001), 96–97; my translation.

33. Marguerite de Navarre, *Chansons*, 4; my translation.

34. Pierre Jourda, *Marguerite de Navarre: Dialogue en vision de forme nocturne* (Paris: Champion, 1926), 35; my translation.

35. Abel Lefranc says, "Tous les intermédiaires, anges ou saints, sont déclarés inutiles avec une insistance surprenante" (All intermediaries, angels or saints, are declared useless with a surprising insistence); *Les Idées religieuses*, 12, my translation.

36. Lefranc states, "Il ne faudrait pas inférer de certains vers que l'auteur incline à reconnaître le culte de la Vierge et des Saints" (It should not be inferred from certain verses that the author is inclined to recognize the cult of the Virgin and the saints); *Les Idées religieuses*, 35, my translation.

37. Saulnier asserts, "tout en faisant de la Foi l'exigence première de son *credo*, [elle] admettait la vénération des reliques, les pèlerinages, le culte des Saints et de la Vierge" (while making Faith the primary requirement of her creed, [she] approved of the veneration of relics, pilgrimages, the cult of Saints and the Virgin); Marguerite de Navarre, *Théâtre Profane*, ed. Verdun L. Saulnier (Geneva: Droz, 1946), 13, my translation.

38. Saulnier, in Navarre, *Théâtre Profane*, 15.

39. Jourda, *Marguerite d'Angoulême*, 1052.

40. Ferguson, *Mirroring Belief*, 106–107.

41. In his introduction to Navarre, *Chansons*, Dottin remarks, "Elle aura soin par ailleurs de rappeler que la bonté des Saints ne peut provenir que de Dieu, seul dispensateur de la Grâce" (She takes care to repeat that the goodness of the saints can come only from God, the sole Bestower of Grace), 25–26, my translation.

42. Brigitte Cazelles remarks, "French hagiographers grounded the value of their narratives in 'historical' truth"; *The Lady as Saint: A Collection of French Hagiographic Romances of the Thirteenth Century* (Philadelphia: University of Pennsylvania Press, 1991), 5.

43. Nancy Frelick notes, "Marguerite's focus is on the almost theatrical dialogues between characters or storytellers. Characterization in the frame-tale is mostly achieved through debates that precede or follow the tales, as if written for the stage"; "In the Eye of the Beholder: The Rhetoric of Beauty and the Beauty of Rhetoric in the *Heptaméron*," in "Women in the World and Works of Marguerite de Navarre," ed. Judy Kem, special issue, *L'Esprit Créateur* 57, no. 3 (2017): 10.

44. Zegura, *Marguerite de Navarre's Shifting Gaze*, 11.

45. Le Gall, "Marguerite de Navarre," 85.

46. Elizabeth Wright remarks that "the European novella genre was practiced almost exclusively by male authors"; "Marguerite Reads Giovanni," 22.

47. See Judy Kem, *Pathologies of Love: Medicine and the Woman Question in Early Modern France* (Lincoln: University of Nebraska Press, 2019), 13–14.

48. For more extensive studies on gender and hagiography, see Cazelles, *Lady as Saint*; Gaunt, *Gender and Genre*; Campbell, *Medieval Saints' Lives*; Blumenfeld-Kosinski and Szell, *Images of Sainthood*; Wogan-Browne and Burgess, *Virgin Lives and Holy Deaths*.

49. Michel de Montaigne, *Essais*, 1.56, ed. Emmanuel Naya, Delphine Reguig, and Alexandre Tarrête (Paris: Gallimard, 2009), 343; my translation.

50. Pierre de Ronsard, *Œuvres complètes: Remonstrance au people de France*, ed. Jean Céard et al. (Paris: Gallimard, 1993), 1033, my translation.

51. Nancy Frelick states, "Readers are thus invited to question and deconstruct conflicting codes and ideologies, as well as discourses of difference (and sameness) that are all too often put forward as truths, especially with respect to women or the so-called 'battle of the sexes'"; "Mirroring Discourses of Difference," *French Forum* 42, no. 3 (2017): 375.

Chapter 2 The Prologue, Pilgrimage, and Prophetesses in the *Heptaméron*

Epigraph: Jacques de Voragine, *La légende dorée en François*, trans. Jean de Vignay, ed. Jean Battalier (Paris: Nicolas de La Barre pour Simon Vostre, 1499), fol. 2. Jacobus de Voragine, *The Golden Legend: Readings on the Saints*, trans. William Granger Ryan (Princeton, NJ: Princeton University Press, 1993), 3.

1. An earlier version of the first section of this chapter was originally published as "Pilgrimage and the Prologue,".

2. See Brantôme, *Recueil des Dames, poésie et tombeaux*, ed. Étienne Vaucheret (Paris: Gallimard, 1991), where Brantôme claims, "Je l'ay ouy ainsin conter à ma grandmere, qui alloyt tousjours avecq'elle dans la lityère, comme sa dame d'honneur, et luy tenoit l'escritoyre" (I heard it from my grandmother, who as her lady-in-waiting always went with her in the litter, and who held the writing desk for her), 183; my translation.

3. Corinne Wilson, "Classroom Tools," in *Approaches to Teaching Marguerite de Navarre's* Heptaméron, ed. Colette H. Winn (New York: Modern Language Association, 2007), 22.

4. See Cholakian and Cholakian, *Marguerite de Navarre*, 47, 147; and Jean-Pierre Duteil, *Marguerite de Navarre* (Paris: Ellipses, 2021), 24.

5. See Michael Alan Anderson, *Saint Anne in Renaissance Music: Devotion and Politics* (New York: Cambridge University Press, 2014), 221.

6. Marie Holban, "François du Moulin de Rochefort and La Querelle de la Madeleine," *Humanisme et Renaissance* 2, no. 1 (1935): 26–43.

7. Wes Williams refers to the "Protestant anti-pilgrimage polemic" that was prevalent in Renaissance France in *Pilgrimage and Narrative in the French Renaissance: "The Undiscovered Country"* (Oxford: Clarendon Press, 1998), 7.

8. Brock, *Visionary Queen*, 61.

9. Ruth Barnes, "Relatives in Faith: Pilgrimage in Judaism, Islam and Christianity," in *Pilgrimage: The Sacred Journey, ed.* Ruth Barnes and Crispin Branfoot (Oxford: Ashmolean Museum, 2006), 38.

10. Kem, *Pathologies of Love*, 149.

11. See Diana Webb, *Medieval European Pilgrimage* (London: Palgrave, 2002), 49–56.

12. Brock, *Visionary Queen*, 61.

13. Marguerite de Navarre, *Heptaméron*, 1, ed. Renja Salminen (Geneva: Droz, 1999), 1.

14. Usuard, *Martyrilogium Usuardi monachi: quod ad karolum magnu[m] scripsit. Cum additionib[us] iam ex diuer . . . martyrilogijs collectis. atq[ue] de nouo adiectis* (Cologne: Landen Johann, 1515).

15. Usuard, *Vsvardi martyrologium, quo Romana ecclesia ac permultae aliae vtuntur: Jussu Caroli Magni conscriptum ex martyrologiis . . . Cum additionibus ex martyr. Rom. Ecclesiae.* (Operâ Ioannis Molani Louaniensis, 1568); trans. George Keynes and ed. William Nugent Skelly, *The Roman Martyrology*, (London: T. Richardson, 1848), 256.

16. Gary Ferguson and Mary B. McKinley, "The *Heptaméron*: Word, Spirit, World," in Ferguson and McKinley, *Companion to Marguerite de Navarre*, 329.

17. For a discussion of repetitive, or recurrent, pilgrimages, see Ian Reader, *Pilgrimage: A Very Short Introduction* (Oxford: Oxford University Press, 2015), 79–82.

18. Judith Perrenoud-Wörner, *Rire et Sacré: La vision humoristique de la vérité dans l'*Heptaméron *de Marguerite de Navarre* (Geneva: Slatkine, 2008), 167.

19. Nicolas Le Cadet, *L'Évangélisme fictionnel: Les livres rabelaisiens, le Cymbalum Mundi, l'Heptaméron (1532–1552)* (Paris: Classiques Garnier, 2010). He remarks, "Dès le Prologue, le narrateur principal utilise à douze reprises le nom de 'Dieu'. Ce lexique suggère, dans un climat biblique de tribulations, que c'est bien la main de Dieu qui guide en secret les devisants, d'abord vers l'abbaye de Sainct-Savin . . . , puis . . . vers ce havre de paix qu'est l'abbaye de Serrance" (From the Prologue, the main narrator uses the name of "God" twelve times. This lexicon suggests, in a biblical climate of tribulations, that it is indeed the hand of God that secretly guides the *devisants*, first toward the abbey of Saint-Savin . . . , then toward this haven of peace that is the abbey of Sarrance), 333; my translation.

20. See Ferguson and McKinley, "*Heptaméron*: Word, Spirit, World," 325–331.

21. Due to textual variants, this is my own translation.

22. Jonathan Sumption, *The Age of Pilgrimage: The Medieval Journey to God* (Mahwah, NJ: Hidden Spring / Paulist Press, 2003), 250.

23. See the image and a summary of the event at "Apparitions et miracles: Quelques saints miraculeux," *Les Hautes-Pyrénées et le village de Loucrup*, http://lieux.loucrup65.fr/apparitionsaints.htm.

24. Perrenoud-Wörner states, "Il est dit explicitement que Dieu intervient pour sauver nos devisants: ce sont donc des miraculés qui trouvent refuge à l'abbaye Notre-Dame de Sarrance" (It is explicitly stated that God intervenes to save our *devisants*: they are therefore miraculous survivors who find refuge at the abbey of Notre-Dame de Sarrance) in *Rire et Sacré*, 168; my translation.

25. Reader notes, "A common image of pilgrimage development relates to the idea of miraculous events" in *Pilgrimage*, 61.

26. Webb notes that "pilgrimage was by no means just the concern of isolated individuals; it was often a shared experience, both in its inspiration and in its performance. Pilgrims travelled together in groups for reasons of security but also out of a desire for conviviality"; *Medieval European Pilgrimage*, 78.

27. Reader, *Pilgrimage*, 84.

28. Wes Williams, "The Diplomat, the *Trucheman* and the Mystagogue: Forms of Belonging in Early Modern Jerusalem," in *Pilgrim Voices: Narrative and Authorship in Christian Pilgrimage*, ed. Simon Coleman and John Elsner (New York: Berghahn, 2003), 19.

29. The final sentence of the English translation is not in McKinley and Russell's version, thus it is my own translation.

30. Jan Miernowski asserts, "Marguerite's fictional stories should replace old devotional images"; "Fiction and Ritual in the *Heptameron*," in Winn, *Approaches to Teaching*, 112.

31. Robert Maniura asserts, "the telling, like the physical offering, also acts as a form of gift; a performance of thanksgiving"; "Pilgrimage into Words and Images: The Miracles of Santa Maria delle Carceri in Renaissance Prato," in *Pilgrim Voices: Narrative and Authorship in Christian Pilgrimage*, ed. Simon Coleman and John Elsner (New York: Berghahn, 2003), 52.

32. Wes Williams refers to pilgrimage as a "journey undertaken with a view of metamorphosis," in *Pilgrimage*, 6.

33. Le Cadet, *L'Évangélisme fictionnel*, 103.

34. Virginia Nixon refers to the "unprecedented popularity Anne enjoyed in the decades between 1470 and 1530"; *Mary's Mother: Saint Anne in Late Medieval Europe* (University Park: Penn State University Press, 2004), 1. Jennifer Welsh evokes "the late fifteenth- and early sixteenth-century heyday of her cult," in *The Cult of St. Anne in Medieval and Early Modern Europe* (New York: Routledge, 2017), 1. David Williams evokes the "enormity of the cult of Saint Anne" in *Saints Alive: Word, Image, and Enactment in the Lives of the Saints* (Montreal: McGill-Queen's University Press, 2010), 47.

35. Anderson remarks, "From a loyal wife and mother to a teacher and widow, St. Anne reflected several core values of the period, seeming to fit the bill at every turn and bringing a sense of empowerment to these sociocultural roles"; *Saint Anne*, 14.

36. Ton Brandenbarg, "Saint Anne: A Holy Grandmother and Her Children," in *Sanctity and Motherhood: Essays on Holy Mothers in the Middle Ages*, ed. Anneke B. Mulder-Bakker (New York: Garland, 1995), 31.

37. See Ann Moss, *Renaissance Truth and the Latin Language Turn* (Oxford: Oxford University Press, 2003), chap. 5, "Paris"; Anderson, *Saint Anne*, 212, 221; Sheila M. Porrer, *Jacques Lefèvre d'Étaples and the Three Marys Debates* (Geneva: Droz: 2009), 113–119.

38. Voragine relates, "Anna is said to have had three husbands, Joachim, Cleophas, and Salome. Of Joachim, her first husband, she gave birth to one daughter, Mary, the mother of our Lord. . . . Joachim died and Anna married Cleophas, Joseph's brother, and of him had another daughter, whom she likewise called Mary. . . . After the death of her second husband Anna took a third, namely Salome of whom she had another daughter, whom she also called Mary"; Voragine, *Golden Legend*, 536.

39. Jacques Lefèvre d'Étaples, *De Maria Magdalena, triduo Christi, et ex tribus una Maria disceptation* (Paris: H. Estienne, 1518).

40. Moss, *Renaissance Truth*, 102.

41. Jacques Lefèvre d'Étaples and François Demoulins de Rochefort, *Petit livret faict à l'honneur de madame saincte Anne et de la royne, sa fille, vierge pure, mere de Jesus-Christ*, MS 4009, BnF, https://gallica.bnf.fr/ark:/12148/btv1b55005729x/f114.item.

42. The beginning of the manuscript features an illustration of Demoulins and Lefèvre offering the text to Louise de Savoie. Lefèvre d'Étaples and Demoulins, "Petit livret," fol. 1v. See https://gallica.bnf.fr/ark:/12148/btv1b55005729x/f6.item.

43. Demoulins refers to "le roy et vous Et madame la duchesse" (the king and you And madame the duchess) in Lefèvre d'Étaples and Demoulins, "Petit livret," fol. 2v.

44. See Duteil, *Marguerite de Navarre*; or Zegura, *Marguerite de Navarre's Shifting Gaze*, 9.

45. Lefèvre d'Étaples and Demoulins, *Petit livret*, fol. 19r.

46. *L'Office de sainte Anne*, MS Fr 1035, BnF, https://gallica.bnf.fr/ark:/12148/btv1b52000991j.

47. Anderson, *Saint Anne*, 216.

48. *Prayer Book of Claude de France*, MS M.1166, Morgan Library and Museum, New York, fols. 16v, 17r, 17v, and 42r.

49. Raymond Ritter, *Les Solitudes de Marguerite de Navarre* (Paris: Honoré Champion, 1953), 161.

50. Charles Vincens, *De l'iconographie de Sainte Anne et de la Vierge Marie à propos d'une statue du XVe siècle* (Paris: Association Française pour l'Avancement des Sciences, 1891), 5.

51. Anderson, *Saint Anne*, 221.

52. Anderson, *Saint Anne*, 216.

53. Nixon, *Mary's Mother*, 56.

54. Nixon, *Mary's Mother*, 18.

55. Philip M. Sodrgel [recte Soergel], "Portents, Disaster, and Adaptation in Sixteenth Century Germany," *Medieval History Journal* 10, no. 1–2 (2006): 312.

56. Florence Montreynaud, Agnès Pierron, and François Suzzoni, *Dictionnaire de proverbes et dictons: La sagesse du monde entier* (Paris: Dictionnaires Le Robert, 1989), 252. The translation is mine. Another adage about Saint Anne's feast also involves rain and storms: "Si les fourmis s'agitent à la Sainte-Anne, l'orage descend de la montagne" (If the ants are restless on Saint Anne's Day, the storm descends from the mountains), *Dicocitations: Le dictionnaire des citations*, https://www.dicocitations.com/citations/citation-16996.php.

57. See Patricia Francis Cholakian, *Rape and Writing in the* Heptaméron *of Marguerite de Navarre* (Carbondale: Southern Illinois University Press, 1991), 34; or Bonnie D. Irwin, "What's in a Frame? The Medieval Textualization of Traditional Storytelling," *Oral Tra-*

dition 10, no. 1 (1995): 12. Christine Scollen-Jimack remarks that "using a sixteenth-century spelling, Oysle is an anagram of Loyse"; "Funeral Poetry in France: From Octovien de Saint-Gelais to Clément Marot," in *Vernacular Literature and Current Affairs in the Early Sixteenth Century: France, England, Scotland,* ed. Jennifer Britnell and Richard Britnell (Aldershot: Ashgate, 2000), 162.

58. Kathleen Ashley and Pamela Sheingorn, eds., *Interpreting Cultural Symbols: Saint Anne in Late Medieval Society* (Athens: University of Georgia Press, 1990), 49.

59. Nixon, *Mary's Mother,* 11–12.

60. Myra D. Orth, "Reconsidering Radical Beauty: Marguerite de Navarre's Illuminated Protestant Catechism and Confession (Arsenal, MS 5096)," in *Le livre évangélique en français avant Calvin: Études originales, publications d'inédits, catalogues d'éditions anciennes,* ed. Jean-François Gilmont and William Kemp (Turnhout: Brepols, 2004), 89.

61. Lefèvre and Demoulins, *Petit livret,* fol. 9v; my translation.

62. Lefèvre and Demoulins, *Petit livret,* fol. 21v; my translation.

63. Anderson, *Saint Anne,* 23.

64. Lefèvre and Demoulins, *Petit livret,* fols. 69v–70r.

65. Lefèvre and Demoulins, *Petit livret,* fol. 17v.

66. Paula Sommers, "Feminine Authority in the *Heptaméron*: A Reading of Oysille," *Modern Language Studies* 13, no. 2 (1983): 54.

67. Nixon, *Mary's Mother,* 69.

68. Anderson, *Saint Anne,* 3.

69. Karin Tilmans refers to Saint Anne as "the first teacher of her daughter Mary, who through her learns to read and at the same time learns of her destiny. The function of the mother as the first and most important teacher and educator of her offspring is a new theme in the humanistic writings of the fifteenth century"; "Sancta Mater versus Sanctus Doctus? Saint Anne and the Humanists," in *Sanctity and Motherhood: Essays on Holy Mothers in the Middle Ages,* ed. Anneke B. Mulder-Bakker (New York: Garland, 1995), 345.

70. *L'Office de Sainte Anne,* Français 1035, fol. 4v, BnF, https://gallica.bnf.fr/ark:/12148/btv1b52000991j/f12.item.

71. See Cholakian and Cholakian, *Marguerite de Navarre,* 17.

Chapter 3 Violence, Sufferings, and Women of Faith

Epigraph: Marguerite de Navarre, *Chansons spirituelles,* 71, my translation.

1. See Cholakian, *Rape and Writing,* 8–19.

2. An earlier version of this section of the chapter first appeared as an article, "Saint Sebastian and the Mule-Driver's Wife,".

3. Mary B. McKinley refers to the tale as "an exemplary hagiographical account of martyrdom"; "Agony, Ecstasy, and the Mulekeeper's Wife," in *A French Forum: Mélanges de littérature française offerts à Raymond C. et Virginie A. La Charité,* ed. Gérard Defaux and Jerry C. Nash (Paris: Klincksieck, 2000), 129. John D. Bernard classifies the narrative as "a quasi saint's legend"; "Sexual Oppression and Social Justice in Marguerite de Navarre's *Heptameron,*" *Journal of Medieval and Renaissance Studies* 19 (1989): 254. He also refers to it as an "exemplum of saintly virtue," 258. Zegura comments on "the strong hagiographic resonances of nouvelle 2"; *Marguerite de Navarre's Shifting Gaze,* 14. André

Tournon argues that it is "a hagiographical and entirely unequivocal story"; "Rules of the Game," in *Critical Tales: New Studies of the* Heptameron *and Early Modern Culture,* ed. John D. Lyons and Mary B. McKinley (Philadelphia: University of Pennsylvania Press, 1993), 189. Dora Polachek offers a persuasive reading of the novella in connection with rape and female saints' vitae and bodily sufferings: "Is It True or Is It Real? The Dilemma of Staging Rape in Marguerite de Navarre's *Heptaméron,*" in *Violence in French and Francophone Literature and Film,* ed. James Day (Leiden: Brill, 2008).

4. Jacques Baudoin, *Grand livre des saints: Culte et iconographie en Occident* (Brioude: Créer, 2006), 219.

5. *Prayer Book of Claude de France,* MS M.1166, fols. 33v–34r, Morgan Library and Museum, New York, http://www.themorgan.org/collection/Prayer-Book-of-Claude-de-France/34.

6. *Hours, Use of Rome,* MS 411, fol. 137r, Beinecke Rare Book and Manuscript Library, Yale University.

7. Cholakian, *Rape and Writing,* 51.

8. Randle Cotgrave, *A Dictionarie of the French and English Tongues* (Columbia: University of South Carolina Press, 1950), http://www.pbm.com/~lindahl/cotgrave/.

9. Jacobus de Voragine, *La légende dorée,* ed. Brenda-Dunn Lardeau (Paris: Honoré Champion, 1997), 234; Voragine, *Golden Legend,* 101.

10. Zegura, *Marguerite de Navarre's Shifting Gaze,* 73. This representation of the heroine also illustrates what Saara Nevanlinna and Irma Taavitsainen describe as a characteristic motif in hagiography when they state, "The prayer before the martyrdom is a typical example of the common stock-in-trade of a hagiographer"; *St. Katherine of Alexandria: The Late Middle English Prose Legend in Southwell Minster MS 7* (Cambridge: D. S. Brewer, 1993), 46.

11. See, for example, Chanson 15, where Marguerite describes death as "heureuse" (happy), "glorieuse" (glorious), and "joyeuse" (joyous), *Chansons spirituelles,* 46.

12. Cholakian, *Rape and Writing,* 53.

13. Simon Gaunt notes, "female virgin martyrs in hagiographical texts die to protect their virginity"; *Gender and Genre,* 185. Brigitte Cazelles refers to the medieval Catholic Church's emphasis on virginity and chastity as "the hallmark of female perfection"; *Lady as Saint,* 48.

14. Leanna Bridge Rezvani, "The Mule-Driver's Wife Meets the Misoygnists: The Second Novella of Marguerite de Navarre's *Heptaméron* and the *Querelle des Femmes,*" *Romance Review* 12 (2002): 11–17.

15. McKinley, "Agony," 132.

16. In his introduction to Marguerite de Navarre's *Chansons,* Georges Dottin remarks, "Enfin, comme tous les Chrétiens du XVI. siècle qui fondaient leur doctrine exclusivement sur les Écritures, Marguerite ne cesse d'insister sur le fait que le Christ est seul à pouvoir nous sauver. . . . Le corollaire bien connu de cette attitude doctrinale sera le refus du culte de la Vierge et des Saints. . . . L'attitude de Marguerite . . . sera plus nuancée. Elle acceptera le dogme de la communion des saints" (Finally, like all the Christians of the sixteenth century who based their doctrine exclusively on the Scriptures, Marguerite never ceases to insist on the fact that Christ alone can save us. . . . The well-known corollary of this doctrinal attitude would be the refusal of the cult of the Virgin and the Saints. . . .

Marguerite's attitude . . . will be more nuanced. She will accept the dogma of the communion of saints), xxvii, my translation.

17. Brigitte Cazelles remarks, "In contrast to the representation of male sanctity, which essentially entails self-assertiveness, female perfection appears to be grounded in bodily pain, silence, and passivity"; *Lady as Saint*, 9.

18. Patricia Grieve notes that, "In hagiography, female saints are usually saved from rape"; "Embroidering with Saintly Threads: María de Zayas Challenges Cervantes and the Church," *Renaissance Quarterly* 44, no. 1 (1991): 95.

19. Raymond Lebègue interprets Floride's mutilation in connection with Saint Lucie's legend in "La femme qui mutile son visage (*Heptaméron* X)," *Comptes rendus des séances de l'Académie des Inscriptions et Belles-Lettres* 103, no. 2 (1959): 176–184. Naomi Baker asserts that the story "is shaped by medieval hagiographic models, most obviously in Florinda's self-disfigurement in a chapel in order to avoid rape"; *Plain Ugly: The Unattractive Body in Early Modern Culture* (Manchester: Manchester University Press, 2010), 173. Sofina Dembruk mentions Saint Marina, Saint Euphrosina, and comments briefly on Saint Eusebia as possible sources for this tale in *"Saincte et precieuse deformité": Expérimentations littéraires de la laideur à la Renaissance* (Paris: Classiques Garnier, 2022), 139.

20. Duteil, *Marguerite de Navarre*, 24; Patricia Eichel-Lojkine, *Marguerite de Navarre: Perle de la Renaissance* (Paris: Perrin, 2021), 59.

21. "Abbey of Saint-Savin-en-Lavedan, Saint-Savin, France," *SpottingHistory*, https://www.spottinghistory.com/view/8853/abbey-of-saint-savin-en-lavedan/.

22. *Prayer Book of Claude de France*, MS M.1166, fol. 27r–27v, https://www.themorgan.org/collection/Prayer-Book-of-Claude-de-France/27.

23. "Amadour du Quercy," *Wikipédia: L'encyclopédie libre*, https://fr.wikipedia.org/wiki/Amadour_du_Quercy; my translation.

24. See Claire Marshall, "The Politics of Self-Mutilation: Forms of Female Devotion in the Late Middle Ages," in *The Body in Late Medieval and Early Modern Culture*, ed. Darryll Grantley and Nina Taunton (Aldershot: Ashgate, 2000); Baker, *Plain Ugly*; and Jane Tibbetts Schulenburg, *Forgetful of Their Sex: Female Sanctity and Society, ca. 500–1100* (Chicago: University of Chicago Press, 1998).

25. Jane Tibbetts Schulenburg, "The Heroics of Virginity: Brides of Christ and Sacrificial Mutilation," in *Women in the Middle Ages and the Renaissance: Literary and Historical Perspectives*, ed. Mary Beth Rose (Syracuse, NY: Syracuse University Press, 1986), 47–48.

26. Schulenburg, "Heroics of Virginity," 48.

27. Victor Verlaque, *Notice sur Sainte Eusébie: Abbesse et Martyre du Diocèse de Marseille* (Marseille: Arnaud, Cayer, 1867), 16; Schulenburg, "Heroics of Virginity," 46–47.

28. Verlaque, *Notice*, 33.

29. Carla Freccero, "Rape's Disfiguring Figures: Marguerite de Navarre's *Heptameron*, Day 1:10," in *Rape and Representation*, ed. Lynn A. Higgins and Brenda R. Silver (New York: Columbia University Press, 1991), 237.

30. "En 1473, d'après la monographie d'Edmond Albe, le lieu fut nommé *la roque de Saint Amadour*" (In 1473, according to Edmond Albe's monograph, the site was named the rock of Saint Amadour), "Rocamadour," *Wikipédia: L'encyclopédie libre*, https://fr.wikipedia.org/wiki/Rocamadour.

31. Nora Martin Peterson, "What Does Rape Look Like? Textual and Visual Representations of Sexual Assault in the *Heptaméron* (1559)," *Explorations in Renaissance Culture* 49, no. 1 (2023): 107.

32. For a discussion of the tale's representation of clerical abuse, see Cholakian, *Rape and Writing*, chap. 12; Dembruk, *Sainte et precieuse deformité*, 118–126.

33. Cotgrave, *Dictionarie*.

34. *Heures de Marguerite de Valois, sœur de François Ier*, NAL 83, BnF.

35. *Hours, Use of Rome*, MS 411, fol. 137r, Beinecke Rare Book and Manuscript Library, Yale University.

36. Damien Plantey, *Les Bibliothèques des Princesses de Navarre au XVIe Siècle: Livres, Objets, Mobilier, Décor, Espaces et Usage* (Lyon: Université de Lyon Portail de l'ENSSIB, 2016), 45, 46; Ritter, *Solitudes de Marguerite de Navarre*, 161.

37. Elsa Kammerer, *Jean de Vauzelles et le creuset Lyonnais: Un humaniste catholique au service de Marguerite de Navarre entre France, Italie, et Allemagne* (Geneva: Droz, 2013), 173–174.

38. Christine de Pizan, *Le livre de la Cité des dames*, ed. and trans. Anne Paupert and Claire Le Ninan (Paris: Honoré Champion, 2023), 727; Christine de Pizan, *The Book of the City of Ladies*, ed. and trans. Rosalind Brown-Grant (New York: Penguin, 1999), 204–205.

39. Virginia Krause, "The *Heptameron*'s Tales 22 and 72 and the Visual Arts: Resisting Temptation," in Winn, *Approaches to Teaching*, 205.

40. Marguerite de Navarre, *Heptaméron*, ed. Salminen, 222. I use Salminen's edition here since the detail of Sister Marie praying to Mary does not appear in Cazauran's version.

41. I have added "to the Virgin Mary" since this detail does not appear in McKinley and Russell's version.

42. Christine de Pizan, *Livre de la Cité*, 726–727.

43. Denis Lynch, *St. Joan of Arc: The Life-Story of the Maid of Orleans* (New York: Benziger Brothers, 1919), 274.

44. Larissa Juliet Taylor, *The Virgin Warrior: The Life and Death of Joan of Arc* (New Haven, CT: Yale University Press, 2009), 181.

45. Taylor, *Virgin Warrior*, 184.

46. Saint Jerome, *Corpus scriptorum ecclesiasticorum Latinorum CSEL* 55 (1912), 52 *Ad Riparium* PL 22, col 907; Saint Jerome, *Ad Riparium*, I (Migne, *Patrologia Latina* 22) 907; NPNF2-06. Jerome: The Principal Works of Saint Jerome, ed. Philip Schaff. https://ccel.org/ccel/schaff/npnf206/npnf206.v.CIX.html

47. Voragine, *Légende dorée*, 1110; *Golden Legend*, 723.

48. Voragine, *Légende dorée*, 1112; *Golden Legend*, 724.

49. Voragine, *Légende dorée*, 606; *Golden Legend*, 369.

50. Voragine, *Légende dorée*, 1111; *Golden Legend*, 724.

51. Voragine, *Légende dorée*, 1111; *Golden Legend*, 724.

52. Voragine, *Légende dorée*, 605; *Golden Legend*, 368.

53. Nevanlinna and Taavitsainen, *St. Katherine*, 18.

54. Michel Gailliard refers to "une lutte entre la vraie croyante et son pérsecuteur"; *L'Heptaméron de Marguerite de Navarre: Analyses Textuelles* (Toulouse: Presses Universitaires du Mirail, 2007), 125.

Chapter 4 Saintly Women Confined and Isolated

Epigraph: Marguerite de Navarre, *Les dernières œuvres de la royne Marguerite de Navarre*, 1501–1600, Français 24298, BnF, https://gallica.bnf.fr/ark:/12148/btv1b90632774, my translation.

1. Mary J. Baker, "Mapping the Moral Domain in the *Heptaméron*," in *Les visages et les voix de Marguerite de Navarre*, ed. Marcel Tetel (Paris: Klincksieck, 1995), 9–18; Emily Thompson, "Shifting Rules and Shifty Wives: A Historical Reading of Three Tales from the *Heptaméron*," *in* "Women in the World and Works of Marguerite de Navarre," ed. Judy Kem, special issue, *L'Esprit Créateur* 57, no. 3 (2017): 67–78; Reinier Leushuis, *Le mariage et l'amitié courtoise dans le dialogue et le récit brief de la Renaissance* (Florence: Leo S. Olschki, 2003); Gérard Defaux, "De la Bonne Nouvelle aux Nouvelles: Remarques sur la structure de l'*Heptaméron*," *French Forum* 27, no. 1 (2002): 23–43.

2. Thompson, "Shifting Rules," 67.

3. John D. Lyons notes, "The aunt's prison makes her a saint"; *Exemplum: The Rhetoric of Example in Early Modern France and Italy* (Princeton, NJ: Princeton University Press, 1990), 98. Emily Thompson remarks that the heroine of tale 40 "chooses to end her life in saintly silence"; "Shifting Rules," 72. António de Ridder-Vignone offers a reading of tale 21 in association with martyrs' tales in "Incoherent Texts? Storytelling, Preaching, and the *Cent nouvelles nouvelles* in Marguerite de Navarre's *Heptaméron* 21," in *Renaissance Quarterly* 68, no. 2 (2015): 465–495.

4. Christine de Pizan, *Livre de la Cité*, 754; *Book of the City*, 216.

5. Scott Francis, "Scandalous Women or Scandalous Judgment? The Social Perception of Women and the Theology of Scandal in the *Heptaméron*," in Kem, "Women in the World and Works of Marguerite de Navarre," 41.

6. Gary Ferguson has remarked on this very phenomenon in Marguerite's devotional poetry, saying, "As the saints have no will but the will of God, they can offer no prayer but the prayer of Christ"; *Mirroring Belief: Marguerite de Navarre's Devotional Poetry* (Edinburgh: Edinburgh University Press, 1992), 100.

7. Thompson notes, "The punishment that the nobleman metes out to both his sister and his daughter constitutes the single most important overlap between novellas 21 and 40. . . . The castle that is used to imprison and silence the defiant Rolandine is what leads Parlamente to recount the story of Rolandine's aunt for whom the enclosure was built"; "Shifting Rules," 71.

8. Catharine Randall states, "Catholic saints' lives . . . customarily included objects in their narratives, populating their portraits with objects that functioned symbolically to illuminate significant aspects of the saint"; *Earthly Treasures: Material Culture and Metaphysics in the* Heptaméron *and Evangelical Narrative* (West Lafayette, IN: Purdue University Press, 2007), 183. In the same work, she also notes, "Marguerite's inclusion of objects situates her within some persistent awareness of, and respect for, this genre," 184.

9. Jacques Chocheyras, *Le Théâtre Religieux en Savoie au XVIe siècle avec des fragments inédits* (Geneva: Droz, 1971), 100–101, my translation.

10. Marguerite de Navarre, *Heptaméron*, 202, emphasis added.

11. Randall, *Earthly Treasures*, 241.

12. Grace Morgan Armstrong, "Crime Is in the Eye of the Beholder: Rebellion and Decriminalization in Marguerite de Navarre's *Heptaméron*," in *Rebelles et criminelles chez les écrivaines d'expression française*, ed. Frédérique Chevillot and Colette Trout (Amsterdam: Rodopi, 2013), 36.

13. Randall, *Earthly Treasures*, 240.

14. Ferguson, "Veritable Histoire," 4.

15. Plantey, *Bibliothèques des Princesses de Navarre*, 44.

16. François Demoulins de Rochefort composes a prayer for Louise asking for Saint Mary Magdalene's intercession for Claude's and Marguerite's pregnancies in *La vie de la belle et clere Magdalene*, MS 24955, fol. 106r, BnF, https://gallica.bnf.fr/ark:/12148/btv1b8529693c.

17. Holban, "François du Moulin de Rochefort," 31; Ferguson, "Veritable Histoire," 4.

18. Demoulins, *La vie*, 1517. The BnF website also lists Marguerite as the "ancien possesseur," or "previous owner," of this work.

19. See Holban, "François du Moulin de Rochefort," 26, my translation.

20. Reid, *King's Sister*, 1.135.

21. Diane Apostolos-Cappadona, *In Search of Mary Magdalene: Images and Traditions* (New York: American Bible Society, 2002), 15.

22. Demoulins, *La vie*, fols. 106v-107r, my translation.

23. Demoulins asks for Saint Mary Magdalene's intercession for the French royal family in *La vie*, fol. 12v. The text includes a prayer from Louise to Saint Mary Magdalene pleading for the saint's intercession for her children and herself, fol. 106r.

24. Rigolot, "*Heptameron* and the 'Magdalen Controversy,'" 228; Rigolot, "Magdalen's Skull," 57–73.

25. Rigolot, "*Heptameron* and the 'Magdalen Controversy,'" 223.

26. Apostolos-Cappadona, *In Search*, 44. For an extensive study on the debate, see Porrer, *Jacques Lefèvre d'Étaples*.

27. Apostolos-Cappadona remarks that a "survey of her iconography in western Christian art demonstrates that the earliest descriptions of the Magdalene in artistic and dramatic narratives were as *the* first witness of the Resurrection and apostle to the apostles"; *In Search*, 9.

28. Katherine Ludwig Jansen, *The Making of the Magdalen: Preaching and Popular Devotion in the Later Middle Ages* (Princeton, NJ: Princeton University Press, 2000), 23.

29. Apostolos-Cappadona argues that the Catholic Church changed its stance on Mary Magdalene because "Gregory the Great concluded that a multiform Magdalene who was both sinful and penitent would prove more salutary to Christianity"; *In Search*, 15.

30. Voragine, *La légende dorée*, 615; Voragine, *Golden Legend*, 375.

31. Voragine, *Légende dorée*, 615; *Golden Legend*, 375.

32. Cazelles, *Lady as Saint*, 33.

33. Christine de Pizan, *Livre de la Cité*, 724; *Book of the City*, 203.

34. Demoulins, *La vie*, fol. 23v.

35. Demoulins, *La vie*, fol. 51v.

36. Paula Sommers, "Marguerite de Navarre as Reader of Christine de Pizan," in *The Reception of Christine de Pizan from the Fifteenth Through the Nineteenth Centuries: Visitors to the City*, ed. Glenda K. McLeod (Lewiston, NY: Edwin Mellen, 1991), 73–74.

37. Sommers, "Marguerite de Navarre as Reader," 76.

38. Marguerite de Navarre, *"Pater Noster" et "Petit Œuvre dévot"*, 96.

39. Rigolot, "Magdalen's Skull," 64.

40. Gabriele Sorice, "The Skull-Cup Motif in *Gerbert de Metz* Between Intertextuality and Ethnography," *Cahiers de recherches médiévales et humanistes* 36 (2018): 377–391.

41. Apostolos-Cappadona, *In Search*, 15.

42. Zegura, *Marguerite de Navarre's Shifting Gaze*, 72.

43. See Henry Percival Biggar, *A Collection of Documents Relating to Jacques Cartier and the Sieur de Roberval* (Ottawa: Publications of the Public Archives of Canada, 1930), 178.

44. Elizabeth Boyer notes that this represents "a memorial of some significance . . . in a man whose life and reputation centered in these navigational documents"; *A Colony of One: The History of a Brave Woman* (Novelty, OH: Veritie, 1983), 5.

45. Cornelius Wytfliet, *Nova Francia et Canada* (Louvain: Jan Bogaert, 1597). For access to Wytfliet's map and other early maps of Canada in McGill Library's Pugsley collection, see the W. H. Pugsley Collection of Early Canadian Maps (La Collection W. H. Pugsley de Cartes Anciennes du Canada), McGill University Libraries, McGill University, https://digital.library.mcgill.ca/pugsley/pugsley.php.

46. Jacques Cartier, *Voyages de découverte au Canada* (Paris: Anthropos, 1968), 96; my translation. Also see Boyer, *Colony of One*, 14.

47. For further exploration of various resources on Marguerite de Roberval, see my website: Leanna Bridge Rezvani, "Marguerite de Roberval: A Web-Based Approach to Teaching a Renaissance Heroine," https://teachingmargueritederoberval.com/.

48. For the most comprehensive study of the sixteenth- and seventeenth-century versions in French, see Michel Bideaux, *Roberval, la Damoiselle et le Gentilhomme* (Paris: Classiques Garnier, 2009). For a study in English, see Arthur Stabler, *The Legend of Marguerite de Roberval* (Pullman: Washington State University Press, 1972).

49. Bideaux, *Roberval*, 74.

50. Frank Lestringant, "La Demoiselle dans l'île: Prolégomènes à une lecture de la Nouvelle 67," in *Lire "l'Heptaméron" de Marguerite de Navarre*, ed. Dominique Bertrand (Clermont Ferrand: Presse Universitaire Blaise Pascale, 2005), 185; Stabler, *Legend of Marguerite*, 5.

51. Margaret W. Ferguson, *Dido's Daughters: Literacy, Gender, and Empire in Early Modern England and France* (Chicago: University of Chicago Press, 2003), 263.

52. Carrie Klaus, "From *désert* to *patrie*: Marguerite de Navarre's Lessons from the New World," in Kem, "Women in the World," 58–66.

53. For more on this topic, see Leanna Bridge Rezvani, "The *Heptaméron*'s 67th Tale: Marguerite de Navarre's Humble Heroine Confronts the *Querelle des Femmes* and Catholic Tradition," *Romance Notes* 52, no. 1 (2012): 43–50.

54. Voragine classifies both men and women as martyrs. However, Saints Paul, Macarius, and Anthony are referred to as hermits. Male saints are also categorized as apostles, doctors, bishops, and confessors. In contrast, women are frequently defined by their sexuality in his work; Voragine refers to them as virgins or he refers to their lack of chastity, defining Saints Mary of Egypt, Magdalene, and Pelagia as "pecheresses." In addition, Saint Thais is labeled as a courtesan.

55. Voragine, *Légende dorée*, 408; *Golden Legend*, 227.

56. Voragine, *Légende dorée*, 409; *Golden Legend*, 227.

57. Voragine, *Légende dorée*, 409; *Golden Legend*, 227.

58. Gaunt, *Gender and Genre*, 228.

59. Ronald Pepin and Hugh Feiss, trans., *Saint Mary of Egypt: Three Medieval Lives in Verse* (Kalamazoo: MI: Cistercian, 2005), 1.

60. Pepin and Feiss, *Saint Mary of Egypt*, 10.

61. Voragine, *Légende dorée*, 410; *Golden Legend*, 228.

62. André Thevet, *La cosmographie universelle* (Paris: Chez P. L'Huilier, 1575), fol. 1019; my translation.

63. Thevet, *Cosmographie universelle*, fol. 1019; my translation.

64. François de Belleforest, *Le cinquiesme tome des Histoires tragiques, contenant un discours mémorable de plusieurs histoires, le succez et evenement desquelles est pour la plus part recueilly des choses advenues de nostre temps* (Paris: Jean Hulpeau, 1572), fol. 185, https://gallica.bnf.fr/ark:/12148/bpt6k8702090b; my translation.

65. Belleforest, *Cinquiesme tome des Histoires tragiques*, fol. 212; my translation.

66. Ferguson refers to the tale's "protest against common views of women's sexual nature and verbal authority"; *Dido's Daughters*, 241.

67. Ferguson, *Dido's Daughters*, 227.

68. For information on the pilgrimage, see Duteil, *Marguerite de Navarre*, 88.

69. Voragine, *Légende dorée*, 410; *Golden Legend*, 228.

70. For more on the connections between nourishment and spirituality, see Leanna Bridge Rezvani, "Nature and Nourishment, Bodies and Beasts: The *Heptaméron*'s Portrayal of Marguerite de Roberval's Marooning," *Dalhousie French Studies* 102 (Summer 2014): 3–7.

71. See, for instance, Stabler, *Legend of Marguerite*, 20n26; Bideaux, *Roberval*, 26n2; Lestringant, "Demoiselle dans l'île," 192–193; Claude La Charité, "Les questions laissées en suspens par le *Brief recit* (1545) de Jacques Cartier et les réponses de la nouvelle 67 de l'*Heptaméron* (1559) de Marguerite de Navarre," *Œuvres & Critiques* 36, no. 1 (2011): 102.

72. Voragine, *Légende dorée*, 411; *Golden Legend*, 228–229.

73. Ferguson, *Dido's Daughters*, 228.

74. Parlamente is correct in arguing that Saint Paul does indeed recognize women's contributions in the church. For instance, 1 Corinthians 7:14 recognizes women's role in the salvation of their husbands: "For the unbelieving husband is made holy through his wife." Moreover, in Saint Paul's second letter to Timothy, he acknowledges that Timothy's faith has been passed from his grandmother to his mother and then to him: "I recall your sincere faith that first lived in your grandmother Lois and in your mother Eunice and that I am confident lives also in you"; 2 Timothy 1:5.

Chapter 5 Holiness and False Sanctity

Epigraph: Saint Francis of Assisi, *Writings of Saint Francis*, ed. Paschal Robinson (Philadelphia: Dolphin, 1908), 21.

1. Jourda, *Marguerite d'Angoulême*, 169–170; Duteil, *Marguerite de Navarre*, 169.

2. Eichel-Lojkine, *Marguerite de Navarre*, 167; Duteil, *Marguerite de Navarre*, 157, 169; Cholakian and Cholakian, *Marguerite de Navarre*, 167.

3. Johanna Vernqvist refers to "the remarkable story of Poline, which has interesting similarities to the legends of Saint Francis and Saint Clare"; "Negotiating Neoplatonism and the Androgyne Metaphor in *Heptaméron* 70 and 19," in Kem, "Women in the World," 98. Romano Nanni alludes to Marie-Madeleine Fontaine's position that "l'origine de la 19e nouvelle pourrait être liée au culte de la sainte Marie-Madeleine, culte devenu, au cours du XVIe siècle, un mythe de la chrétienté catholique, et plus particulièrement du roi 'très chrétien'" (the origin of the 19th tale could be linked to the cult of Saint Mary Magdalene, a cult that became, in the course of the 16th century, a myth of Catholic Christianity, and more specifically, of the "very Christian" king); "Au temps d'Isabelle: en relisant l'*Heptaméron* de Marguerite ('nouvelle dixneufiesme')," in *Louise de Savoie, 1476–1531*, ed. Pascal Brioist, Laure Fagnart, and Cédric Michon (Tours: Presse Universitaire François Rabelais; Rennes: Presse Universitaire de Rennes, 2015), 277.

4. Voragine, *La légende dorée*, 950; Voragine, *Golden Legend*, 607.

5. Joan Mueller remarks that in her writings, Clare often argued that "the one thing necessary . . . was the attainment of the so-called privilege of poverty"; *The Privilege of Poverty: Clare of Assisi, Agnes of Prague, and the Struggle for a Franciscan Rule for Women* (University Park: Pennsylvania State University Press, 2006), 9.

6. Saint Francis of Assisi, and Saint Clare, *Francis and Clare: The Complete Works*, ed. and trans. Regis J. Armstrong and trans. Ignatius C. Brady (New York: Paulist Press, 1982), 40.

7. Nanni, "Au temps d'Isabelle," 282.

8. Jacques Le Goff notes, "Francis took part in the battle between . . . two cities in 1202 at the Ponte San Giovanni on the Tiber. He was captured there by the Perugians and remained in prison in Perugia for over a year"; *Saint Francis of Assisi* (New York: Routledge, 2004), 24–25.

9. Voragine, *Légende dorée*, 948; *Golden Legend*, 606.

10. See Donald Spoto, *The Reluctant Saint: The Life of Francis of Assisi* (London: Penguin, 2003), 28.

11. Lezlie S. Knox remarks, "Francis already had heard of her reputation as a pious young woman and so sought an introduction to her"; *Creating Clare of Assisi: Female Franciscan Identities in Later Medieval Italy* (Leiden: Brill, 2008), 21.

12. See Regis J. Armstrong, ed., *Clare of Assisi: Early Documents* (Mahwah, NJ: Paulist Press, 1988).

13. Vernqvist, "Negotiating," 102.

14. Marco Bartoli refers to the "extremely unusual" and "extraordinary" circumstances of the event, noting that Francis "was not even a priest but only a layman, and yet he took upon himself the right to consecrate Clare to the Lord," in *Clare of Assisi* (Quincy, IL: Franciscan Press, 1993), 45. Paul Sabatier makes a similar argument about Francis's

actions toward Clare when he asserts, "He, a simple deacon, arrogated to himself the right to receive Clara's vows and admit her to the Order without the briefest novitiate"; *Life of Saint Francis of Assisi* (London: Hodder and Stoughton, 1894), 151.

15. Philip Ford, "Sexual Equality and Evangelical Neoplatonism in the *Heptameron*," in Winn, *Approaches to Teaching*, 72.

16. Vernqvist, "Negotiating," 102.

17. Katherine Ludwig Jansen remarks on the important connections between these two saints, saying, "Mary Magdalen is invoked as the example whom Francis followed in following Christ. Following in her footsteps, he became a contemplative recluse, as well as the naked follower of Christ, preaching and suffering for the faith"; "Penitent Sinner, Apostolic Saint: The Mary Magdalene Cult Emerges," in *Secrets of Mary Magdalene: The Untold Story of History's Most Misunderstood Woman*, ed. Dan Burstein and Arne J. De Keijzer (London: Weidenfeld and Nicolson, 2006), 142.

18. Bartoli refers to the "dearth of historical studies on Clare of Assisi," saying, "the number is small, but particularly so when we compare it to the amount written about Francis of Assisi"; *Clare of Assisi*, 5.

19. Margaret Carney, *The First Franciscan Woman: Clare of Assisi and Her Form of Life* (Quincy, IL: Franciscan Press, 1993), 21.

20. Carney, *First Franciscan Woman*, 62.

21. Le Gall remarks, "Pope Clement VII granted her [i.e., Marguerite] the right, with 12 noblewomen of her choice, to enter the enclosure of any convent of Poor Clares, to speak and eat with the sisters, and even, accompanied by four ladies, to spend the night. We know that Marguerite paid frequent visits to the Poor Clares in Nérac"; "Marguerite de Navarre," 76. Duteil remarks, "A 1546 letter to the chancellor of Navarre, charging him with the reform of the Franciscan convent at Tarbes and the 'sœurs clarisses' of Mont-de-Marsan, demonstrates Marguerite's ongoing concern about the Franciscan and Poor Clare orders"; *Marguerite de Navarre*, 169.

22. Marguerite de Navarre, *"Pater noster" et "Petit Œuvre dévot"*, 96; Pizan, *Livre de la Cité*, 724; Pizan, *Book of the City*, 203.

23. See Ford, "Sexual Equality."

24. Nicolas Le Cadet remarks, "les Frères mineurs de Saint François d'Assise . . . Marguerite de Navarre raille leur avarice, leur luxure et leur orgueil . . . trois péchés capitaux qui font évidemment contraste avec les trois vœux religieux des mendiants : pauvreté, chasteté, et obéissance" (the Friars Minor of Saint Francis of Assisi . . . Marguerite de Navarre mocks their avarice, their lust and their pride . . . three cardinal sins which obviously contrast with the three religious vows of the mendicants: poverty, chastity, and obedience); *Évangélisme fictionnel*, 415, my translation.

25. See Ferguson and McKinley, *Companion to Marguerite de Navarre*, 333–338; or Cholakian, *Rape and Writing*, 158–166.

26. Marguerite de Navarre, *"Pater noster" et "Petit Œuvre dévot"*, 97.

27. Judith Perrenoud-Wörner notes, "Ce n'est pas saint François qui est visé ici par l'illusion ironique, mais les prétendus imitateurs du saint" (It is not Saint Francis who is targeted here by the ironic illusion, but the so-called imitators of the saint); *Rire et Sacré*, 376, my translation.

28. "The Saint Whose Hair Was Cut by St Francis of Assisi," *Catholic Herald*, August 7, 2014, https://catholicherald.co.uk/the-saint-whose-hair-was-cut-by-st-francis-of-assisi/.

29. Voragine, *Légende dorée*, 956; *Golden Legend*, 611.

30. For an example of an Italian manuscript from Marguerite's lifetime, see the BnF manuscript *Opera gentilissima, et utilissima a tuti li fideli christiani: laqual se chiama li fioreti de miser santo Francesco*, 1480. The legend of the wolf of Gubbio can be found online at page view 61: https://gallica.bnf.fr/ark:/12148/bpt6k59175b/f61.item.

31. See *Opera gentilissima . . . santo Francesco*, 1480, BnF, https://gallica.bnf.fr/ark:/12148/bpt6k59175b/f62.item.

32. Cholakian posits, "There is an important difference, however, in the treatment of clerical as opposed to secular rape. Gentlemen like Bonnivet who try to dishonor women are never apprehended or punished, but when clerics commit sex crimes, they are subjected to horrible forms of retribution"; *Rape and Writing*, 159.

33. Gary Ferguson, "All in Knots: Teaching the *Heptameron* with *Les Prisons*," in Winn, *Approaches to Teaching*, 135–140; Ferguson, "Péchés capitaux et 'vices italiens': L'avarice et ses complices dans l'*Heptaméron* de Marguerite de Navarre," *Seizième Siècle* 4 (2008): 73–87; and Ferguson, "Mal vivre, mal croire: L'anticléricalisme de l'*Heptaméron* de Marguerite de Navarre," *Seizième Siècle* 6 (2010): 151–163.

34. Ronda De Sola Chervin, *Quotable Saints* (Oak Lawn: IL: CMJ Marian Publishers, 1992), 139.

35. André Tournon, "Doublets et hybrides dans l'*Heptaméron*," in *Études sur l'Heptaméron de Marguerite de Navarre*, ed. Christine Martineau-Génieys (Nice: Université de Nice-Sophia Antipolis, 1993), 7–19.

36. Carrie Klaus, "Shaping the Legacy of Louise de Savoie: A New Reading of the *Heptaméron*," *Romance Notes* 60, no. 3 (2020): 564.

37. Jan Miernowski, "Le Miracle de la Pentecôte à Sarrance: Cohérence narrative et vérité religieuse dans la septième journée de l'*Heptaméron*," in *Narrations brèves: Mélanges de littérature ancienne offerts à Krystyna Kasprzyk*, ed. Piotr Salwa and Teresa Zółkiewska (Geneva: Droz, 1993), 177–196.

38. In the commentary of tale 61 Renja Salminen asserts, "le péché capital de la femme adultère est d'avoir indignement reçu le Saint Sacrement et l'Extrême Onction" (the capital sin of the adulterous woman is to have taken the Blessed Sacrament and Extreme Unction in a disgraceful manner); Navarre, *Heptaméron*, 775, my translation.

39. Pierre Jourda, "Marguerite de Navarre: Lettres inédites," *Revue du Seizième-Siècle* 15 (1928): 100–133.

40. See the website of France's Minister of Culture for details on the cathedral's history: "Église paroissiale Saint-Solenne, actuellement cathédrale Saint-Louis," Ministère de la Culture, https://pop.culture.gouv.fr/notice/merimee/IA00141115.

41. Brenda Gardenour notes that "The ideal pilgrim . . . would wear only a simple tunic and walk completely barefoot. For the pilgrim, walking long distances through harsh climates was a form of suffering, both a penance imposed on the contrite of heart, as well as a purgation of the body and soul"; "Barefootedness," in *Encyclopedia of Medieval Pilgrimage*, ed. Larissa J. Taylor et al. (Leiden: Brill, 2009; online ed. 2012).

42. Navarre, *L'Heptaméron* (ed. Cazauran and Lefèvre), 3.1022n17, my translation.

43. On Marguerite's representation of herself in this tale and her other cameo appearances in the *Heptaméron*, see Claudie Martin-Ulrich's insightful work, *La persona de la princesse au XVIe siècle: Personnage littéraire et personnage politique* (Paris: Champion, 2004), especially part 4, chap. 3, "Marguerite dans l'*Heptaméron*."

44. Cotgrave, *Dictionarie*.

45. See Kem, *Pathologies of Love*, 13–14, where she discusses the *querelle des femmes* and texts deriding women's "loquaciousness," 13–14.

46. François Rabelais, *Tiers Livre* (Paris: Éditions du Seuil, 1997), 337, my translation.

Conclusion

Epigraph: Christine de Pizan, *Livre de la Cité*, 801; *Book of the City*, 236.

1. Le Gall, "Marguerite de Navarre," 84.

2. Plantey, *Bibliothèques des Princesses de Navarre*, 44.

3. Ferguson remarks that "the Virgin Mary . . . stands out above all others, appearing again and again throughout Marguerite's poetry"; *Mirroring Belief*, 106.

4. Thomine-Bichard and Montagne, *Marguerite de Navarre*, 61, my translation.

5. François Cornilliat, "Pas de miracle : La Vierge et Marguerite dans l'*Heptaméron*," *Études littéraires* 27, no. 2 (1994): 81, my translation.

6. Mary B. McKinley, "Telling Secrets: Sacramental Confession and Narrative Authority in the *Heptameron*," in *Critical Tales: New Studies of the* Heptameron *and Early Modern Culture*, ed. John D. Lyons and Mary B. McKinley (Philadelphia: University of Pennsylvania Press, 1993), 159.

7. Jen Percy, "What People Misunderstand about Rape," *New York Times*, August 22, 2023, https://www.nytimes.com/2023/08/22/magazine/immobility-rape-trauma-freeze.html.

8. Percy, "What People Misunderstand."

9. Percy, "What People Misunderstand."

10. See Ella Torres, "Why Assault Victims Stay in Touch with Attackers, in Light of Weinstein Defense," *ABC News*, January 23, 2020, https://abcnews.go.com/US/sexual-assault-victims-continue-relationships-assailants/story?id=68460398.

11. McKinley, "Telling Secrets," 160.

12. Cornilliat, "Pas de miracle," 81.

13. Dmitri Zakharine notes that "lying prostrate was interpreted as an extreme expression of devoutness in Catholic worship"; "Medieval Perspectives in Europe: Oral Culture and Bodily Practices," in *Body—Language—Communication: An International Handbook on Multimodality in Human Interaction*, ed. Cornelia Müller et al. (Berlin: De Gruyter Mouton, 2013), 349.

14. Cornilliat, "Pas de miracle," 82.

15. Cholakian and Cholakian, *Marguerite de Navarre*, 50.

16. Dariusz Krawczyk notes, "Les figures d'autorité spirituelle féminine dans les œuvres de Marguerite de Navarre ne manquent pas . . . et elles sont certainement plus nombreuses que les figures masculines équivalentes" (The feminine spiritual authority figures in the works of Marguerite de Navarre are not lacking . . . and they are certainly

more numerous than the equivalent masculine figures); "Figures féminines d'autorité spirituelle dans les œuvres de Marguerite de Navarre," in *L'Autorité de la parole spirituelle feminine en français au XVIe siècle*, ed. Michèle Clément et al. (Leiden: Brill, 2023), 202, my translation.

17. Butterworth, *Marguerite de Navarre*, 39.

18. Robert Cottrell, "Inmost Cravings: The Logic of Desire in the *Heptameron*," in Lyons and McKinley, *Critical Tales*, 3–24. He remarks, "Nearly all the men in the *Heptameron* are driven by 'la fureur de la concupiscence' . . . by a peculiarly masculine 'malice' that compels them to satisfy their desire in a paroxysm of what the text calls 'jouissance' . . . on the conquered and humiliated, often raped and wounded female body," 10.

19. Sommers, "Feminine Authority," 58.

20. Catherine Porter and Ségolène Le Stradic, "France's Horrifying Rape Trial Has a Feminist Hero," *New York Times*, September 25, 2024, https://www.nytimes.com/2024/09/25/world/europe/france-rape-trial-gisele-pelicot.html.

21. Aurelien Breeden, "Sexual Abuse Allegations Shatter a Crusading Priest's Legacy," *New York Times*, September 14, 2024, https://www.nytimes.com/2024/09/14/world/europe/abbe-pierre-sexual-abuse-france.html; Jenny Gross and Emma Bubola, "Pope Francis Is Met with Anger over Sexual Abuse on Visit to Belgium," *New York Times*, September 27, 2024, https://www.nytimes.com/2024/09/27/world/europe/pope-francis-belgium-sex-abuse.html; Norimitsu Onishi, "Angry Catholics Wanted to Burn the Church: He Came to Save It," *New York Times*, June 13, 2024, https://www.nytimes.com/2024/06/13/world/canada/catholic-church-canada-indigenous-people.html; Ruth Graham and Orlando Mayorquin, "Archdiocese of Los Angeles Agrees to Pay $880 Million to Settle Sex Abuse Claims," *New York Times*, October 16, 2024, https://www.nytimes.com/2024/10/16/us/archidiocese-los-angeles-abuse-settlement.html. For scandals involving the Church of Jesus Christ of Latter-day Saints or Southern Baptists, see Amanda Taub, "What's Behind the Pileup of Sex Abuse Scandals?," *New York Times*, September 1, 2022, https://www.nytimes.com/2022/09/01/world/americas/whats-behind-the-pileup-of-sex-abuse-scandals.html.

Bibliography

Archival Sources

Bibliothèque nationale de France, Paris

d'Albret, Jeanne to the Vicomte de Gourdon, August 22, 1555. Français 17,044, Portefeuilles Vallant, fol. 446, Bibliothèque nationale de France.

Houghton Library, Harvard University, Cambridge, MA

Thevet, André. *La cosmographie universelle.* Paris: Chez P. L'Huilier, 1575, Typ. 515.75.831F v.2.

Primary Sources

Albèri, Eugenio. *Relazioni degli ambasciatori veneti.* 1st series, vol. 4. Florence, 1860. https://babel.hathitrust.org/cgi/pt?id=hvd.32044019262674&seq=9.

Belleforest, François de. *Le cinquiesme tome des Histoires tragiques, contenant un discours mémorable de plusieurs histoires, le succez et evenement desquelles est pour la plus part recueilly des choses advenues de nostre temps.* Paris: Jean Hulpeau, 1572. https://gallica.bnf.fr/ark:/12148/bpt6k8702090b.

Brantôme. *Recueil des dames, poésies et tombeaux.* Edited by Etienne Vaucheret. Paris: Gallimard, 1991.

Briçonnet, Guillaume, and Marguerite d'Angoulême. *Correspondance (1521–1524).* 2 vols. Edited by Christine Martineau and Michel Veissière. Geneva: Droz, 1975–1979.

Calvin, Jean. *Institution de la religion chrestienne, en laquelle est comprinse une somme de pieté, et quasi tout ce qui est necessaire a congnoistre en la doctrine de salut.* Geneva: Michel du Bois, 1541. https://www.e-rara.ch/gep_g/content/titleinfo/1751445.

———. *Traité des reliques suivi de l'excuse à messieurs les Nicodémites.* Edited by Albert Autin. Paris: Bossard, 1921.

Calvin, John. *Institutes of the Christian Religion: 1541 French Edition.* Translated by Elsie Ann McKee. Grand Rapids, MI: William B. Eerdmans, 2009.

———. *Treatise on Relics.* Amherst, NY: Prometheus, 2008.

Cartier, Jacques. *Voyages de découverte au Canada.* Paris: Anthropos, 1968.

Chocheyras, Jacques. *Le Théâtre Religieux en Savoie au XVIe siècle avec des fragments inédits.* Geneva: Droz, 1971.

Clare of Assisi: Early Documents. Edited by Regis J. Armstrong. Mahwah, NJ: Paulist Press, 1988.

Cotgrave, Randle. *A Dictionarie of the French and English Tongues.* Columbia: University of South Carolina Press, 1950. http://www.pbm.com/~lindahl/cotgrave/.

Demoulins de Rochefort, François. *La vie de la belle et clere Magdalene.* 1517. Français 24955, Bibliothèque nationale de France. https://gallica.bnf.fr/ark:/12148/btv1b8529693c.

Fantazzi, Charles. "The Handbook of the Christian Soldier / Enchiridion Militis Christiani." In *Spiritualia: Enchiridon / De Contemptu Mundi / De Vidua Christiana,* vol. 66, edited by John W. O'Malley, 1–128. Toronto: University of Toronto Press, 1988.

Francis of Assisi, Saint. *Writings of Saint Francis.* Edited by Paschal Robinson. Philadelphia: Dolphin, 1908.

Francis of Assisi and Clare of Assisi. *Francis and Clare: The Complete Works.* Edited and translated by Regis J. Armstrong and translated by Ignatius C. Brady. New York: Paulist Press, 1982.

Heures de Marguerite de Valois, sœur de François Ier. NAL 83, Bibliothèque nationale de France. https://gallica.bnf.fr/ark:/12148/btv1b105127516/f15.item.

Horae ad usum Parisiensem, dites Heures de Charles d'Angoulême. MS Latin 1173, Bibliothèque nationale de France. https://gallica.bnf.fr/ark:/12148/btv1b52502694t/f113.item.

Horae ad usum Romanum. 1488–1492. MS 2842, Bibliothèque municipale de Toulouse. https://arca.irht.cnrs.fr/ark:/63955/md62f7626358.

Hours, use of Rome. 1500–1515. MS 411, General Collection, Beinecke Rare Book and Manuscript Library, Yale University Library. https://collections.library.yale.edu/catalog/2029198.

Hours of Francis I. 1539–1540. 2011.353, Metropolitan Museum of Art, New York. https://www.metmuseum.org/art/collection/search/238581.

La vie de Sainte Marie L'Égyptienne: Versions en ancien et en moyen français. Edited by Peter F. Dembowski. Geneva: Droz, 1977.

Lefèvre d'Étaples, Jacques. *De Maria Magdalena, triduo Christi, et ex tribus una Maria disceptatio.* Paris: H. Estienne, 1519. https://gallica.bnf.fr/ark:/12148/bpt6k8718979j.

Lefèvre d'Étaples, Jacques, and François Demoulins de Rochefort. *Petit livret faict à l'honneur de madame Saincte Anne et de la royne, sa fille, vierge pure, mere de Jesus-Christ.* MS 4009, Bibliothèque nationale de France. https://gallica.bnf.fr/ark:/12148/btv1b55005729x/f114.item.

L'Office de sainte Anne. Français 1035, Bibliothèque nationale de France. https://gallica.bnf.fr/ark:/12148/btv1b52000991j.

Luther, Martin. *Selected Political Writings.* Philadelphia: Fortress, 1974.

Mills, Léonard, ed. *Le Mystère de Saint Sébastien.* Geneva: Droz, 1965.

Montaigne, Michel de. *Essais.* Edited by Emmanuel Naya, Delphine Reguig, and Alexandre Tarrête. Paris: Gallimard, 2009.

Navarre, Marguerite de. *Chansons spirituelles.* Edited by Georges Dottin. Geneva: Droz, 1971.

———. *Les Comédies Bibliques.* Edited by Barbara Marczuk. Geneva: Droz, 2000.

———. *Les dernières poésies de Marguerite de Navarre.* Edited by Abel Lefranc. Paris: Armand Colin, 1896.

———. *Dialogue en forme de vision nocturne entre très noble et excellente princesse Madame Marguerite de France, . . . et l'âme saincte de défuncte Madame Charlote de France, . . . Le Miroir de l'âme pécherresse. . . . Discord estant en l'homme par la contrariété de l'esperit et de la chair, et sa paix par vie spirituelle. Une oraison à Nostre Seigneur Jésus Christ*. Alençon: S. Du Bois, 1533, https://gallica.bnf.fr/ark:/12148/bpt6k706153.

———. *Heptaméron*. Edited by Renja Salminen. Geneva: Droz, 1999.

———. *The Heptameron*. Edited and translated by Mary B. McKinley and Nicolas Russell. Toronto: Iter, Centre for Reformation and Renaissance Studies, forthcoming.

———. *Le miroir de l'âme pécheresse*. Edited by Joseph L. Allaire. Munich: Wilhelm Fink, 1972.

———. *Les dernières œuvres de la royne Marguerite de Navarre*, 1501–1600. Français 24298, Bibliothèque nationale de France. https://gallica.bnf.fr/ark:/12148/btv1b90632774.

———. *Marguerites de la Marguerite des princesses, tresillustre royne de Navarre*. Lyon: Jean de Tournes, 1547. RES-YE-1629, Bibliothèque nationale de France. https://gallica.bnf.fr/ark:/12148/btv1b86095677/f184.item.

———. *Œuvres complètes*. Vol. 1: *"Pater Noster" et "Petit Œuvre dévot"*. Edited by Nicole Cazauran and Sabine Lardon. Paris: Honoré Champion, 2001.

———. *Œuvres complètes*. Vol. 8: *Chrétiens et mondains: Poèmes épars*. Edited by Nicole Cazauran and Richard Cooper. Paris: Honoré Champion, 2007.

———. *Œuvres complètes*. Vol. 10: *L'Heptaméron*. Edited by Nicole Cazauran and Sylvie Lefèvre. 3 vols. Paris: Honoré Champion, 2013.

———. *Théâtre Profane*. Edited by Verdun L. Saulnier. Geneva: Droz, 1946.

Opera gentilissima, et utilissima a tuti li fideli christiani: laqual se chiama li fioreti de misersanto Francesco, 1480. Bibliothèque nationale de France. https://gallica.bnf.fr/ark:/12148/bpt6k59175b/f1.item.

Pizan, Christine de. *The Book of the City of Ladies*. Edited and translated by Rosalind Brown-Grant. New York: Penguin, 1999.

———. *La Cité des Dames*. Français 1178, Bibliothèque nationale de France. https://gallica.bnf.fr/ark:/12148/btv1b8448971t/f1.item.

———. *Le livre de la Cité des dames*. Edited and translated by Anne Paupert and Claire Le Ninan. Paris: Honoré Champion, 2023.

Prayer Book of Claude de France. Tours, France, ca. 1517. MS M.1166, The Morgan Library and Museum, New York. https://www.themorgan.org/collection/Prayer-Book-of-Claude-de-France.

Rabelais, François. *Tiers Livre*. Paris: Éditions du Seuil, 1997.

Ronsard, Pierre de. *Œuvres complètes: Remonstrance au people de France*. Edited by Jean Céard, Daniel Ménager, and Michel Simonin. Paris: Gallimard, 1993.

Saint Jerome, *Corpus scriptorum ecclesiasticorum Latinorum* 55, 1912. *Ad Riparium*, I (Migne, *PL* 22).

———. The Principal Works of Saint Jerome. Edited by Philip Schaff. https://ccel.org/ccel/schaff/npnf206/npnf206.v.CIX.html.

Saint Mary of Egypt: Three Medieval Lives in Verse. Translated by Ronald Pepin and Hugh Feiss. Kalamazoo, MI: Cistercian Publications, 2005.

Usuard. *Martyrilogium Usuardi monachi: quod ad karolum magnu[m] scripsit. Cum additionib[us] iam ex diuer . . . martyrilogijs collectis. atq[ue] de nouo adiectis.* Cologne: Landen Johann, 1515.

———. *The Roman Martyrology. Translated by George Keynes and Edited by William Nugent Skelly.* London: T. Richardson, 1848. https://archive.org/details/romanmartyrology oocath_1/page/256/mode/2up.

———. *Vsvardi martyrologium, quo Romana ecclesia ac permultae aliae vtuntur: Jussu Caroli Magni conscriptum ex martyrologiis . . . Cum additionibus ex martyr. Rom. Ecclesiae.* Operâ Ioannis Molani Louaniensis, 1568.

Vignay, Jean de. *Le miroir historial.* Edited by Mattia Cavagna. Paris: Société des Anciens Textes Français, 2017.

Voragine, Jacobus de. *The Golden Legend: Readings on the Saints.* Translated by William Granger Ryan. Princeton, NJ: Princeton University Press, 1993.

———. *La légende dorée.* Edited by Brenda-Dunn Lardeau. Paris: Honoré Champion, 1997.

———. *La légende dorée en François.* Translated by Jean de Vignay, edited by Jean Battalier. Paris: Nicolas de la Barre for Simon Vostre, 1499. https://gallica.bnf.fr/ark:/12148 /btv1b8604282b.

Wytfliet, Cornelius. *Nova Francia et Canada.* Louvain: Jan Bogaert, 1597. https://digital .library.mcgill.ca/pugsley/pugsley.php.

Secondary Sources

Anderson, Michael Alan. *Saint Anne in Renaissance Music: Devotion and Politics.* New York: Cambridge University Press, 2014.

Apostolos-Cappadona, Diane. *In Search of Mary Magdalene: Images and Traditions.* New York: American Bible Society, 2002.

Archibald, Elizabeth. *Incest and the Medieval Imagination.* Oxford: Oxford University Press, 2001.

Armstrong, Grace Morgan. "Crime Is in the Eye of the Beholder: Rebellion and Decriminalization in Marguerite de Navarre's *Heptaméron.*" In *Rebelles et criminelles chez les écrivaines d'expression française*, edited by Frédérique Chevillot and Colette Trout, 29–43. Amsterdam: Rodopi, 2013.

Armstrong, Regis J., ed. *Clare of Assisi: Early Documents.* Mahwah, NJ: Paulist Press, 1988.

Ashley, Kathleen, and Pamela Sheingorn, eds. *Interpreting Cultural Symbols: Saint Anne in Late Medieval Society.* Athens: University of Georgia Press, 1990.

Badir, Patricia. *The Maudlin Impression: English Literary Images of Mary Magdalene, 1550–1700.* Notre Dame, IN: University of Notre Dame Press, 2009.

Baine Campbell, Mary. *Wonder and Science: Imagining Worlds in Early Modern Europe.* Ithaca, NY: Cornell University Press, 1999.

Baker, Mary J. "Mapping the Moral Domain in the *Heptaméron.*" In *Les visages et les voix de Marguerite de Navarre*, edited by Marcel Tetel, 9–18. Paris: Klincksieck, 1995.

Baker, Naomi. *Plain Ugly: The Unattractive Body in Early Modern Culture.* Manchester: Manchester University Press, 2010.

Barnes, Ruth. "Relatives in Faith: Pilgrimage in Judaism, Islam and Christianity." In *Pilgrimage: The Sacred Journey*, edited by Ruth Barnes and Crispin Branfoot, 14–41. Oxford: Ashmolean Museum, 2006.

Barnes, Ruth, and Crispin Branfoot, eds. *Pilgrimage: The Sacred Journey*. Oxford: Ashmolean Museum, 2006.

Bartoli, Marco. *Clare of Assisi*. Translated by Sister Frances Teresa. Quincy, IL: Franciscan Press, 1993.

Baudoin, Jacques. *Grand livre des saints: Culte et iconographie en Occident*. Brioude: Créer, 2006.

Becker, Marie-France, ed. *Claire d'Assise: Écrits*. Paris: Les Éditions du Cerf, 2003.

Bené, Charles. "La Querelle des Trois Maries et Erasme." In *Visages de la Madeleine dans la littérature européenne (1500–1700)*, edited by Jacques Chocheyras, 13–21. Grenoble: ELLUG, 1990.

Bernard, John D. "Realism and Closure in the *Heptaméron:* Marguerite de Navarre and Boccaccio." *Modern Language Review* 84, no. 2 (1989): 305–318.

———. "Sexual Oppression and Social Justice in Marguerite de Navarre's *Heptameron*." *Journal of Medieval and Renaissance Studies* 19, no. 2 (1989): 251–281.

Bideaux, Michel. *Roberval, la Damoiselle et le Gentilhomme*. Paris: Classiques Garnier, 2009.

Biggar, Henry Percival. *A Collection of Documents Relating to Jacques Cartier and the Sieur de Roberval*. Ottawa: Publications of the Public Archives of Canada, 1930.

Blumenfeld-Kosinski, Renate, and Timea Szell, eds. *Images of Sainthood in Medieval Europe*. Ithaca, NY: Cornell University Press, 1991.

Bodo, Murray. *Simple Way: Meditations on the Words of Saint Francis*. Cincinnati, OH: Saint Anthony Messenger, 2009.

Boinet, Amédée. "Le livre d'heures de Marguerite de Valois." *Memoires de la Société Nationale des antiquaires de France* 65 (1904–1905): 273–90.

Boyer, Elizabeth. *A Colony of One: The History of a Brave Woman*. Novelty, OH: Veritie, 1983.

Brandenbarg, Ton. "Saint Anne: A Holy Grandmother and Her Children." In *Sanctity and Motherhood: Essays on Holy Mothers in the Middle Ages*, edited by Anneke B. Mulder-Bakker, 31–65. New York: Garland, 1995.

———. "St. Anne and Her Family: The Veneration of St. Anne in Connection with Concepts of Marriage and the Family in the Early-Modern Period." In *Saints and She-Devils: Images of Women in the 15th and 16th Centuries*, edited by Lène Dresen-Coenders,101–127. London: Rubicon, 1987.

Breeden, Aurelien. "Sexual Abuse Allegations Shatter a Crusading Priest's Legacy." *New York Times*, September 14, 2024. https://www.nytimes.com/2024/09/14/world/europe/abbe-pierre-sexual-abuse-france.html.

Brock, Theresa. *The Visionary Queen: Justice, Reform, and the Labyrinth in Marguerite de Navarre*. Newark: University of Delaware Press, 2024.

Bromilow, Pollie. "The Case of Lucretia: Female Exemplarity in Boaistuau and Belleforest's *Histoires tragiques* and Marguerite de Navarre's *Heptaméron*." In *Female Saints and Sinners: Saintes et mondaines (France 1450–1650)*, edited by Jennifer Britnell and Ann Moss, 163–178. Durham: University of Durham, 1992.

Brunel, Jean. "La 'faute' d'Amadour et la signification de la Xème nouvelle de l'Heptaméron." *La Licorne* 20 (1991): 5–30.

Butterworth, Emily. *Marguerite de Navarre: A Critical Companion.* Martlesham, UK: Boydell and Brewer, 2022.

Campbell, Emma. *Medieval Saints' Lives: The Gift, Kinship and Community in Old French Hagiography.* Cambridge: D. S. Brewer, 2008.

Capgrave, John. *The Life of Saint Katherine of Alexandria.* Translated by Karen A. Winstead. Notre Dame, IN: University of Notre Dame Press, 2011.

Carney, Margaret. *The First Franciscan Woman: Clare of Assisi and Her Form of Life.* Quincy, IL: Franciscan Press, 1993.

Cazauran, Nicole. "L'*Heptaméron* face au *Décaméron.*" In *La Nouvelle: Boccace, Marguerite de Navarre, Cervantès*, edited by Jean Bessière and Philippe Daros, 69–108. Paris: Honoré Champion, 1996.

———. *Variétés pour Marguerite de Navarre, 1978–2004.* Paris: Honoré Champion, 2005.

Cazelles, Brigitte. *The Lady as Saint: A Collection of French Hagiographic Romances of the Thirteenth Century.* Philadelphia: University of Pennsylvania Press, 1991.

Chervin, Ronda De Sola. *Quotable Saints.* Oak Lawn: IL: CMJ Marian Publishers, 1992.

Cholakian, Patricia Francis. *Rape and Writing in the* Heptaméron *of Marguerite de Navarre.* Carbondale: Southern Illinois University Press, 1991.

Cholakian, Patricia Francis, and Rouben Charles Cholakian. *Marguerite de Navarre: Mother of the Renaissance.* New York: Columbia University Press, 2006.

Colombin, Marie-Pierre. "Rolandine ou la 'vérité' du romanesque dans la vingt-et-unième nouvelle de l'Heptaméron." In *Figures féminines et roman*, edited by Jean Bessière, 49–57. Paris: Presses Universitaires de France, 1987.

Cornilliat, François. "Pas de miracle : La Vierge et Marguerite dans l'*Heptaméron.*" *Études littéraires* 27, no. 2 (1994): 77–96.

Cottrell, Robert. "Inmost Cravings: The Logic of Desire in the *Heptameron.*" In *Critical Tales: New Studies of the* Heptameron *and Early Modern Culture*, edited by John D. Lyons and Mary B. McKinley, 3–24. Philadelphia: University of Pennsylvania Press, 1993.

Davis, Betty J. *The Storytellers in Marguerite de Navarre's "Heptaméron".* Lexington, KY: French Forum, 1978.

Defaux, Gérard. "De la Bonne Nouvelle aux Nouvelles: Remarques sur la structure de l'*Heptaméron.*" *French Forum* 27, no. 1 (2002): 23–43.

Delègue, Yves. "Autour des deux prologues: L'*Heptaméron* est-il un anti-Boccace?" *Travaux de linguistique et de littérature* 4, no. 2 (1966): 23–37.

Delieuvin, Vincent, ed. *La Sainte Anne: L'ultime chef-d'œuvre de Léonard de Vinci.* Paris: Louvre Éditions, 2012.

Dembowski, Peter F., ed. *La Vie de Sainte Marie l'Egyptienne.* Geneva: Droz, 1977.

Dembruk, Sofina. *"Sainte et precieuse deformité" : Expérimentations littéraires de la laideur à la Renaissance.* Paris: Classiques Garnier, 2022.

Dicocitations: Le dictionnaire des citations. https://www.dicocitations.com/citations/citation-16996.php.

Diffley, P. B. "From Translation to Imitation and Beyond: A Reassessment of Boccaccio's Role in Marguerite de Navarre's *Heptaméron*." *Modern Language Review* 90, no. 2 (1995): 345–362.

Donaldson-Evans, Lance K. "The Narrative of Desire: Boccaccio and the French *Decamerons* of the 15th and 16th Centuries." *Neophilologus* 77, no. 4 (1993): 541–552.

Duffy, Eamon. Introduction to *The Golden Legend: Reading on the Saints* by Jacobus de Voragine, translated by William Granger Ryan. Princeton, NJ: Princeton University Press, 2012.

Dünninger, J. "Fourteen Holy Helpers," in *New Catholic Encyclopedia*, 2nd ed. Detroit, MI: Gale, 2003, 5:836–837.

Duteil, Jean-Pierre. *Marguerite de Navarre*. Paris: Ellipses, 2021.

Dzero, Irina. "From Exile to Escape: Frame Narratives of the *Decameron* and the *Heptameron*." In *Topodynamics of Arrival: Essays on Self and Pilgrimage*, edited by Gert Hofman and Snjezana Zoric, 169–183. Amsterdam: Rodopi, 2012.

Eichel-Lojkine, Patricia. *Marguerite de Navarre: Perle de la Renaissance*. Paris: Perrin, 2021.

Farmer, David. *The Oxford Dictionary of Saints*. Oxford: Oxford University Press, 1997.

Febvre, Lucien. *Amour sacré, amour profane: Autour de l'Heptaméron*. Paris: Gallimard, 1944.

Ferguson, Gary. "All in Knots: Teaching the *Heptameron* with *Les Prisons*." In *Approaches to Teaching Marguerite de Navarre's* Heptameron, edited by Colette H. Winn, 135–140. New York: Modern Language Association, 2007.

———. "Mal vivre, mal croire: L'anticléricalisme de l'*Heptaméron* de Marguerite de Navarre." *Seizième Siècle* 6 (2010): 151–163.

———. *Mirroring Belief: Marguerite de Navarre's Devotional Poetry*. Edinburgh: Edinburgh University Press, 1992.

———. "Péchés capitaux et 'vices italiens': L'avarice et ses complices dans l'*Heptaméron* de Marguerite de Navarre." *Seizième Siècle* 4 (2008): 73–87.

———. "'Veritable Histoire': L'*Heptaméron* et la Madeleine." *Le Verger* 20 (January 2021): 1–21.

Ferguson, Gary, and Mary. B. McKinley. "The *Heptaméron*: Word, Spirit, World." In *A Companion to Marguerite de Navarre*, edited by Gary Ferguson and Mary B. McKinley, 323–371. Leiden: Brill, 2013.

———, eds. *A Companion to Marguerite de Navarre*. Leiden: Brill, 2013.

Ferguson, Margaret W. *Dido's Daughters: Literacy, Gender, and Empire in Early Modern England and France*. Chicago: University of Chicago Press, 2003.

Fiore, Silvia Ruffo. "Boccaccio in Marguerite de Navarre's *Heptaméron*: The Muted Confronts the Dominant." *Rivista di Studi Italiani* 14, no. 2 (1996): 54–63.

Fontaine, Marie-Madeleine. "Marie Madeleine, une sainte courtisane pour les dames de cour." In *Female Saints and Sinners: Saintes et mondaines (France 1450–1650)*, edited by Jennifer Britnell and Ann Moss, 1–37. Durham: University of Durham Press, 2002.

Ford, Philip. "Neo-Platonic Themes of Ascent." In *A Companion to Marguerite de Navarre*, edited by Gary Ferguson and Mary B. McKinley, 89–107. Leiden: Brill, 2013.

———. "Sexual Equality and Evangelical Neoplatonism in the *Heptameron*." In *Approaches to Teaching Marguerite de Navarre's* Heptaméron, edited by Colette H. Winn, 70–75. New York: Modern Language Association, 2007.

Francis, Scott. "'Cheminer apres les plus parfaictz': Les pèlerinages et le culte des saints dans les *Comédies Profanes* et l'*Heptaméron*." *Le Verger* 20 (January 2021): 1–22.

———. "Cross-Dressed Monks in Saints' Lives and Their Parodies: A Source for *Heptaméron* 31." In *Subject/Object and Beyond: Women in Early Modern France*, edited by Nancy M. Frelick and Edith Benkov, 167–188. New York: Iter, 2023.

———. "Scandalous Women or Scandalous Judgment? The Social Perception of Women and the Theology of Scandal in the *Heptaméron*." In "Women in the World and Works of Marguerite de Navarre," edited by Judy Kem. Special issue, *L'Esprit Créateur* 57, no. 3 (2017): 33–45.

Freccero, Carla. "Rape's Disfiguring Figures: Marguerite de Navarre's *Heptameron*, Day 1:10." In *Rape and Representation*, edited by Lynn A. Higgins and Brenda R. Silver, 227–247. New York: Columbia University Press, 1991.

Frelick, Nancy. "In the Eye of the Beholder: The Rhetoric of Beauty and the Beauty of Rhetoric in the *Heptaméron*." In "Women in the World and Works of Marguerite de Navarre," edited by Judy Kem. Special issue, *L'Esprit Créateur* 57, no. 3 (2017): 8–20.

———. "Mirroring Discourses of Difference." *French Forum* 42, no. 3 (2017): 375–392.

Gailliard, Michel. *L'Heptaméron de Marguerite de Navarre: Analyses Textuelles*. Toulouse: Presses Universitaires du Mirail, 2007.

Gardenour, Brenda. "Barefootedness." In *Encyclopedia of Medieval Pilgrimage*, edited by Larissa J. Taylor, Rita W. Tekipspe, Thomas Izbicki, Leigh Anne Craig, and John B. Friedman. Leiden: Brill, 2009. Online ed. 2012.

Garnier, Isabelle, with Isabelle Pantin. "Opening and Closing Reflections: The *Miroir de l'âme pécheresse* and the *Miroir de Jésus-Christ crucifié*." In *A Companion to Marguerite de Navarre*, edited by Gary Ferguson and Mary B. McKinley, 109–160. Leiden: Brill, 2013.

Gaunt, Simon. *Gender and Genre in Medieval French Literature*. Cambridge: Cambridge University Press, 1995.

Gomez-Géraud, Christine. "Fortunes de l'Infortunée Demoiselle de Roberval." In *La Nouvelle Définitions, Transformations*, edited by Bernard Alluin and François Suard, 181–192. Lille: Presses Universitaires de Lille, 1990.

Graham, Ruth, and Orlando Mayorquin. "Archdiocese of Los Angeles Agrees to Pay $880 Million to Settle Sex Abuse Claims." *New York Times*, October 16, 2024. https://www.nytimes.com/2024/10/16/us/archidiocese-los-angeles-abuse-settlement.html.

Grieve, Patricia E. "Embroidering with Saintly Threads: María de Zayas Challenges Cervantes and the Church." *Renaissance Quarterly* 44, no. 1 (1991): 86–106.

Gross, Jenny and Emma Bubola. "Pope Francis Is Met with Anger over Sexual Abuse on Visit to Belgium." *New York Times*, September 27, 2024. https://www.nytimes.com/2024/09/27/world/europe/pope-francis-belgium-sex-abuse.html.

Harvey, Carol J. *Medieval French Miracle Plays: Seven Falsely Accused Women*. Dublin and Portland: Four Courts, 2011.

Hayes, Bruce. "De rire ne me puys tenir: Marguerite de Navarre's Satirical Farces." In *La Satire dans tous ses états : Le "meslange satyricque" à la Renaissance française*, edited by Bernd Renner, 183–202. Geneva: Droz, 2009.

Holban, Marie. "François du Moulin de Rochefort and La Querelle de la Madeleine." *Humanisme et Renaissance* 2, no. 1 (1935): 26–43.

Irwin, Bonnie D. "What's in a Frame? The Medieval Textualization of Storytelling." *Oral Tradition* 10, no. 1 (1995): 27–53.

Jansen, Katherine Ludwig. *The Making of the Magdalen: Preaching and Popular Devotion in the Later Middle Ages*. Princeton, NJ: Princeton University Press, 2000.

———. "Penitent Sinner, Apostolic Saint: The Mary Magdalene Cult Emerges." In *Secrets of Mary Magdalene: The Untold Story of History's Most Misunderstood Woman*, edited by Dan Burstein and Arne J. De Keijzer, 148–154. London: Weidenfeld and Nicolson, 2006.

Jean, J. S., ed. *Simple Notice sur les reliques de Sainte-Anne d'Apt*. Vaucluse: 1859.

Jenkins, Jacqueline, and Katherine J. Lewis, eds. *St Katherine of Alexandria: Texts and Contexts in Western Medieval Europe*. Turnhout: Brepols, 2003.

Jourda, Pierre. *Marguerite de Navarre: Dialogue en vision de forme nocturne*. Paris: Champion, 1926.

———. "Marguerite de Navarre: Lettres inédites." *Revue du Seizième-Siècle* 15 (1928): 100–133.

———. *Marguerite d'Angoulême, duchesse d'Alençon, reine de Navarre (1492–1549): Étude biographique et littéraire*. 2 vols. Paris: Honoré Champion, 1930.

Kammerer, Elsa. *Jean de Vauzelles et le creuset Lyonnais: Un humaniste catholique au service de Marguerite de Navarre entre France, Italie, et Allemagne*. Geneva: Droz, 2013.

Kasprzyk, Krystyna. "Marguerite de Navarre, lecteur du *Décaméron*." *Studi francesi* 34 (1990): 1–11.

Kem, Judy. *Pathologies of Love: Medicine and the Woman Question in Early Modern France*. Lincoln: University of Nebraska Press, 2019.

———, ed. "Women in the World and Works of Marguerite de Navarre." Special issue, *L'Esprit Créateur* 57, no. 3 (2017): 1–131.

Klaus, Carrie. "From *désert* to *patrie*: Marguerite de Navarre's Lessons from the New World." In "Women in the World and Works of Marguerite de Navarre," edited by Judy Kem. Special issue, *L'Esprit Créateur* 57, no. 3 (2017): 58–66.

———. "Shaping the Legacy of Louise de Savoie: A New Reading of the *Heptaméron*." *Romance Notes* 60, no. 3 (2020): 563–574.

Knox, Lezlie S. *Creating Clare of Assisi: Female Franciscan Identities in Later Medieval Italy*. Leiden: Brill, 2008.

Kong, Katherine. "Writing Love in the Thirteenth Nouvelle: Marguerite de Navarre's Epistolary Fictions." *Romance Quarterly* 58, no. 2 (2011): 144–157.

Krause, Virginia. "The Heptameron's Tales 22 and 72 and the Visual Arts: Resisting Temptation." In *Approaches to Teaching Marguerite de Navarre's* Heptaméron, edited by Colette H. Winn, 198–205. New York: Modern Language Association, 2007.

Krawczyk, Dariusz. "Figures féminines d'autorité spirituelle dans les œuvres de Marguerite de Navarre." In *L'Autorité de la parole spirituelle feminine en français au XVIe siècle*, edited by Michèle Clément, Isabelle Garnier, and Darius Krawczyk, 188–207. Leiden: Brill, 2023.

La Charité, Claude. "Les questions laissées en suspens par le *Brief recit* (1545) de Jacques Cartier et les réponses de la nouvelle 67 de l'*Heptaméron* (1559) de Marguerite de Navarre." *Œuvres & Critiques* 36, no. 1 (2011): 91–109.

Lebègue, Raymond. "La femme qui mutile son visage (*Heptaméron* X)." *Comptes rendus des séances de l'Académie des Inscriptions et Belles-Lettres* 103, no. 2 (1959): 176–184.

Le Cadet, Nicolas. *L'Évangélisme fictionnel: Les livres rabelaisiens, le Cymbalum Mundi, l'Heptaméron (1532–1552)*. Paris: Classiques Garnier, 2010.

Lefebvre, Lucien. *Autour de l'Heptaméron : Amour sacré, amour profane*. Paris: Gallimard, 1944.

Lefranc, Abel. *Les idées religieuses de Marguerite de Navarre d'après son œuvre poétique*. Paris: Fischbacher, 1898. Reprint, Geneva: Slatkine, 1969.

Le Gall, Jean-Marie. "Marguerite de Navarre: The Reasons for Remaining Catholic." In *A Companion to Marguerite de Navarre*, edited by Gary Ferguson and Mary B. McKinley, 59–87. Leiden: Brill, 2013.

Le Goff, Jacques. *Saint Francis of Assisi*. New York: Routledge, 2004.

Lestringant, Frank. *L'atelier du cosmographe : Ou l'image du monde à la Renaissance*. Paris: Albin Michel, 1991.

———. "La Demoiselle dans l'île: Prolégomènes à une lecture de la Nouvelle 67." In *Lire l'Heptaméron de Marguerite de Navarre*, edited by Dominique Bertrand, 183–196. Clermont-Ferrand: Presses Universitaires de Blaise Pascale, 2005.

Leushuis, Reinier. *Le mariage et l'amitié courtoise dans le dialogue et le récit brief de la Renaissance*. Florence: Leo S. Olschki, 2003.

Lewis, Katherine J. *The Cult of St. Katherine of Alexandria in Late Medieval England*. Rochester, NY: Boydell, 2000.

Long, Sarah Ann. *Music, Liturgy, and Confraternity Devotions in Paris and Tournai, 1300–1550*. Rochester, NY: University of Rochester Press, 2021.

Losse, Deborah N. "Authorial and Narrative Voice in the *Heptaméron*." *Renaissance and Reformation/Renaissance et Réforme* 11, no. 3 (1987): 223–242.

Loysen, Kathleen. *Conversation and Storytelling in Fifteenth- and Sixteenth-Century French Nouvelles*. New York: Peter Lang, 2004.

Luro, Victor. *Marguerite d'Angoulême, Reine de Navarre et la Renaissance: Étude historique et littéraire*. Paris: Michel Lévy Frères, 1866.

Luther, Martin. *Selected Political Writings*. Philadelphia: Fortress, 1974.

Lynch, Denis. *St. Joan of Arc: The Life-Story of the Maid of Orleans*. New York: Benziger Brothers, 1919.

Lyons, John D. *Exemplum: The Rhetoric of Example in Early Modern France and Italy*. Princeton, NJ: Princeton University Press, 1990.

Lyons, John D., and Mary B. McKinley, eds. *Critical Tales: New Studies of the* Heptameron *and Early Modern Culture*. Philadelphia: University of Pennsylvania Press, 1993.

Maniura, Robert. "Pilgrimage into Words and Images: The Miracles of Santa Maria delle Carceri in Renaissance Prato." In *Pilgrim Voices: Narrative and Authorship in Christian Pilgrimage*, edited by Simon Coleman and John Elsner, 40–60. New York: Berghahn, 2003.

Marshall, Claire. "The Politics of Self-Mutilation: Forms of Female Devotion in the Late Middle Ages." In *The Body in Late Medieval and Early Modern Culture*, edited by Darryll Grantley and Nina Taunton, 11–22. Aldershot: Ashgate, 2000.

Martin-Ulrich, Claudie. *La persona de la princesse au XVIe siècle: Personnage littéraire et personnage politique*. Paris: Champion, 2004.

Martineau-Génieys, Christine. "La *lectio divina* dans l'*Heptaméron*." In *Études sur l'Heptaméron de Marguerite de Navarre*, edited by Christine Martineau-Génieys, 21–42. Nice: Publications de la Faculté des Lettres, Arts, et Sciences Humaines de Nice, 1996.

McKinley, Mary B. "Agony, Ecstasy, and the Mulekeeper's Wife." In *A French Forum: Mélanges de littérature française offerts à Raymond C. et Virginie A. La Charité*, edited by Gérard Defaux and Jerry C. Nash, 129–142. Paris: Klincksieck, 2000.

———. "Telling Secrets: Sacramental Confession and Narrative Authority in the *Heptameron*." In *Critical Tales: New Studies of the* Heptameron *and Early Modern Culture*, edited by John D. Lyons and Mary B. McKinley, 146–171. Philadelphia: University of Pennsylvania Press, 1993.

Miernowski, Jan. "Fiction and Ritual in the *Heptameron*." In *Approaches to Teaching Marguerite de Navarre's* Heptaméron, edited by Colette H. Winn, 106–112. New York: Modern Language Association, 2007.

———. "Le Miracle de la Pentecôte à Sarrance : Cohérence narrative et vérité religieuse dans la septième journée de l'*Heptaméron*." In *Narrations brèves: Mélanges de littérature ancienne offerts à Krystyna Kasprzyk*, edited by Piotr Salwa and Teresa Zółkiewska, 177–196. Geneva: Droz, 1993.

Montreynaud, Florence, Agnès Pierron, and François Suzzoni, *Dictionnaire de proverbes et dictons : La sagesse du monde entier*. Paris: Dictionnaires Le Robert, 1989.

Moroldo, Arnaldo. "Réception du *Decameron* à la Renaissance française." In *Études sur "l'Heptaméron" de Marguerite de Navarre*, edited by Christine Martineau-Génieys, 97–108. Nice: Publications de la Faculté des Lettres, Arts, et Sciences Humaines de Nice, 1996.

Moss, Ann. *Renaissance Truth and the Latin Language Turn*. Oxford: Oxford University Press, 2003.

Mueller, Joan. *The Privilege of Poverty: Clare of Assisi, Agnes of Prague, and the Struggle for a Franciscan Rule for Women*. University Park: Pennsylvania State University Press, 2006.

Mulder-Bakker, Anneke B., ed. *Sanctity and Motherhood: Essays on Holy Mothers in the Middle Ages*. New York: Garland, 1995.

Nanni, Romano. "Au temps d'Isabelle : En relisant l'*Heptaméron* de Marguerite ('nouvelle dixneufiesme')." In *Louise de Savoie, 1476–1531*, edited by Pascal Brioist, Laure Fagnart, and Cédric Michon, 277–288. Tours: Presse Universitaire François Rabelais; Rennes: Presse Universitaire de Rennes, 2015.

Nevanlinna, Saara, and Irma Taavitsainen, eds. *St. Katherine of Alexandria: The Late Middle English Prose Legend in Southwell Minster MS 7*. Cambridge: D. S. Brewer, 1993.

Nixon, Virginia. *Mary's Mother: Saint Anne in Late Medieval Europe*. University Park: Pennsylvania State University Press, 2004.

Onishi, Norimitsu. "Angry Catholics Wanted to Burn the Church: He Came to Save It." *New York Times*, June 13, 2024. https://www.nytimes.com/2024/06/13/world/canada/catholic-church-canada-indigenous-people.html.

Orth, Myra D. "Radical Beauty: Marguerite de Navarre's Illuminated Protestant Catechism and Confession." *Sixteenth Century Journal* 24, no. 2 (1993): 383–427.

———. "Reconsidering Radical Beauty: Marguerite de Navarre's Illuminated Protestant Catechism and Confession (Arsenal, MS 5096)." In *Le livre évangélique en français avant Calvin : Études originales, publications d'inédits, catalogues d'éditions anciennes*, edited by Jean-François Gilmont and William Kemp, 86–97. Turnhout: Brepols, 2004.

Parkin, John. *The Humor of Marguerite de Navarrre in the* Heptaméron: *A Feminist Author before Her Time*. Lewiston, NY: Edwin Mellen, 2008.

Percy, Jen. "What People Misunderstand about Rape." *New York Times*, August 22, 2023. https://www.nytimes.com/2023/08/22/magazine/immobility-rape-trauma-freeze.html.

Perrenoud-Wörner, Judith. *Rire et Sacré: La vision humoristique de la vérité dans l'Heptaméron de Marguerite de Navarre*. Geneva: Slatkine, 2008.

Peterson, Nora Martin. *Involuntary Confessions of the Flesh in Early Modern France*. Newark: University of Delaware Press, 2016.

———. "What Does Rape Look Like? Textual and Visual Representations of Sexual Assault in the *Heptaméron* (1559)." *Explorations in Renaissance Culture* 49, no. 1 (2023): 82–120.

Petsalis-Diomidis, Alexia. "Narratives of Transformation: Pilgrimage Patterns and Self-Presentation in Three Pilgrimage Texts." In *Pilgrim Voices: Narrative and Authorship in Christian Pilgrimage*, edited by Simon Coleman and John Elsner, 84–109. New York and Oxford: Berghahn, 2003.

Plantey, Damien. *Les Bibliothèques des Princesses de Navarre au XVIe Siècle : Livres, Objets, Mobilier, Décor, Espaces et Usage*. Lyon: Université de Lyon Portail de l'ENSSIB, 2016.

Polachek, Dora. "Is It True or Is It Real? The Dilemma of Staging Rape in Marguerite de Navarre's *Heptaméron*." In *Violence in French and Francophone Literature and Film*, edited by James Day, 15–26. Leiden: Brill, 2008.

———. "Recasting the *Heptaméron* Novellas in Brantôme's *Vie des dames galantes*." In *Storytelling in Sixteenth-Century France: Negotiating Shifting Forms*, edited by Emily E. Thompson, 170–192. Newark: University of Delaware Press, 2022.

Porrer, Sheila M. *Jacques Lefèvre d'Étaples and the Three Marys Debates*. Geneva: Droz, 2009.

Porter, Catherine and Ségolène Le Stradic. "France's Horrifying Rape Trial Has a Feminist Hero." *New York Times*, September 25, 2024. https://www.nytimes.com/2024/09/25/world/europe/france-rape-trial-gisele-pelicot.html.

Randall, Catharine. *Earthly Treasures: Material Culture and Metaphysics in the* Heptaméron *and Evangelical Narrative*. West Lafayette, IN: Purdue University Press, 2007.

Reader, Ian. *Pilgrimage: A Very Short Introduction*. Oxford: Oxford University Press, 2015.

Reid, Jonathan A. *King's Sister—Queen of Dissent: Marguerite of Navarre (1492–1549) and Her Evangelical Network*. 2 vols. Leiden: Brill, 2009.

———. "Marguerite de Navarre and Evangelical Reform." In *A Companion to Marguerite de Navarre*, edited by Gary Ferguson and Mary B. McKinley, 29–58. Leiden: Brill, 2013.

Reinburg, Virginia. *French Books of Hours: Making an Archive of Prayer, c. 1400–1600*. Cambridge: Cambridge University Press, 2012.

Rezvani, Leanna Bridge. "The *Heptaméron*'s 67th Tale: Marguerite de Navarre's Humble Heroine Confronts the *Querelle des Femmes* and Catholic Tradition." *Romance Notes* 52, no. 1 (2012): 43–50.

———. "Marguerite de Roberval: A Web-Based Approach to Teaching a Renaissance Heroine." https://teachingmargueritederoberval.com.

———. "The Mule-Driver's Wife Meets the Misogynists: The Second Novella of Marguerite de Navarre's *Heptaméron* and the *Querelle des femmes*." *Romance Review* 12 (2002): 11–17.

———. "Nature and Nourishment, Bodies and Beasts: The *Heptaméron*'s Portrayal of Marguerite de Roberval's Marooning." *Dalhousie French Studies* 102 (Summer 2014): 3–7.

———. "Pilgrimage and the Prologue of Marguerite de Navarre's *Heptaméron*." *Romance Notes* 61, no. 3 (2022): 451–461.

———. "Saint Sebastian and the Mule-Driver's Wife: Marguerite de Navarre's Renaissance Martyr." In "Women in the World and Works of Marguerite de Navarre," edited by Judy Kem. Special issue, *L'Esprit Créateur* 57, no. 3 (2017): 46–57.

Ridder-Vignone, António de. "Incoherent Texts? Storytelling, Preaching, and the *Cent nouvelles nouvelles* in Marguerite de Navarre's *Heptaméron* 21." *Renaissance Quarterly* 68, no. 2 (2015): 465–495.

Rigolot, François. "The *Heptameron* and the 'Magdalen Controversy': Dialogue and Humanist Hermeneutics." In *Critical Tales: New Studies of the* Heptameron *and Early Modern Culture*, edited by John D. Lyons and Mary B. McKinley, 218–231. Philadelphia: University of Pennsylvania Press, 1993.

———. "Magdalen's Skull: Allegory and Iconography in *Heptameron* 32." *Renaissance Quarterly* 47, no. 1 (1994): 57–73.

Ritter, Raymond. *Les Solitudes de Marguerite de Navarre*. Paris: Honoré Champion, 1953.

Robertson, Duncan. *The Medieval Saints' Lives: Spiritual Renewal and Old French Literature*. Lexington, KY: French Forum, 1995.

Roelker, Nancy Lyman. *Queen of Navarre: Jeanne d'Albret*. Cambridge, MA: Belknap Press of Harvard University Press, 1968.

Rothstein, Marian. *The Androgyne in Early Modern France: Contextualizing the Power of Gender*. New York: Palgrave Macmillan, 2015.

Russell, Nicolas. *Transformations of Memory and Forgetting in Sixteenth-Century France: Marguerite de Navarre, Pierre de Ronsard, Michel de Montaigne*. Newark: University of Delaware Press, 2011.

Sabatier, Paul. *Life of Saint Francis of Assisi*. London: Hodder and Stoughton, 1894.

Scaglione, Aldo. "From the *Decameron* to the *Heptaméron*." In *Approaches to Teaching Boccaccio's* Decameron, edited by James H. McGregor, 127–133. New York: Modern Language Association, 2000.

Schulenburg, Jane Tibbetts. *Forgetful of Their Sex: Female Sanctity and Society, ca. 500–1100.* Chicago: University of Chicago Press, 1998.

———. "The Heroics of Virginity: Brides of Christ and Sacrificial Mutilation." In *Women in the Middle Ages and the Renaissance: Literary and Historical Perspectives*, edited by Mary Beth Rose, 29–72. Syracuse, NY: Syracuse University Press, 1986.

Scollen-Jimack, Christine. "Funeral Poetry in France: From Octovien de Saint-Gelais to Clément Marot." In *Vernacular Literature and Current Affairs in the Early Sixteenth Century: France, England, Scotland*, edited by Jennifer Britnell and Richard Britnell, 153–170. Aldershot: Ashgate, 2000.

Simon, Anne. *The Cult of Saint Katherine of Alexandria in Late-Medieval Nuremberg: Saint and the City*. Farnham: Ashgate, 2012.

Sodrgel [*recte* Soergel], Philip M. "Portents, Disaster, and Adaptation in Sixteenth Century Germany." *Medieval History Journal* 10, no. 1–2 (2006): 303–326.

Sommers, Paula. "Feminine Authority in the *Heptaméron*: A Reading of Oysille." *Modern Language Studies* 13, no. 2 (1983): 52–59.

———. "Marguerite de Navarre and the Humanistic Tradition." *Language Quarterly* 24, nos. 1–2 (1985): 217–226.

———. "Marguerite de Navarre as Reader of Christine de Pizan." In *The Reception of Christine de Pizan from the Fifteenth Through the Nineteenth Centuries: Visitors to the City*, edited by Glenda K. McLeod, 71–82. Lewiston, NY: Edwin Mellen, 1991.

———. "Marguerite de Navarre's *Heptaméron*: The Case for the Cornice." *French Review* 57, no. 6 (1984): 786–793.

Sorice, Gabriele. "The Skull-Cup Motif in *Gerbert de Metz* Between Intertextuality and Ethnography." *Cahiers de recherches médiévales et humanistes* 36 (2018): 377–391.

Spoto, Donald. *The Reluctant Saint: The Life of Francis of Assisi*. London: Penguin, 2003.

Stabler, Arthur. *The Legend of Marguerite de Roberval*. Pullman: Washington State University Press, 1972.

Stephenson, Barbara. *The Power and Patronage of Marguerite de Navarre*. Aldershot: Ashgate, 2004.

Sumption, Jonathan. *The Age of Pilgrimage: The Medieval Journey to God*. Mahwah, NJ: Hidden Spring / Paulist Press, 2003.

Suzuki, Mihoko. "Gender, Power, and the Female Reader: Boccaccio's *Decameron* and Marguerite de Navarre's *Heptameron*." *Comparative Literature Studies* 30, no. 3 (1993): 231–252.

Taub, Amanda. "What's Behind the Pileup of Sex Abuse Scandals?" *New York Times*, September 1, 2022. https://www.nytimes.com/2022/09/01/world/americas/whats-behind-the-pileup-of-sex-abuse-scandals.html.

Taylor, Larissa Juliet. *The Virgin Warrior: The Life and Death of Joan of Arc*. New Haven, CT: Yale University Press, 2009.

Telle, Émile. *L'œuvre de Marguerite d'Angoulême, reine de Navarre et la Querelle des Femmes*. Toulouse: Lion et Fils, 1937.

Thomine-Bichard, Marie-Claire, and Véronique Montagne. *Marguerite de Navarre, L'Heptaméron*. Neuilly-sur-Seine: Atlande, 2020.

Thompson, Augustine, *Francis of Assisi: A New Biography*. Ithaca, NY: Cornell University Press, 2012.

Thompson, Emily E. "Shifting Rules and Shifty Wives: A Historical Reading of Three Tales from the *Heptaméron*." In "Women in the World and Works of Marguerite de Navarre," edited by Judy Kem. Special issue, *L'Esprit Créateur* 57, no. 3 (2017): 67–78.

Thysell, Carol. *The Pleasure of Discernment: Marguerite de Navarre as Theologian*. Oxford: Oxford University Press, 2000.

Tilmans, Karin. "Sancta Mater versus Sanctus Doctus? Saint Anne and the Humanists." In *Sanctity and Motherhood: Essays on Holy Mothers in the Middle Ages*, edited by Anneke B. Mulder-Bakker, 331–351. New York: Garland, 1995.

Torres, Ella. "Why Assault Victims Stay in Touch with Attackers, in Light of Weinstein Defense." *ABC News*, January 23, 2020. https://abcnews.go.com/US/sexual-assault-victims-continue-relationships-assailants/story?id=68460398.

Tournon, André. "Doublets et hybrides dans l'*Heptaméron*." In *Études sur l'Heptaméron de Marguerite de Navarre*, edited by Christine Martineau-Génieys, 7–19. Nice: Université de Nice-Sophia Antipolis, 1993.

———. "Rules of the Game." In *Critical Tales: New Studies of the* Heptameron *and Early Modern Culture*, edited by John D. Lyons and Mary B. McKinley, 188–199. Philadelphia: University of Pennsylvania Press, 1993.

Vance, Jacob. *Secrets: Humanism, Mysticism, and Evangelism in Erasmus of Rotterdam, Bishop Guillaume Briçonnet, and Marguerite de Navarre*. Leiden: Brill, 2014.

Verlaque, Victor. *Notice sur Sainte Eusébie: Abbesse et Martyre du Diocèse de Marseille*. Marseille: Arnaud, Cayer, 1867.

Vernqvist, Johanna. "Negotiating Neoplatonism and the Androgyne Metaphor in *Heptaméron* 70 and 19." In "Women in the World and Works of Marguerite de Navarre, edited by Judy Kem. Special issue, *L'Esprit Créateur* 57, no. 3 (2017): 93–104.

Viet, Nora. "*Caméron, Décaméron, Heptaméron* : La genèse de l'*Heptaméron* au miroir des traductions françaises de Boccace." *Seizième Siècle* 8 (2012): 287–302.

Vincens, Charles. *De l'iconographie de Sainte Anne et de la Vierge Marie à propos d'une statue du XVe siècle*. Paris: Association Française pour l'Avancement des Sciences, 1891.

Walsh, Christine. *The Cult of St Katherine of Alexandria in Early Medieval Europe*. Aldershot: Ashgate, 2007.

Webb, Diana. *Medieval European Pilgrimage*. London: Palgrave, 2002.

Weed, Stanley. "Venerating the Virgin Martyrs: The Cult of the 'Virgines Capitales' in Art, Literature, and Popular Piety." *Sixteenth Century Journal* 41 no. 4 (2010): 1065–1091.

Welsh, Jennifer. *The Cult of St. Anne in Medieval and Early Modern Europe*. New York: Routledge, 2017.

Williams, David. *Saints Alive: Word, Image, and Enactment in the Lives of the Saints*. Montreal: McGill-Queen's University Press, 2010.

Williams, Wes. "The Diplomat, the *Trucheman* and the Mystagogue: Forms of Belonging in Early Modern Jerusalem." In *Pilgrim Voices: Narrative and Authorship in Christian*

Pilgrimage, edited by Simon Coleman and John Elsner, 17–39. New York: Berghahn, 2003.

———. *Pilgrimage and Narrative in the French Renaissance: "The Undiscovered Country"*. Oxford: Clarendon Press, 1998.

Wilson, Corinne. "Classroom Tools." In *Approaches to Teaching Marguerite de Navarre's* Heptaméron, edited by Colette H. Winn, 22–25. New York: Modern Language Association, 2007.

Winstead, Karen A. *Virgin Martyrs: Legends of Sainthood in Late Medieval England*. Ithaca, NY: Cornell University Press, 2018.

Wogan-Browne, Jocelyn. "The Virgin's Tale." In *Feminist Readings in Middle English Literature: The Wife of Bath and All Her Sect*, edited by Ruth Evans and Lesley Johnson, 61–85. London: Routledge, 1994.

Wogan-Browne, Jocelyn, and Glyn S. Burgess, trans. and eds. *Virgin Lives and Holy Deaths: Two Exemplary Biographies for Anglo-Norman Women*. London: J. M. Dent, 1996.

Wolf, Kenneth Baxter. *The Poverty of Riches: Saint Francis of Assisi Reconsidered*. Oxford: Oxford University Press, 2003.

Wright, Elizabeth C. "Marguerite Reads Giovanni: Gender and Narration in the *Heptaméron* and *Decameron*." *Renaissance and Reformation / Renaissance et Réforme* 15, no. 1 (1991): 21–36.

Zakharine, Dmitri. "Medieval Perspectives in Europe: Oral Culture and Bodily Practices." In *Body—Language—Communication: An International Handbook on Multimodality in Human Interaction*, edited by Cornelia Müller, Alan Cienki, Ellen Fricke, Silva Ladewig, David McNeill, and Sedinha Teßendorf, 343–364. Berlin: De Gruyter Mouton, 2013.

Zegura, Elizabeth Chesney. *Marguerite de Navarre's Shifting Gaze: Perspectives on Gender, Class, and Politics in the* Heptaméron. New York: Routledge, 2017.

Index

Note: Page numbers in italics indicate illustrative material.

About the Author

Leanna Bridge Rezvani is a lecturer in French at MIT. She received a PhD from Boston College and has published articles on Marguerite de Navarre, Madame de Lafayette, and Marguerite de Roberval. In addition, she has developed websites on Marguerite de Roberval, the *Heptaméron,* and *La Princesse de Clèves.* She also created and maintains the website for the Marguerite de Navarre Society.